# TEILHARD

# TEILHARD

by Mary Lukas
and Ellen Lukas

McGraw-Hill Book Company

New York   St. Louis   San Francisco   Bogotá   Guatemala
Hamburg   Lisbon   Madrid   Mexico   Montreal
Panama   Paris   San Juan   São Paulo   Tokyo   Toronto

*For our Father*

Reprinted by arrangement with
Doubleday and Company, Inc.

First McGraw-Hill Paperback edition, 1981

1 2 3 4 5 6 7 8 9 0    FGFG    8 7 6 5 4 3 2 1

Library of Congress Cataloging in Publication Data

Lukas, Mary.
  Teilhard.

  (McGraw-Hill paperbacks)
  Includes bibliographical references and index.
  1. Teilhard de Chardin, Pierre.
2. Philosophers—France—Biography.  I. Lukas,
Ellen, joint author.  II. Title.
B2430.T374L836    1981        194        80-26353
ISBN 0-07-039047-9

# Preface to the Paperback Edition

In the dog days of the 1980 summer, those of us with a continuing interest in Teilhard de Chardin were startled to read in our newspapers one morning that the famous 1913–1915 forgery of "prehistoric human remains" at Piltdown, Sussex, had produced a new culprit in the person of Teilhard himself. The charge, leveled by *Natural History* magazine columnist Stephen Jay Gould, was based on nothing stronger than the following: in a 1953 letter to one of the investigators of the fraud, Teilhard volunteered that, two years before any public announcement was made of the second of the two "finds" at Piltdown, he had been privately shown a "second site" some distance from the first where, he was told, a new cache of fossils had turned up. Undeterred by the fragility of this evidence, Gould took the unsolicited observation by Teilhard that he had known about the site before the public did, as the basis for denouncing him as co-conspirator with Charles Dawson, since 1953 the generally recognized single perpetrator of the crime. Gould even seized upon Teilhard's hesitation about the date Dawson had pointed the spot out to him as further proof of guilt.

Subsequent research in the British Museum archives by Professor J. S. Weiner (one of the original Piltdown detectives), and by us, has turned up other documents which to our satisfaction completely clear Teilhard. As Dawson, ever since the exposure of the hoax, has been notorious for having prepared his faked fossils years before announcing them in public, we were not surprised when we discovered in the collected correspondence with his British Museum patron Arthur Smith Woodward two letters of July 1913 in which he discussed "bones" that he had found in a "new place, a long way from Piltdown"—a "plough field" whose topography corresponds to the description of the "discovery" site publicly announced in 1915. We recognized at once the likelihood that Dawson had pointed out his "new" locality to the young Teilhard when he visited him during a brief passage through England in August 1913.

Over the last autumn, the nasty squall over Teilhard's alleged complicity in Piltdown continued. From August 1980, newspapers which had repeated the magazine charge were troubled with emotional rebuttals from his partisans, and in a subsequent issue of *Natural History*, the same writer who first made the accusation launched a new attack, this time on Teilhard's philosophy, and thus provoked a new round of complaints.

It was thus in January 1981, and after a period of relative calm, that Teilhard in the centennial year of his birth was almost as controversial a figure as he had been when first his works were published in the 1950s. Inasmuch as new research over the past quarter century in particle physics, microbiology, thermodynamics, and astronomy have only served to vindicate and clarify the scientific aspect of his vision, and given the fact that his nonjudgmental attitude toward other people's ideas and lifestyles (despite the strength of his personal convictions) has now become the common courtesy of clerics, his continued power to attract or irritate is something of a wonder in itself.

Those afternoons in London last autumn when we leafed through columns of old letters in museum files, we had time to think about why he should still have power to touch a nerve. Neither the unusually caloric quality of his personality, which qualifies him as the kind of "shining target" which, according to French proverb, "death and scandal love," nor the bizarre details of his life of high adventure seem enough to justify his staying power as a hub of controversy.

In the end, the only explanation we could find for his particular magnetism as man and thinker was the same we gave when we first introduced this book: the fact that everything he did and wrote articulated in so contemporary a voice the old question of the purpose (or lack of it) to the entire human enterprise.

If four years ago, in an era of social and political disillusionment, Teilhard's challenge found as deep an echo in the minds of readers as it did, in our own time of even greater insecurity, the challenge is more relevant still.

It is therefore with considerable satisfaction that we see this book returned to print. We are grateful to Tim Yohn of the McGraw-Hill Book Company for giving us this opportunity to append to this edition the considerable annotation that the hardcover edition lacked. In 1977, certain problems arising from interpersonal relationships among the witnesses who had admitted us to their confidence, coupled with our solicitude for the professional security of the churchmen who had helped us with their recollections, made it impossible for us to annotate the text in great detail. Today for various reasons, these proscriptions do not hold. Furthermore, many of the letters which we read long ago as original documents have since been printed *in toto* or in excerpts, and remaining letters are now in the process of being recovered by the Teilhard family or the Fondation Teilhard de Chardin in Paris for the use of future scholars.

In this annotation, therefore, complementing as it does the slim bibliography of the previous edition of this book, the reader will find listed the most important of the book sources we used, the private testimony of witnesses to individual events most useful to us, and the dates and names of addressees of the various letters on which this book is based. Though we read these letters in Teilhard's own hand or typescript, we have tried as best we can to note which of them are now available in published collections, and those which are still in the possession of their owners.

By completing this new bibliography, we hope, of course, to satisfy those readers of our book who have asked to follow our own voyage of discovery more closely. But more important, we hope that by the act of listing the wide range of material relating to Teilhard still unexplored by scholars, we can, especially in this centennial year of his birth, assist in widening the field of Teilhardian studies.

—M.L.
—E.L.

January 1981

# Contents

# Acknowledgments

It would be a hopeless task to try to name all the people who contributed to the making of this book over the years we worked on it. Nevertheless, we wish to express our indebtedness to:

The Teilhard Family, particularly to M. and Mme. Joseph Teilhard de Chardin, without whose continuing kindness and encouragement this book could never have come to term; to M. and Mme. Henri du Passage, to M. and Mme. François-Régis Teilhard de Chardin, to Mme. Victor Teilhard de Chardin, and to Mme. Gonzague de Lavergnie.

We also wish to express our gratitude to La Fondation Teilhard de Chardin, particularly to Mlle. Jeanne Mortier and M. Claude Cuénot, Docteur ès Lettres.

We acknowledge our great indebtedness to the French, American, Belgian, English, and Italian Jesuit Fathers who provided us with details of Père Teilhard's life and relations with the Society as well as invaluable documentary and illustrative material: René Arnou, Christian d'Armagnac, Louis Barjon, Henry Bertels, Robert Bosc, Georges Bottereau, Henri Bouillard, Emmanuel de Breuvery, James Brodrick, J. Edward Coffey, Francis K. Drolet, Joseph Donceel, Henri Dopp, J. Franklin Ewing, Gaston Fessard, Robert Gannon, Martin Geraghty, François Graffin, Robert Graham, James Hennessey, Charles Hoefner, Henri Holstein, John LaFarge, Edmund Lamalle, Joseph Lecler, Henri de Lubac, Pierre Leroy, Louis Maleves, Paolo Molinari, Christopher Mooney, Vincent O'Keefe, Raymond O'Pray, René d'Ouince, André Ravier, François Russo, Roberto Tucci, and William Walsh.

We thank Père Teilhard's friends and associates, all of whom contributed their time, their souvenirs, and their memories of

## Acknowledgments

Père Teilhard: Professor and Mrs. George B. Barbour, Colonel David D. Barrett, USA (Ret.), Comte and Comtesse Robert de Beaumont du Repaire, Ambassador and Mrs. Jules-Gabriel Beauroy, Comte Max-Henri de Begouën, Mrs. Ida Treat Bergeret, Miss Mary E. Boyle, Mrs. Otto Burchart, Professor Paul Chauchard, Mr. and Mrs. O. Edmund Clubb, Major General Carl S. Day, USMC (Ret.), Dr. Alan Drummond, Mr. Robert Drummond, Mr. William Drummond, Monseigneur Xavier Ducros, Miss Mary Ferguson, Dr. William Foley, Mrs. Mary W. Gilbert, Ambassador Guillaume Georges-Picot, Miss Gulborg K. Gröning, Mrs. Olga Hempel Gowan, Comtesse Roger d'Hauteville, M. Jacques Havet, Miss Malvina Hoffman, Ambassador Henri Hoppenot, Sir Julian Huxley, l'Abbé Albert de Lapparent, Mr. and Mrs. Cecil B. Lyon, Ambassador and Mme. Roland de Margerie, Professor and Mrs. Hallam Movius, Dr. Kenneth Oakley, Mrs. Lita Fejos Osmundsen, Frère Déodat Pennereth, O.S.J.D., Professor Jean Piveteau, Miss Ida Pruitt, Mme. Françoise Raphael, Mrs. Bernard Read, Comtesse Raoul de Sercey, Dr. Harry L. Shapiro, Dr. Albert Simard, Monseigneur Bruno de Solages, Mr. Roger L. Straus, Jr., Mrs. Lucile Swan, Dr. and Mrs. Edgar Taschdjian, Mlle. Alice Teillard-Chambon, Mme. Marthe Vaufrey, Mr. and Mrs. John Carter Vincent, Mrs. Irena Wiley, and General William A. Worton, USMC (Ret.).

Finally, for background information, for details on personalities or subjects in science, history, and philosophy that are covered in this book, our thanks in particular to Mr. Joseph Barnea, Mr. and Mrs. Carl Barnett, Dr. Junius Bird, Mr. Henry Simon Bloch, Francis Cardinal Brennan, Dr. William Foley, R.P. Paul Dupire, Monsignor Alberto Giovanetti, Dr. Abraham J. Heschel, Mrs. Charles Hoffman, Mr. Alfred Jenkins, Mr. Jonathan Norton Leonard, Mr. Robert G. Muller, Miss Ann M. Murphy (Director of Libraries, Fordham University), Rev. Francis X. Murphy, C.S.S.R., Dr. Malcolm McKenna, Rev. Paul Philibert, O.P., Rev. John Quinn, R.P. Philippe de la Trinité, O.C.D., Miss Terry Sampson, M. Philippe de Seynes, Rev. Wilfrid J. Thibodeau, S.S.S., Mr. P. K. Yu; the Press & Information Division, Embassy of France, New York; and the Historical Branch, G-3 Division Headquarters, United States Marine Corps.

# PROLOGUE

The ancient province of Auvergne is a five-hundred-square-mile platform in the center of the Massif Central, bounded by the Marche on the west and Burgundy on the east. One of the earliest landmasses of Europe to emerge from the sea in the Secondary Geologic Era, it was the scene of intense volcanic activity in the late Tertiary and early Quaternary. Today the landscape is rough, cicatrized, rude enough to scratch the retina, and marked by two different chains of conical or mound-shaped *puys* (burnt-out volcanos), which meet at a right angle near the principal city of Clermont-Ferrand. Nearby lakes lie glassy in enormous craters. Petrified lava-flows overhang cliffs like the pipes of some demonic organ.

There is a small amount of pasturage in the Auvergne but, discounting the north-south alluvial plain of the Limagne, little or no farm production. The economic benefits of the Michelin tire factory in Clermont are mostly confined to the city. Except for the sketchy industry resulting from quartzite mining near the *puys*, the mineral yield is negligible. And the inhabitant of this rough land has grown stony in its image.

To this day, the province of Auvergne remains one of the most stolid and old-fashioned in France. Unlike those romantically green, pastoral, or sea-tossed regions where art and imagination have always flourished, even the folklore that it has produced is rude and inconsiderable. What little legendry exists generally falls into four categories: half-remembered history embroidered with a turgid fancy, homespun tales of commonsensical country bumpkins who outwit sophisticated rascals, *fades* (the ancient, earthy peasant jokes), and a few sorties into fantasy.

In that slim literature of the marvelous which does exist, one single theme recurs with curious frequency. It is the story of the Innocent Seeker who leaves his land and all he has to look for the Secret at the Heart of Reality—the Magus who seeks the Single Truth behind the veil of multiple illusion. In different stories the theme takes different forms. Sometimes it is a gnosticism that is sought, sometimes a trick of alchemy. In one tale the prize is the acquisition of a Magic Bird of Paradise, the shattering beauty of whose song will ravish anyone who hears it.

Because the Auvergnat folklorists were plain men, they knew there must be some coherence between rock and flower and beast. Because they were patient and hardy, they had always believed that, with industry and determination, the secret of their relationship could be uncovered. But because they were realists, they knew that such things must be paid for, often dearly. In all their tales, therefore, the Searcher-Protagonist who finds what he is looking for is wounded in the conquest. He inevitably ends either by abandoning the Power of the Secret he has so dearly won, or by being forced to walk alone to the end of his life, without being able to communicate it to another living soul.

There is an intriguing parallel between the theme of those Auvergnat tales of the marvelous and the real-life story of the Jesuit paleontologist Pierre Teilhard de Chardin, who was born near the city of Clermont in 1881. In true mythic tradition, he made himself both priest and scientist, steeped himself as deeply as he could in the disciplines of both callings, crossed continents and still-uncharted regions of the world in an anguished effort to work out a synthesis of science and religion. After seventy-five years of searching, he had (at least to his own satisfaction) the answer he was looking for. But when he died in 1955, in a little apartment in New York City, three thousand miles away from the land that first awakened his passion for the Quest, he was almost unknown and alone, and his Answer seemed about to perish with him.

Teilhard, however, built one bulwark against oblivion. Before his exile to America, he had the foresight to bequeath his philosophical papers to his Paris secretary, Jeanne Mortier. A few months after his death, she took her courage in her hands and brought his major book to a French publisher. The manuscript, which he had called *Le Phénomène Humain* and which summed up his basic philosophical position, became an overnight sensation. For a moment, Teilhard seemed about to be raised to the pantheon of French philosophers. But the light went out almost at once; and from then on, despite his partisans' efforts on his behalf, Teilhard's writings became the property of a cabal of admirers, quite outside the mainstream of modern thought.

By the beginning of the seventies, it seemed certain that the implacable Fate of the Auvergnat folktales had triumphed over Teilhard, too. While cultists doted on his half-explained generalities, the great wave of mankind continued—quite oblivious to them—on the very march he had predicted, overthrowing stifling social orders, suffering the death of old illusions, and staring transfixed at the new scientific view of their own psychological and biological origins, completely unable to wrestle with the larger question of the purpose of it all.

At the same time, just as Teilhard had predicted, some men began to shake off the alienation that separated them from other men. Growing shortages of resources brought about a recognition of human interdependence, and the sudden proliferation of the techniques of communication made clear not only the necessity of cultivating and caring for these goods but the necessity of caring for and cultivating the precious human cargo of the spinning world itself.

Still, the only guarantee that such progress would continue

was the apparently insatiable quality of human curiosity. The deeper question "Why?" remained unanswered, and a new question arose. Since man is rational, how long will he keep pushing forward into a future which is closed before him—how long can he resist being driven to come to terms at last with this tormenting question? Is it not possible that just as the great human migration across the world stopped dead on Easter Island for lack of a polestar to guide it, today's continuing human march will one day stop before the barrier of despair for lack of any reason to go farther?

It is not the intention of the authors of this book to present Teilhard's philosophy as the *only* viable solution to this "Why?" We simply offer it as a solution that merits serious consideration. We do not here propose to present a finished analysis of all the scientific ramifications of Teilhard's intuitions, a task we leave to specialists. What we have undertaken is to narrate his extraordinary story as accurately and graphically as possible, drawing on primary sources, putting his philosophic work in its psychological, historical, and political environment, translating into common speech as clearly as we can his groping neologisms, so that Teilhard's hard-won "solution" to the Purpose and End of the human adventure can be, as it was meant to be, re-examined and reinstated into its place as a part of the common human heritage.

# 1

# THE
# BURNING
# BUSH

# CHAPTER
# ONE

Clermont-Ferrand is an autumn city—one not to be visited in the seasons of promise. Its economy is built around the Michelin tire factory at the city's edge. All spring and summer it stretches dry and dusty under a critical sun. Iron deer poised on bits of rock stare out of cloudy souvenir-shop windows. Scraps of rose gardens struggle to live between stone walls. Shops and cafés have little charm. Flying ants rise with every breeze.

But with the approach of winter, Clermont is transformed. A medieval town still sleeps under its newer stones, and with the first sharp wind it shakes awake again. Under an iron sky full of moving clouds, houses hacked out of ancient rock lean over the streets of the old quarter. A Civil Guard, with sword and cocked hat out of the Second Empire, still appears on holiday occasions. Old ladies wearing skirts that brush their shoe-tops scurry with market baskets along the Rue du Port, a street that was old when the young Pascal walked there with his sister Jacqueline. In the Place DeLille, where Peter the Hermit preached the First Crusade, tree branches shiver in winds that gust at every corner.

By November the first snow garnishes the old buildings, and old Clermont assumes an almost hallucinatory air. In fountain after fountain, water clatters into stone basins or freezes into lovely tracery. Leather heels clap on cobblestones like the rattle of remembered carriages. Sundays are kept with

old-fashioned solemnity, with bell chimes in the air all morning long; and in the afternoon, small knots of people slowly
pass and nod to one another on the way to Vespers.

It was thus, from shadow and into shadow, in the last decade of the nineteenth century that the country squire Emmanuel Teilhard de Chardin and his family walked through
the winter twilight on their way to evening prayer. They
came, as many Clermontois still do, out of the gloom of a city
courtyard into a little plaza, through narrow streets, then ten
feet down stone steps as into a mine, to the twelfth-century
church of Notre Dame du Port. There, in a mineral blur,
under a cage of Romanesque arches and clerestory windows
that gleam like pockets of amethyst, they bowed before a
Host, in a radiance of gold, raised in the great floating gesture
of Benediction.

In the Clermont of the 1890s, the Teilhard name was an
important one. It had twice been honored for service to the
crown and to the Duchy of Berry. Monsieur Teilhard, a tall,
taciturn man with a drooping moustache *à la Gauloise,* was
one of the largest landholders in the province. All his life he
had lived in the shadow of the *puys,* riding, fishing, and hunting on his little fief, carrying home to his various châteaux
samples of flora and fauna, which he assembled into a respectable amateur collection. He was a member of all the local
learned societies; and when the scholarly fit was on him, he
sometimes spent whole days closeted in his study, with his
dogs asleep beneath his desk, shuffling through yellow maps
and charts, new French and English stud books, and back
copies of *The Field—The English Country Gentleman's
Newspaper.*

Berthe Adèle de Dompierre d'Hornoy, his wife, was a
Picarde from a well-connected family, a great-grandchild of a
sister of Voltaire. Though always a bit too long in the face to
be really pretty, she was graceful, grave, and gentle, and her
gray-blue eyes never lost the soft reflections of the marshy
lowland of her birthplace. She took her place as mistress of

the Teilhard châteaux in Auvergne as though she had been made for it. In twenty years, she presented her husband with eleven children, and she created for them a closed, Pascalian world, so somber, strict, and pious that acquaintances referred to it as "la Grande Grille."

Wherever the family lived—at the turreted barony of Sarcenat in the hills outside the town among the young oaks, fountains, and gray walls hung with portraits of royalist ancestors; at Murol, the sprawling farmhouse where they went to hunt and fish; or in winter quarters at their low-vaulted *hôtel* in the city—the Teilhards carried with them a characteristic atmosphere of piety and plenty. There was a rigidly scheduled regimen of study and devotional exercises, games with their cousins the Teillard-Chambons, and plain, gigantic meals that often began with bowls of hard-boiled eggs and ended with three kinds of dessert. Though the children always had an English or German governess, it was Maman herself who taught them catechism, sitting stiffly in the upstairs parlor of Sarcenat on the edge of a big, blue chair between an oleograph of the Sacred Heart and a statue of the Infant Christ with his wardrobe of little dresses.

Like all French piety of this period, that of the Teilhards was inextricably mixed with politics. When Berthe Adèle and Emmanuel were married in 1875, most practicing French Catholics were *légitimistes*, or supporters of the Bourbon pretender, the Comte de Chambord. Prayer books of the era were covered with the fleur-de-lis, and often with the Chambord coat of arms circled by a crown of thorns. But in 1878, when Leo XIII replaced Pius IX on the papal throne, church politics took off in a new direction, discomforting many of the faithful who tried to follow it. Not only did the new pontiff ask the French nobility to rally to the Republic, which they had always regarded as their natural enemy, but he expressed the hope that they would participate in it, perhaps as a kind of "Tory" party.

For Monsieur Teilhard, obedience to papal directives was

always carried out with military dispatch. He therefore immediately dropped official allegiance to the Bourbon pretender, and later, when the pope's famous labor encyclical appeared, even began a conscientious study of the paternalistic socialism of the Catholic political reformer Albert de Mun. Though the setting that produced the children of the "Grille" was a fairly pedestrian one, it offered them a curious blend of the best of both the old and the new traditions; and they grew up bright, proud, romantic, inquisitive, and adventurous.

Among the Teilhard children, there was one who always seemed to stand a bit apart from the rest. It was the second son, Pierre, the pensive one. Born on May 1, 1881, he was preceded by one brother, Albéric, and two sisters, the dark-eyed Françoise (whose high spirits and iron will earned her the family nickname "Mademoiselle J'ordonne") and Marielle, who died in infancy. He was followed by a noisy troop of younger children: Marguerite-Marie, whom the family called "Guiguite," Gabriel, Olivier, Joseph, Louise, Gonzague, and Victor.

Like the stereotyped protagonists of the Auvergnat legends of the marvelous, Pierre never quite seemed to fit into the tight-knit company in which his character was formed. Photos of him as a boy show him standing among his brothers like a figure superimposed on the film, or a creature newly arrived from another planet. Even the much-reproduced pastel portrait of him as a baby has something disquieting about it. Though it has all the trappings of the Wordsworthian innocent—golden curls, rosy cheeks, lacy dress—something in that face seems to have wrenched away from the anonymous artist's fingers; and the eyes that stare from it are veiled, the whole expression, thoughtful, uneasy, even adult.

From the beginning, Pierre was the complete tempermental opposite of his high-spirited and handsome older brother, Albéric, so accomplished in the gentlemanly arts, a naval cadet at the age of seventeen, who, while still in his early twenties, served as an attaché to the French ambassador to Constantinople. And though Pierre tried, he could not really share his younger brothers' interests, either. Even when his father presented him with his own dog and gun, he could not summon up much more than a dutiful, distracted interest in the chase. "We never knew what he was thinking," his brother Joseph has said. "Even our governesses understood Pierre better than we did."

Only the home leaves of the splendid Albéric, back from mysterious oceans and exotic shores, seemed to draw his younger brother into moments of genuine unity with the family. When Albéric's periodic visits were celebrated in the house, while oriental silks were unpacked in the salon, Pierre was always there, hanging back perhaps, his narrow face a bit out of the light, his eyes bright with dreaming.

Pierre's real passion, something he inherited from his father, was natural history: exploring the countryside, climbing mountains, and collecting mineral and wildlife specimens. But almost from the awakening of his consciousness, something else had made him turn inside himself to make another, deeper kind of exploration that was to engage him all his life.

If his family *had* known what really went on in his head at that time, they might have been a little shocked. In the short spiritual autobiography which he wrote when he was an old man,[1] Teilhard clearly explains why he never was the docile, pious child he seemed to be. Behind the opaque gaze of those eyes was an inner life so full of agitation that he felt compelled to keep it to himself for self-protection.

According to that document, Pierre's first clear memory was of sitting at the age of five by the fireplace at Sarcenat while his mother cut his hair. Under her scissors, a snippet fell into the fire, darkened, and disappeared. The child was seized with horror and disgust. What was disappearing, he suddenly realized, was part of himself—curling like an autumn leaf, turning into nothing. "An awful feeling came on me at that moment," he later wrote. "For the first time in my life I *knew* that I was perishable!"

Madame Teilhard crooned and held the child until his sobs subsided. But lying against her breast, Pierre seemed traumatized, and there, he wrote, he really knew, for the first time, he had to find some personal security in a world that fell to dust and ash so easily.

Very soon afterward, he secretly began to hide away little pieces of iron—the hardest thing he could think of—and when he was alone, to take them out to look at with a kind of "adoration." The very thought of them, he found, was somehow pacifying. At Sarcenat there was the key of a plow in the corner of the garden; at Murol, empty shell casings that he could pick up from the shooting range and jingle in his pocket; at Clermont, the metal top of a banister that stood at the level of his nursery floor, which he chose to think of as his personal property. So intense was his fascination with these symbols of durability that in his autobiography he explicity speaks of them as his "Dieu de Fer."

Pierre's "Iron God," however, was not faithful. One morning, when he was ten, he discovered on the chaste surface of the plow a stripe of rust. Terror overtook him once again. Now shaken twice at the spectacle of the unreliability of a physical world of which he was a part, he threw himself down on the garden grass and sobbed.

Then stumbling to his feet, he sought another durable "god." This time he looked at stone, the fragments of amethyst, citrine, and chalcedony which still lie in clusters all through that volcanic countryside, objects his father had told him were older than people, animals, or even the oaks around the house. For him, the stones became the nearest thing that his childish mind could grasp to that "Unum Necessarium" which would never break, decay, fade, or die, the hoardable treasure which "neither moth nor rust could destroy, nor thieves break in and steal."

While secretly engaged in his curious "idolatry," Pierre was always (he has himself protested) conventionally "pious." He was regular at his prayers, constant in his devotion to the Virgin Mary, and "though the Flesh of Christ always seemed too fragile to me," he later declared, he always practiced a dutiful devotion to a vaguely disembodied "Baby Jesus."

It was the custom in the Teilhard household to send the boys when they were about eleven to the Jesuit school of Notre Dame de Mongré at Villefranche-sur-Saône. In 1893 Pierre went there as a boarder. The experience completely changed his life. At Mongré, for the first time, he found a place where he could exploit his special virtues of diligence and piety to the fullest. In his five years there, he was always near the top of his class. He was elected secretary, then president of the school sodality; and though, expectably, he made good marks in science, he also did quite well in religious subjects. He won the respectable grade of *proxime accessit* in Religious Devotion every year, except the year in which he won first prize.

Mongré had the predictable effect on him. "Here," he wrote of the geology of the place, "the land is not very interesting. I went prospecting for stones the other day, but it was hardly worth the trouble." But from morning till night, the Jesuit fathers talked about the conventional God his mother prayed to—a God Immutable, Eternal, Imperishable, well beyond the reach of any destructive forces; and in Him Pierre discovered a new, more satisfying focus for his life.

In his boarding-school years, in fact, Pierre's interior pendulum swung a full 180 degrees; searching for security in stones lost its appeal entirely. He became an ascetic who rose at dawn each morning out of his curtained dormitory bed and went to sit in one of the school's often bitterly cold chapels and read the repeated "vanitas vanitatis," of Thomas à Kempis's *Imitation of Christ*. As time went on, and an institutional religiosity closed firmly over his old Mystique of the Tangible, it came as no surprise to his family to receive a let-

ter from him near graduation time announcing that he too
wanted to be a Jesuit.

Pierre's father was a little less precipitous about accepting
the decision. When the boy left school in August 1897, he
took with him almost every prize Mongré had to offer. But he
left it so exhausted that Monsieur Teilhard insisted on his
staying home a year to rest. To the annoyance of his more ex-
troverted brothers and sisters, Pierre moved about the house
recollected as a monk; and in February 1899, when he accompanied his father to an old, little-used family property, the
castle of Roquet near the Cantal, he closed the ornithology
notebook he had brought with him with a comment that
would have pleased the author of the *Imitation:* "All things
pass away."

The next month, in still-blustery weather, he set out with
his mother for the Jesuit novitiate in the southern city of Aix-
en-Provence. While the dashing Albéric, back from a stint in
Indochina and waiting for his assignment to Constantinople,
followed the social round at Clermont; while the gypsy-eyed
Françoise memorized essays from the French philosophers
and attended local dances on her brother's arm, Pierre sank
slowly and determinedly into the regimen of prayer, self-
examination, and the simplest kind of manual labor that was
at that time the rule in the Jesuit novitiate. Among his classmates, he made two close friends: another Auvergnat, named
Victor Fontoynont, and Auguste Valensin, a red-haired, lan-
tern-jawed boy from Marseille who had studied under the
philosopher Maurice Blondel.

In 1901 the French Republic was sliding into one of its periodic anticlerical nervous breakdowns. the emotional back-
lash following the Dreyfus scandal had left confusion everywhere behind it. "Free-thinking" was the fashion, and
political unrest grew among the members of the lower orders
of society. Though in the Dreyfus affair, the government and
the army had shown themselves every bit as anti-Semitic as
had the Church, it was considered that domestic tranquillity
could best be served by demanding satisfaction only of the

Catholic bloc. Politicians fastened their particular attention on the question of separation of Church and State in education. In 1901 Premier René Waldeck-Rousseau pushed through a law driving most religious from their schools, and the next year his successor, the passionately antireligious ex-seminarian Premier Émile Combes, implemented it.

Together with most other religious orders, the Jesuits were formally expelled from France. City mayors affixed seals to the doors of schools and seminaries; superiors received their sentences with highly ceremonial protest; and one by one, the proscribed religious communities were dispersed, either across the border to live openly in more hospitable lands, or to anonymous lives as parish priests or "lay" teachers in the vicinity of their old schools.

In 1900 the personnel of the Aix novitiate, where Pierre was studying, had moved into a diocesan seminary near Paris. Early that year, Albéric, on home leave, and returning from a family wedding in Picardy, had stopped off to see Pierre. In the frost and blowing snow, the seminary stood forbidding as a fort, but Albéric was pleased to note how easily Pierre had taken to the ascetic life. "You wouldn't believe how well he looks!" he wrote their younger brother Gabriel. "He is tall, bony, self-contained—completely changed from a boy into a man. . . ."

On March 26, 1902, Pierre took first vows in the Society of Jesus. But in his heart he still had not really broken with his childhood cloister at Sarcenat. The year had been a painful one for him. Discouraging letters about the chronic illness of the Teilhards' third daughter, "Guiguite," began piling up on his worktable—Guiguite, his adoring younger sister who, until her health failed during adolescence, had tagged along behind him on his walks "to see what lay at the bottom of the volcanoes." A rest cure with cousins in Cannes that previous summer had left her in worse health than ever, and doctors were then talking about immobilizing her completely in a cast that would extend from her neck to the base of her spine.

Then, suddenly out of the blue, came a real shock. The splendid Albéric, only twenty-eight and at the height of his promise, fell hopelessly ill. Since 1901 he had been serving as a junior naval officer preparing for a permanent post on the General Staff of the French Navy. All year long his letters had shown evidence of lassitude and fatigue. The following April, after a tour of duty in the Mediterranean, he suddenly collapsed. Though the ship's doctor reassured him, he put him off at a hospital at the port of Rochefort, where he stayed a week.

On the first of July 1902 Albéric came home. He was flushed, feverish, so thin as to be almost unrecognizable. The ominous collection of black silk hats that in those days signaled the arrival of medical specialists appeared on the hall table. The doctors' diagnosis: advanced tuberculosis. When someone suggested that the patient might benefit from a stay at the nearby watering place of La Bourboule, the doctor nodded sadly and said, "Well, if it will give him pleasure . . ." Albéric remained a week in that *fin de siècle* glass palace in the mountains, and came home hemorrhaging badly. Plainly, the illness was terminal. Pierre, caught as he was in the midst of the Jesuit exodus, was not permitted to go home; but the other younger sons, Joseph, Gabriel, and Olivier, were summoned back from school to join Guiguite and little Gonzague and Victor and their parents.

For the next few months, Albéric managed to hold on to life. Most of the time he sat propped upright in a chair in a second-floor bedroom at Sarcenat—gray-faced, emaciated, coughing weakly, and repeating pious maxims entirely foreign to his usual tone of conversation. On September 27 he died. Three days later, while Pierre and some of his classmates were making final preparations for their exile from France, Albéric's body was dressed in one of his gorgeous uniforms, an anchor device was affixed to his catafalque, and he was borne away to Clermont to be buried from the feet of the little Black Virgin of Notre Dame du Port.

# CHAPTER
# TWO

The almost simultaneous explosions of the scientific revolution and the Protestant Reformation in the sixteenth century forced the Roman Chuch into a retrenchment from which she still has not fully recovered. While, from that time on, Western civilization has become increasingly identified with individualism and with inductive reasoning, the Roman Church has consistently depended on the use of deductive reasoning to explore and "explain" her Mysteries of Faith. The Council of Trent, convoked as much to defend itself against the threat of changing intellectual attitudes as it was to reform abuses in the Church, was built on the twin pillars of canon law and the exposition of doctrine in terms of the deductive Aristotelian philosophy of Thomas Aquinas.

From the Renaissance divorce between the two ways of looking at reality have stemmed most of the problems that have shaken the Church over the last four hundred years. By the end of the ninetenth century, new republican nation states were challenging the Church's temporal power; the lower classes were opposing her hierarchical view of society and demanding as their "rights" the things they had once begged as favors; and science was unveiling a new picture of the genesis of the universe that at first glance seemed at odds with the biblical account of creation—all because experience became the common man's criterion of judgment. Orthodox

Christianity, however, managed to stand immobile exactly
where it had always stood.

In his early years, Leo XIII had indeed attempted to cope
with some of the challenges raised by the anticlerical reaction.
He gave a panegyric praising scientific progress; he issued
landmark social encyclicals; he blessed L'École Biblique de
Jérusalem, which applied scientific methods to Scripture
studies; he tried to breathe new life into Catholic theology
and philosophy, which had been much neglected in the nineteenth century. Expectably, the method he chose to accomplish this last end was a return to the directives of Trent and
an appeal to teachers to make a serious re-examination of the
deductive thought of Thomas Aquinas.

The papal endorsement of Thomism only added to the
confusion. Its immediate effect was to divide already per-
plexed Catholic intellectuals even further, into Thomist and
anti-Thomist factions. On the Thomist side stood one of the
longest continuous power conduits in the Western world—
the Roman Curia, with all its favorites and hangers-on.

By 1902, Leo was ninety-two years old, quite deaf, and so
physically weak that he had to be supported at the altar to say
Mass. As his health failed, the power of the Curial party grew
to the point that, ultimately, more liberal Catholics angrily
complained that Italian clerics were attempting to confer infallibility on their own ideas by letting it be believed they
were the ideas of the pope himself.

At first, the fleeing Jesuits were too busy organizing their
departure to be much preoccupied with the ideological struggle then breaking out in the Church. Their migration to
Maison St. Louis on the English Channel island of Jersey in
the autumn of 1902 was conducted with order and even a certain *brio*. The House of Studies, on a leafy hill just outside
the fishing village of St. Helier, stood across the road from the
French consulate, and for over a year the diplomatic staff
watched the arrival of crowds of top-hatted, beknickered,

hunting-jacketed priests and brothers, costumed to dramatize the suddenness of their expulsion.

When Teilhard came to Jersey, his "juniorate" was almost completed and his "scholasticate"(the years of specialization in philosophy, with supplementary courses to prepare the candidate for the work he is to do in the Society) was about to begin. For months, Pierre had been aware of the illness of his brother Albéric, but this awareness had done little to prepare him for the shock of his death when it came. Once again he fell into his old blind panic. Would it not be better, he suddenly asked himself, to renounce his work in science altogether, and devote himself to a purely pastoral career? At that moment, with Albéric gone, with his sister Françoise talking about entering a convent and his brother Olivier shipping off to Mexico to see the world, the "glass case" security of Sarcenat, as Albéric once called it, seemed to have been shattered.

Teilhard took his problem to Paul Troussard, his former novice-master, who encouraged him to follow science, and vaguely promised that, if he trusted his instincts faithfully, someday all would come right for him. Pierre obeyed, and in the first week of November 1902 submerged himself in the intellectual work of the scholasticate with the same enthusiasm which he had once applied to the medieval pious practices of Mongré. In the confusion of those days Pierre never studied under a particularly persuasive Thomist philosophy teacher to stamp his mind with the various "body-soul," "spirit-matter" dichotomies of Aristotelianism. Like many mystical souls before him, he slaked his thirst for the Absolute in Nature.

Pierre's science courses, though (and physics in particular), delighted him. There he discovered a demonstrable physical basis for the fundamental unity of Reality which he had always sensed. In this "world of electrons, waves, and ions" where all matter, at least, was reducible to the same elementary stuff, he later wrote, he felt "strangely at home." The "mysterious" law of gravity, by which each thing seemed drawn to every other thing in an impulse of Heraclitean love, held a secret, "that at twenty-two," he naïvely promised himself, "I'd one day force."

Pierre was lucky in his classmates. The sudden emptying of so many seminaries at once had, as a side effect, the tossing of many young men with minds of real distinction all together on a foreign beach. Since they inevitably sought friends of their own intellectual level, circles formed where the thought and conversation were of an unusually high order. In Jersey little companionable groups came into being that were not unlike the small communities of devoted brothers Ignatius Loyola had envisioned for his Society before successive centuries had monasticized it into the large houses and schools that existed throughout Europe. Teilhard and his peers dreamed their futures and distributed their roles in what seems almost a time-reversal of "The Boys" in the Holmes poem. Valensin would be the philosopher; Huby, Rousselot, and Pierre Charles would be the theologians; and Teilhard would be the "Apostle to the Gentiles." The game (if game it really was) completely absorbed its players. Often during recreation, when Teilhard drew away into one of his more introspective moods, a companion's challenging voice awoke him. "Pierre . . . Come, talk! . . . What have you got to give us today?"

In 1905, sporting his first stubble of missionary beard, Teilhard was sent to do his teaching internship at a Jesuit *collège* in Cairo. The night of his arrival, he stood on the school terrace and stared through a forest of minarets, past the pyramids of Giza, to where the desert shone like an uncharted planet under a white moon. Until that moment, the monist view of reality, which his Jersey physics courses had reinforced, had been highly intellectual. But there, in the pacifying sea of rock and sand, was a monism that he could taste with his senses. Every weekend he made excuses to go off to the desert to look for shells of fossilized bones for friends he had carefully cultivated at the Cairo Museum. In his autobiography he has described the sweet and gently drugged feeling he experienced as he stopped and stared over the expanse of desert —the purple steps of the uplands rising against a horizon of exotic wilderness. "Like a wave of exoticism," he explained, "the Orient swept over me. I drank it thirstily."

Within three years Teilhard returned to England and to an entirely different environment, assigned to finish his theological training at Hastings in Sussex on England's southeast coast. From the chalk-cliffed coast near his new home, contoured downs which changed patterns with the movement of clouds sloped softly to the west. Behind them, in the great basin of Wealdian clay, luxuriant forests of pine, oak, and chestnut trees held sunlight in their branches like nets. Cattle and sheep grazed in the "parks"; game animals peered from the brush. Into that cool and pleasant land, Pierre almost stumbled, his inner eye still burnt by the dizzying glare of measureless space. As he walked along the heaving downs or through the wood under spatters of soft light, he began to sense in the world of living things the same unity or "Single Soul" that he had long since discovered in the inorganic world.

At just about that moment, too, a copy of Bergson's newly published *Creative Evolution* fell into his hands. He seized upon its ideas as a providence. In Bergson's thought, he found, or thought he found, a rationale for his new feeling of union with the vegetable and animal world. As he made Bergson's notion of *durée* his own, using the age of various beings as a slide rule to measure the rise of the Tide of Life, Teilhard's mysticism of Space deepened into a mysticism of Time, as well.

While Pierre rejoiced and wrestled with his new discoveries, the ideological imbalance which had so long been troubling the Church finally touched the student priests of Jersey. A real storm had begun gathering in 1903, when Pius X (Giuseppe Sarto, a bailiff's son from the superauthoritarian province of Veneto) replaced Leo on the papal throne. A ferociously devout, though not an especially cultured man, Pius passionately defended the Aristotelian-Thomist outlook of his predecessors. With the support of a coterie of Italian monsignori (the young Rafael Merry del Val, his Secretary of State, acting as his "right arm" and both Cardinal De Lai, his Secretary for Foreign Affairs, and the brilliant, eccentric Cardinal Vives y Tutó acting as his "left arm") Pius issued one pained statement after another decrying the dangers of all the new developments which he lumped together under the single heading "Modernism."

Secretive old bureaucrats and eager young careerists rallied to his cause. No method seemed too disproportionate or absurd for them to take in order to restore conformity—not even the "Sodalitium Pianum," an elaborate international spy system complete with secret periodicals and codes devised to search out secret unorthodoxy. The Sarto pope set up new boards of censors in every diocese, charged with reporting to Rome all local infractions of orthodoxy. Clerics and teachers in Catholic universities were required to sign a carefully worded "anti-Modernist" oath, which, if understood exactly as its authors intended, imposed return to a religious attitude practicable only before the scientific revolution.

At Hastings, Pierre Teilhard, clean-shaven now and looking more and more like an English schoolmaster, might easily have been shaken by the conversations in the common room, had he not been so preoccupied with the demands of his own scientific pursuits. But providentially, in contrast to his philosophically or theologically oriented friends, he had chosen to devote himself to science. For him "Matter" and "Spirit" were rapidly becoming only two faces of the same coin. Of the Roman restrictions, the worst he is recorded as having written is, "I do wish that they'd let us alone!"

Many of his classmates suffered visibly. In an attempt to regain his intellectual balance, the brilliant neo-Thomist Pierre Rousselot—a young man who in his childhood had exhibited so stubborn a temperament that he once actually jumped from a second-story window rather than be tagged in a nursery game of hide-and-seek—made an abrupt right turn and joined the jingoist Action Française. The owlish Belgian Pierre Charles masked his distress in humor, and composed a "Catechism of the Pharisees" and a "Set of False Beatitudes." ("Blessed are the numbskulls for they shall be called reliable souls.") The devout young Auguste Valensin suffered perhaps most of all. During his novitiate, when he had discovered at his father's deathbed that he was the son of a converted Jew and hence ineligible for admission to the Society,[*] it had been a papal dispensation which permitted him to stay. Valensin's preserved diaries document his anguish. They are full of self-exhortations to "see Jesus Christ in the Pope and the word of Jesus Christ in that of the Pope . . . To stifle bit by bit the 'Modernist' me, exhaust it . . . starve it . . . kill it." After an agonizing summer of giving theology lectures in Holland, Valensin suffered a nervous collapse. "I felt as though a lead cap had dropped down over my head," he wrote in his diary. "I could not read so much as a post card!"

But even in his moments of greatest pain, Valensin found time to talk with Teilhard. At that time, with the aid of Bergson's notion of *durée*, Teilhard was still examining in his mind the progress by which the elements of Earth had moved from brute matter to living things. On free days he went out and tested his conclusions in the field. Since he then had so little contact with secular students of his subject outside the seminary, he sorely needed someone to come home and talk to.

Amateur paleontology in England, however, was just becoming a fad. Almost a century earlier, one Sussex naturalist, at least, had dug bones from his back garden which he declared to be the complete skeleton of an iguanodon. By the beginning of the century everyone seemed to feel that the chalk cliffs outside Hastings and the forested clay of the Weald were still unexplored mines of fossilized prehistoric

[*] This law was abrogated in 1946.

bones and shells. There was much to study in the city museum and nearby municipal libraries. In order to slip into the world of minor adepts in paleontology in England at that time, in fact, all one really needed was a proper show of enthusiasm—a thing Teilhard had in abundance.

As early as 1908 his industry in digging in the area around the theologate had entirely won him the admiration of W. R. Butterfield, director of the Hastings museum. Then, during the Whitsun vacation of 1909, he fell into a strange adventure that was to open even more doors to him.

Teilhard and a Jesuit friend, Felix Pelletier, were poking about a gravel pit near the theologate, where they found another dig in progress. Suddenly, up popped a round-faced, bouncy man in straw hat, vest, and shirt sleeves, wielding a trowel. Spectacles glinting and ruddy face aglow, he rushed to pump the visitors' hands. "You're geologists!" he exclaimed. Though Pierre was hardly a certified scholar in that field, neither was his new acquaintance. He was a solicitor from Uckfield, an antiquarian extraordinary, a hobbyist in several sciences. His name was Charles Dawson.

Despite his lack of academic training and the curious turns his research often took, Dawson's protean activity had already made a noise in semiscientific circles in the neighborhood. In years of puttering, he had discovered a vein of natural gas in Heathfield, turned up a specimen of fish that was a "cross between a goldfish and a carp," discovered "a cart horse with an incipient horn," and observed the "sea serpent" in the English Channel on Good Friday in 1906. By the time he met Teilhard, his exploits had already earned him the appellation of "the Sussex Wizard."

Naturally quite flattered by Dawson's interest, Teilhard began a correspondence with him which lasted nearly up until the Wizard's death. Dawson regularly visited Teilhard at Hastings, once hauling off to the British Museum one of Pierre's geological finds: a block of chalk bearing the imprint of a prehistoric fern. He introduced his young protégé to the ichthyologist Dr. Arthur Smith Woodward of London's South Kensington Museum, whose patronage opened even more doors to him.

That summer of 1911 had its shadows, too. Pierre had managed to cope admirably with the death from meningitis of his younger sister Louise some years earlier; but that June, when his brilliant older sister Françoise (his "second mother"), by then superioress of a missionary convent of the Little Sisters of the Poor in China, succumbed to smallpox, Pierre staggered under the blow. Still, the comfort he derived from the new sense of Divine Immanence in Nature and the prospect of his approaching ordination to the priesthood gave him peace and even a certain sense of his saintly sister's invisible presence near him. As the month of August and the date for the ceremony approached, he felt more sharply each day a sense of her presence near him and of her joy in his joy.

A few days before the ordination, Pierre's parents and younger brothers came to Hastings. They arrived at "the English Cannes" to find the weather salt and sunsweet. Gentlemen in boaters escorted ladies in pastel gowns and hats like birthday cakes in glittering sunshine along the Parade. To his family, for whose lodging Teilhard had made arrangement, he looked the model of the elegant young Jesuit. The evening they arrived, he came to conduct them all (Papa in his frock coat, Maman in black silk and sapphires, the boys bright-eyed and curious) to dinner at the fashionable Marine Palace. The next day, prostrate before a gleaming altar in the colored sunlight of the stained-glass chapel, he received the holy oils of consecration from Bishop Amigo of Southwark, and in the afternoon, he accompanied his family on a tour of nearby estates. The following morning Pierre's brothers served his first Mass; and two days later, refreshed and comforted, the family set out for Auvergne.

# CHAPTER
# THREE

With the pacifying growth of private plenty, anticlericalism in France subsided and the Jesuits slowly began regrouping there. In the summer of 1912 Pierre returned to Paris. He moved into the little Jesuit community on the Rue de Rennes with commissions to study geology with Georges Boussac at the Institut Catholique and to apply for acceptance as a student in paleontology under Marcellin Boule at the Paris Museum of Natural History.

At that time in France the study of paleontology had just begun to establish itself as a discipline separate from its parent science, geology. Cuvier had been its pioneer. After him had come Albert Gaudry and his most famous followers; Charles Déperet of Lyon and the great Boule.

When Teilhard approached him, Boule was probably the most accomplished French scholar in the field. Born in Teilhard's home province, he often seemed to some the embodiment of the cliché Auvergnat: plain-spoken, corpulent, and constitutionally close with his purse strings. A possibly apocryphal but wholly characteristic story of him, still cherished by his friends, concerns his acquisition of the Chinese dinosaur egg which is still proudly displayed on a red velvet backing in the great hall of the Museum of Paleontology. It had been brought to him one day by a missionary who hoped to sell it to get money to support his work. To the priest's confusion, Boule simply accepted the gift as though it were the museum's due, and sent him packing with the thanks of French science. Then, just as the missionary was approaching the door, the old lion, taken with a cramp of conscience, bellowed down the staircase to his secretary, "Madeleine! That fellow who's going out. Stop him! Give him a franc!"

Teilhard first met Boule on a summer afternoon in his laboratory in the glass-domed, red-brick museum which still crouches like a mythical animal among the seasonal flowers of the Jardin des Plantes. Boule was just packing for vacation. The master's reputation for gruffness and his declared agnosticism as much as his eminence as a teacher filled Teilhard with apprehension, and the diffidence of the museum's besmocked old caretaker, sloshing along in carpet slippers to protect the floors, then mounting meekly to the master's sanctum to announce him, did not help to put him at his ease. But perhaps because of their mutual connection with Auvergne, perhaps because of the young Jesuit's personal charm, Boule seemed to take an immediate liking to Teilhard. Not only did he agree to take him as a student; he even offered to let him try his hand in the fall at classifying a drawerful of vertebrate fossils which he had collected from the rivulet-streaked gravel of Quercy near Toulouse.

Boule's easy acceptance of Teilhard was just as surprising to most of his other pupils as it was to the new student. Though he never bothered to restrain his profanity or his articulate anticlericalism, he made no secret of his respect for his new pupil's obvious talents. Daily, he stopped in the little workroom where Teilhard was sorting fossils to drink the bitter tea brewed in the museum basement and to chat. He gave Teilhard easy access to his own laboratory and rarely showed annoyance when the young man charged up the stairs at odd hours to share some problem or discovery with him.

From the window of his room at the museum, Teilhard could hear the rumble of the wine barrels on the streets of Les Halles du Vin, and sometimes even the roar of the sorry

beasts in the zoo. In fair weather he walked with the preco-
cious Rousselot (by then a celebrated philosophy teacher at
the Institut Catholique) down sunshiny avenues, past seasonal flower beds to the vine-laced maze where stands the famous cedar of Lebanon reputedly brought back by the botanist Jussieu in his hat. Demanding as his studies and his lab
work may have been, Teilhard still found time to exercise a
kind of chaplaincy to the glass-factory apprentices at Le Bour-
get and to seek out family connections living in the vicinity.

It was a wonderful time to be alive in Paris. The city was
never more brilliant or more prestigious than it was just then.
Its parks, its fountains, its nobly proportioned buildings, its
high standards of thought and conversation made it a magnet
for everything that was witty and graceful in Europe. American hostesses engaged in "duels of diamonds" with the
grandes dames of the Faubourg St.-Germain. Social climbers
vied for invitations to the salons of Julia Daudet or the ebullient Comtesse de Noailles. The Opéra, where Melba sang,
Paderewski played, and Nijinsky danced, was the artistic
crossroad of Europe. In Paris just before the war, the nineteenth-century dream called "progress" seemed finally to have
materialized. The Métro, acclaimed as a futuristic marvel, was
just finished. Complete electric light had almost entirely
replaced gas. Motor taxis had replaced the city's seventeen
thousand fiacres. The telephone system was already just about
as good as it is now.

That autumn, Pierre rediscovered the family of his father's
first cousin Cirice Teillard-Chambon, who had come to work
in a Paris suburb when his land in the Cantal ceased to be
sufficiently productive to keep up his old standard of living.
Pierre may have had difficulty remembering some of "uncle's"
younger children, but none at all in remembering his oldest
daughter, Marguerite.

At the time of that meeting, Marguerite seemed already a
*demoiselle d'un certain âge,* a formidable creature with high-
boned collar and determinedly topknotted hair, who had for

six years been directress of the Institut de Notre Dame de
Sion, a girls' school in Montparnasse. Intimidating though
she may have been to others, she never was so to him. Behind
her defensive feminism, she was romantic, high-strung, and
unhappy with her spinster's lot and she made no secret of it.
She tried with some success to be a literary hostess. She
nourished the idea that she might have a talent for writing
which perhaps would lift her from obscurity; but she never
felt she had the time nor even the right to neglect her job and
test it.

When Pierre appeared that October of 1912, Marguerite
was delighted. Though the Jesuit had by then become the
protégé of the savants of Paris, his newly acquired façade of
self-confidence barely disguised the touching introversion of
the boy with whom as an adolescent, she (like Guiguite before her) had roamed the *puys* near Sarcenat. In Pierre, Marguerite told herself almost as soon as they met again, she had
found a confidant barred by choice from the kind of life she
had been denied by circumstances—a friend with whom she
could have a spiritual relationship analogous to the warm,
human friendships that filled the lives of the "ordinary Christian women" she professed to envy.

Pierre and Marguerite met frequently, at "Uncle" Cirice's
and at the Paris home of other cousins, the Teilhard d'Eyrys.
Eyes piously downcast, Pierre presided over the ceremonies of
his cousin's school, while Marguerite plied him with tickets
to lectures and introduced him to her circle of acquaintances—
to the geologist Emmanuel de Margerie, to her assistants at
the Institut, and to a few of her old teachers from the Sorbonne. Like the "last duchess" in the Browning poem, Teilhard let his innocent gaze go everywhere, and everything he
saw gave him equal pleasure.

In those days he also followed Georges Boussac on geology
field trips connected with his work at the Institut Catholique
—trips that had an almost picnic air about them. With his
more accomplished friends, Pierre sifted the gravels of the

Seine basin, where Pliocene hippopotami and straight-tusked elephants once roamed. He searched the sediments near Caen where once had been the bed of an inland sea. When he was assigned to give Lenten sermons at Gap near the Swiss border, he arced down through the Midi, then crossed up to Montauban, near the homeground of the little protomonkey Quercy fossils which he had worked on for Boule.

But of all the excursions he made then, the one that impressed him most was one he took in June 1913 in the company of a new museum acquaintance, the Abbé Henri Breuil. With the English prehistorian Dorothy Garrod, Hugo Obermaier, and other friends, Breuil took him off to explore the Cro-Magnon caves of northern Spain. Crawling about the clammy tunnels that the local people believed to be the haunt of goose-footed witches, Teilhard and Breuil made an unlikely-looking pair. Breuil, squat, quick, and dark-eyed, mantled with the authority that his recently published magistral study *The Subdivisions of the Upper Paleolithic and Their Significance* had given him; Teilhard, tall, thin as a crane, and boyishly eager as he bent nearly double to peer into the low, shaggy, vine-hung openings of the caves.

Although in the Jersey sea caves Teilhard had seen gravel deposits washed there sometime in the Tertiary, this was his first venture onto the hearth of early man. To Breuil's amusement, he seemed unable to get enough of it. Time and time again, he returned to a cave near Puente Viesgo to sit all alone in a silence punctuated only by the dripping of the stalactites, and to contemplate its yellow walls covered with red and white tracings of human hands made perhaps thirty thousand years earlier. At Santander and once again at Altamira, he examined, in deepest awe, animal bones charred from cooking and worked tools that had been used there millennia before the emergence of Egyptian civilization. He beamed his acetylene lamp over the upper surface of grottoes decorated with accomplished, stylized paintings of bison, horses, and mountain goats. The little low ceilings, covered with pictures from a world of men just born, had something about them more evocative than a Sistine Chapel ceiling.

Soon afterward, still starry-eyed from his visit to the Spanish caves, Pierre went to England to make his yearly retreat. En route, he dropped in unexpectedly at Lewes to see Dawson. The Wizard was himself in the middle of a remarkable adventure at the moment. He had recently presented to the British Museum parts of a mandible and skull fragments that he had for many years (once in Pierre's presence) been picking out of a gravel field near a cluster of monkey puzzle trees at Piltdown, and which, he suggested, might very well be part of a cranium of the much-discussed "missing link." For some time the controversy raged over whether Dawson's bone fragments even came from the same creature. In contrast to other reconstructed and officially authenticated prehistoric skulls—all of which had receding foreheads and large, meat-tearing jaws—Dawson's "fossil man" had the forehead of a modern Englishman and the sharply receding chin of an ape. It seemed to fit into no known line of human development, and even Boule had called the specimen "monstrueux." Still, the evidence was there: a piece of jawbone and a skull fragment, both of the same color, found at approximately the same geological level, all within a few feet of one another.

Though Pierre had arrived at Lewes a bit precipitously, the Wizard and his menage received him with smothering hospitality. The morning after his arrival, in a light rain, Smith Woodward and Dawson took him down to Piltdown to inspect the pit. They found nothing.

When his eight-day retreat was over, though, Pierre rushed back to Lewes. This time, a search of the area proved more productive. While his companions poked about another part of the pit, Pierre suddenly noticed, peeping from the rain-washed gravel, something he had somehow missed before. It was a lower canine tooth of the same antique brown color as Dawson's other piece, worn to an inclination that made it fit exactly between the upper and lower jaws of the specimen.

There seemed no denying now that the face bones came from the same cranium.

The find enhanced Teilhard's celebrity not only in Britain, but in France as well. He lectured at the National Geological Society and at the Société de France. His field trips were made in ever more impressive company—Breuil; Boussac; Baron Alberto Blanc, the Inspector of the Museum of Rome; the geologist Victor Commont, renowned for his classification of the various paleolithic glaciations of the Somme basin; and Comte Henri de Begouën, an amateur prehistorian who lived near the Pyrenees and who, with his sons, had discovered remarkable Magdalenian clay bison figures in the grotto of Trois Frères on his own property of Las Espas.

But while Teilhard was being drawn ever deeper into a round of work and entertainment, underneath the glittering and tinkling of the formal and old-fashioned social pavilion that was prewar Europe, beams long-rotted swayed and sank. Old nationalistic quarrels, the wrangling of the crowned progeny of Queen Victoria, the general acceptance of the idea that conquest somehow added to a nation's glory—that for the Nietzschean German Soul at least, it was a "biological necessity"—seemed to feed on the pomposity, the ease, the fatness of the time. For at least a decade in all major Continental countries, a huge build-up of armaments was in progress; and a tangle of alliances evolved, so complex that the smallest incident could bring the whole thing crashing down.

By the spring of 1914, anticipation of war was almost lyric. In April French ciphers, codes, and regimental billets had already been arranged down to the last detail. By June General von Moltke was jubilantly declaring, "We are ready. And the sooner it comes, the better." The Austrian archduke was assassinated at Sarajevo on June 28. On August 3 war came.

In 1904 Pierre, like most French clerics, had been classified for "auxiliary service," a category of men who could be called up only in national emergencies, and then only as chaplains or stretcher-bearers. Though, in the patriotic fever of that first month of siege, many patriotic priests ignored the prohibitions of canon law and volunteered for combat, Pierre decided not to defy Church authority.

When the war broke out, Teilhard was on a mountain-climbing trip. Like a sleepwalker caught in a mine field, he rushed back at once to Paris, where Marguerite had turned her school into a hospital for the wounded who were already piling into the city. Pierre was glad to be of use there. He also worked with Boule at the museum, storing away its treasures. He knew that it was only a matter of time before he would be mobilized.

Though accurate news in those days was hard to come by, every hour it became more clear that the main troop concentrations of the opposing armies, slavishly following unrelated battle plans, had simply missed each other like crowds in a revolving door. The French, wearing their glorious red breeches, set out to retake Alsace; and in a meticulous execution of the Schlieffen Plan, the Germans crashed purposefully across Belgium and the Pas de Calais, leaving desolation in their wake. By the end of August, they had reached Compiègne, thirty-odd miles from Paris.

On the thirty-first of that month, the French government departed for Bordeaux, leaving the capital as quiet as an unvisited museum. No vehicles moved in the streets; hypertense people walked quickly by without greeting one another. An occasional voice bawling the "Marseillaise" from a café broke the unnatural stillness. Once in a while a German *Taube* lazily dropped leaflets. Prospects for a turn in France's bad fortunes seemed unlikely.

Then, the next month, the tide of battle turned. French troops rallied at the Marne and began to roll the Germans back. Since Pierre had still not been inducted, his superiors decided it would be a good time to hurry him off to a Jesuit house in England to begin his tertianship, his last preparatory year before attaining full status in the Society.

The exercise, however, was never finished. Two months

after Teilhard crossed the Channel, news came that his younger brother Gonzague had been killed in a battle near Soissons. The next week, his own order to report for duty came. He packed a few necessities and went home.

The train that bore him from Paris to Auvergne, where a new regiment was forming, was a bedlam. Refugees carried children and huge bundles; soldiers crowded back to back in the corridors. The news of the Marne victories had somewhat raised the travelers' spirits. They shared their sausages and wine; they sang; they talked to strangers about the prospect of success in a war they now seemed to have a chance of winning.

Like most young soldiers of his time, Pierre seemed to have been quite untroubled at the prospect of the horror that lay before him. He was eager to see action before "it was all over." Though an apprentice scientist of thirty-three who had already made a good reputation for himself in his field, he was still in many ways a boy. His mysticism and his philosophy had stopped more or less at the plateau they reached in Hastings. Though in his mind the idea of "Spirit" had, of course, quite replaced that of "Stone" as the Security he had looked for all his life, it was only a comforting private intuition whose meaning and consequences he had not worked out even in his conversations with his theologian friends. If, as Pierre had concluded, Spirit (or the faculty for reflection) was indeed the "Ultimate Indestructible," how to explain the uncounted variety of organized forms—nonliving as well as living—between Stone and Spirit that became more destructible and improbable as they grew more individual in their evolution toward what Bergson had called "full Personalization"?

And even more important, how to escape the conclusion that the end of this long labor was only that lonely, fragile thing whose disturbing material perishability had always troubled him: the human being?

On his lab table over the last two years, Pierre had handled hundreds of pieces of fossilized bones. But like the "dry bones" of Ezekiel, they were mute. Motionless, eyeless, tongueless, they did little to explain the paradox that troubled him. As his train lumbered down past Nevers, Moulins, Vichy, and Riom, it covered the old route to Auvergne that he had so often traveled before. But this time it was different. That bleak December afternoon, his destination was not an old château warmed by memory and affection. It was confrontation with the multitude of the dying and the ready-to-die—an "army" not unlike that of Ezekiel, "sinewed, fleshed, and covered with skin," which would stand before him and challenge him to find his answers with a terrible lingering cry.

# CHAPTER
# FOUR

It did not take long for the Glorious Adventure of the war to show itself for what it really was: a pointless exercise in bloodletting. As long as Teilhard lived, the sick taste of it stayed in his mouth, and the vision of it in his mind.

Attached as a stretcher-bearer to a colonial regiment of North African Zouaves and light infantry, he saw action in the Marne before the end of his first year. Then Zouaves were moved northeast to Ypres in Belgium.

When they arrived, the town was already a monstrous devastation. Its buildings were skeletons; its poplars, burnt-out matchsticks. In the mud flats behind the town ("the Zone of the Dead"), bodies hung across barbed wire like scarecrows; and wounded men, slipping in and out of consciousness, tried to hold their blood inside them with their hands, while they prayed for help to come. When, after a long siege, the Germans saw that conventional weapons could not push the Allies out, they turned to poison gas. One April evening, just at dusk, it came across the trenches, a green mist smelling faintly of jasmine. The soldiers screamed as their throats burned. Then as the gas split their lungs, they coughed up a little pinkish foam and died.

After several more months at Ypres, Pierre's regiment was moved to Artois to join a French attack against the Germans entrenched there. When it was over, the French had been victorious; but the Zouaves lost nearly one half of their complement. In November 1915, while the regiment was being reconstituted, Pierre went home on his first leave.

Half giddy with relief at being out of it, Pierre first rushed down to see his parents at Sarcenat. The gloom he found there was unbearable. Guiguite was there, as sick and brave as ever, but all his brothers were now at the front. Papa sat about brooding and silent; and though pain played frequently across his mother's face, she did not speak of her distress. After a short time there, Pierre went north to Paris, to lose himself in the company of his museum friends and of his cousin Marguerite Teillard-Chambon.

When in early 1916 he returned to his regiment, it had moved to the Belgian coast. In midwinter everything was at a stalemate. Flanders was glazed with ice like a Canadian prairie; a gray sea thick with mines lapped at the shore line; sandstorms were as frequent as snowstorms. All winter long, two armies nearly paralyzed with cold watched each other across canals only a few meters wide and waited for the spring.

Billeted in the drafty salon of a ruined villa near Nieuport, Pierre suffered from boredom—the soldier's old malaise. His turn to make the three-mile trip to an aid post at the front to look for occasional casualties came up only once a month. Otherwise, except for his religious exercises, he had very little to do. With time so heavy on his hands, he set himself the task of making philosophic sense of the nightmare world around him. More, perhaps, than many of his comrades, he recognized his need to find some shield against the nausea that took him when he reached into a hole to pull out the blasted, weeping remains of a man whom he had known—something to keep his purpose firm when, as he made his way back to his lines, he felt the thing he carried on his shoulders grow slowly slack with death—some thought to calm him when he woke at night, cold, sweating, and bolt upright on his pallet after a dream that was necessarily less dreadful than reality.

In a schoolboy's notebook, he put down his thoughts. In

time the "thoughts" turned into essays. Toward the end of
April 1916 he finished a paper he called "La Vie Cosmique,"
which he declared might well turn out to be his "final testament," to justify what was still a "passionate vision of the
earth."

The statement issued from the deepest part of him. Over
the landscape of loss and disintegration that stretched out on
every side, he superimposed the vision of another world—
healthy, whole, and growing, a world whose rise from the
abyss of complete dispersion to stunning heights of power
and stability was of a single piece. Directing the lower forces
of nature, he posited the existence of a Cosmic Organizing
Energy (very like Bergson's *élan vital*), which caused subatomic particles to come together into atoms, the atoms to
draw together into molecules, and the molecules to join other
molecules—some of which became so complex that ultimately
they broke through into Life. At the end of a procession of
animal species, which showed ever-heightening self-awareness,
Man at last appeared, and he began to join with other men to
make a kind of simple organism with a single Personal Goal.
That Goal, Teilhard believed, would one day be reached; and
when it was, he concluded, "Everything that is hard, crusty,
or rebellious . . . all that is false and reprehensible . . . all
that is physically or morally evil will disappear. . . . Matter
will be absorbed into Spirit."

Soon after he had finished the essay, a bit astonished at his
own boldness, Teilhard packed up several copies of it, and
sent them off to Léonce de Grandmaison, editor of the Jesuit
journal *Études*, to his invalid sister Guiguite, and to Marguerite Teillard-Chambon.

In those first years at the front, Pierre's correspondence
with his cousin was extensive. Emerging, as he was, from the
attenuated adolescence of the cloister, he found Marguerite
Teillard-Chambon's admiration very satisfying. Even at the
age of thirty-four, he was still painfully shy. His own brothers
at Sarcenat had never been interested in his awkward specula-

tion, and now even some of his Jesuit superiors were beginning to look oddly at him when he talked about philosophy.
Among the Moslem infantrymen, the plain-spoken, irreverent
*poilus*, or the often cynical officers of his regiment, he found
little companionship. Only Marguerite gave him the kind of
sounding board he needed in his effort to reconcile the idea of
the directed Creative Process that he felt was working in the
world with the destruction he saw all around him.

His letters to his cousin clearly show his psychological development. At first he struck the attitude of director of her
conscience; passages from some of his letters sound as though
they had been copied whole from the platitudes written to
"Philotheas" by the spiritual directors of other centuries.*
But as time went on, the correspondence changed its tone. In
the sharply telescoped exchange that took place between
Pierre and Marguerite during the young soldier's first leave,
he began to recognize certain facts about Marguerite's steely
nature (and—by extension—about human nature in general).
From this moment, his advice to her became more individual
and personal.

In May of 1916 the Zouaves were ordered to Verdun,
where an action was in progress that surpassed even the horror of Ypres the year before. The terrain around the city was a
sea of mud that swallowed men, animals, vegetation, and
matériel without distinction. All summer long, Teilhard's regiment camped on the left side of the Meuse in a hollow
below Mort Homme and the legendary Hill 304. It was during this nerve-wracking détente, in the yellow flash of German guns, that Teilhard dreamed a pious literary triptych,
"Three Stories in the Style of Benson,"† in which he tried to
illustrate the way God permeates creation as His influence
radiates from three centers: the consecrated Host displayed in

---

* Example: "Introduction to a Devout Life" by Francis de Sales (1567–
1622) for Jane Frances de Chantal, foundress of the Visitandine Nuns. The
first chapter begins, "My dearest Philothea. . . ."
† Robert Hugh Benson (1881–1914), British Roman Catholic apologist and
novelist.

its golden halo in a church, the light emanating from the Heart of Christ such as Teilhard had seen repeated in so many paintings and oleographs throughout his youth,‡ and the Eucharistic Presence closed in the pocketwatch-size pyx that a chaplain (himself dying) carried to give to other dying men.

The same month that Teilhard finished his "Three Stories," the Zouaves attacked the fort of Douaumont. They crossed a moat in an opaque fog, and after fighting from turret to turret, took their objective and six thousand German prisoners in one day's time.

After Douaumont, came Louvement, the last remaining German-held fort near Verdun. Once it had fallen too, the Zouaves were moved slowly toward the Marne, where the Allies were preparing their spring offensive. By then, Teilhard had been promoted from stretcher-bearer to chaplain in the regiment—a change that gave him even more empty time, which he filled writing all alone in empty rooms in Meusian peasant houses, in the sacristies of abandoned churches, and in rectory attics isolated enough to discourage visits from "bores and undesirables."

In the first essay he wrote during this period, "La Lutte contre la Multitude,"[1] Teilhard analyzed the tormenting tendency of matter in organized states to disintegrate until it stabilizes at a level of complete dispersion. All that existed, he felt, was simultaneously held together by a "psychic tension" and pulled apart by the backward drift of matter toward nonbeing. When evolution passed from one living stage to a higher living stage, the "psychic tension" of evolving beings increased (as, paradoxically, did their fragility). And when evolution crossed the great threshold in the human stage, the change was so profound that the psychic force then generated was strong enough to continue in existence, even when its ma-

‡ The much older devotion to the Sacred Heart of Jesus (symbol of His love for men), was revived in the Church in the seventeenth century by the nun Marguerite-Marie Alacoque and the Jesuit Claude de la Colombière, and promulgated as a kind of religious manifestation of the Romantic rebellion.

terial matrix was destroyed. In the case of Man, Teilhard therefore maintained, "The countless factors which generate Spirit melt into such a perfect point that nothing can dissolve their fusion; and consequently, the human soul can detach itself and continue to subsist even after the body has disintegrated."

By autumn 1917, with his regiment again behind the lines, Pierre fell into the habit of taking lonely walks at dusk. Each evening he climbed a nearby hill to look across the valley at the limestone chain of the Chemin des Dames, rising sharp as a blade against the graying sky. From there, he could see the flares and shellfire of what he liked to call "the warm and living line of the front." The contemplation of this flash-point meeting place of two enormous, internally cohesive, though mutually destructive, collectivities, stirred feelings that he did not fully understand.[2] Standing on the hill, he felt he was watching the explosion of some kind of "critical point in human history." If only these two passionate energies could be melded into one, he concluded, what a world of new achievement could be Man's!

Sometimes Teilhard stayed there until moonrise. When that pale satellite showed its face over the battlefield and the shadows changed, his fancy did the same. That old globe had looked down over so many different earthscapes and so many seemingly senseless evolutionary struggles, ranging from the soup of blindly moving life to the monstrous world of reptiles to the world of brutish human hunters; and now it looked down upon a planet in which one sixth of the human mass was pitted against another in a "war to end all wars." In writing on this particular battle Teilhard wondered, Was this bright "death's head" really only the blind witness of horror without meaning? Or was it, perhaps, a warning that if mankind did not unite and work for its own betterment, it, too, would end as a dead planet, "carrying the bones of all that once had animated it, through an eternal night?"[3]

With the fall of Malmaison to the Allies on October 23,

1917, the myth of German invincibility in World War I was finally shattered. By mid-March 1918 a desperate Ludendorff sent out seventy crack divisions along an S-shaped curve from Amiens to Château-Thierry, and the quiet countryside blazed up again. Caught by surprise in an advance attempt near Rheims, Pierre's regiment underwent a brutal three-week battering, until it stopped the German push at Épernay.

During the rest period that followed, Teilhard had time to think about his future and what still remained for him to do before he could be received for final profession in the Society.

Though the tertianship remained unfinished, Pierre was quite aware that war service was considered an acceptable substitute. Père Vuilliez-Sermet, the Jesuit who had supervised his abbreviated tertianship in England and was now master of novices at Lyon, knew a true religious temperament when he met one, and wanted to see Pierre professed.

But there were obstacles. Since finishing "La Vie Cosmique" in April 1916, Teilhard had often sent his essays on to Vuilliez-Sermet. By that same act he was, of course, also sending them to his provincial, Père Claude Chanteur, and to the censors he appointed.

That spring of 1918 the provincial's desk (and the desks of the censors as well) were littered with poetic, neologism-studded, utterly un-Thomistic, and perhaps even pantheistic papers written by the candidate for profession. Unlike Vuilliez-Sermet, the censors found the decision of whether or not to admit Pierre to full profession quite difficult to make. They adjusted their eyeglasses, ran their fingers through their thinning hair, and tried to follow the young priest's logic. But no matter how long they studied the papers, they could only see a confirmation of the strange impression they always had of him. Was not "La Lutte contre la Multitude" a direct denial of creation *ex nihilo*. What about "L'Union Créatrice"[4]— which could easily be read as a challenge to the traditional distinction between "body" and "soul?" And what about "L'Ame du Monde"[5] or "La Grande Monade," which both seemed to be more concerned with some kind of *group* beatitude than with the salvation of the individual? If anything saved Teilhard's essays from being dubbed clearly heretical, it was the simple fact that they were so bizarrely phrased.

While his provincialate continued to review his case, he waited with his regiment in the forest country outside Rheims. On May 5, news came that another brother, Olivier, had been killed in action on the northern front. To his parents, Pierre wrote the usual pained and helpless platitudes. In Olivier's case—even more than usual—there was nothing to be said. Ever since his participation in the bloody engagement in the Argonne in 1915, the young officer, for all his courage, expertise, and devotion to duty, had seemed sick with weariness. In a note he wrote to his brother Joseph on the morning of his death, Olivier had concluded, "I no longer hope for anything. I regret nothing. Neither my conscience nor my memory is burdened. In the mud of Flanders, I have found a formidable foe."

Quite unexpectedly that month, Pierre's superiors simply decided to give in on the matter of his full profession. They notified him he was to take the step on May 26 at Ste.-Foy-lez-Lyon. When the ceremony was over, he went down to Sarcenat on leave to comfort his parents, still grieving for the lost Olivier.

Meanwhile, the Germans continued to bear down harder along the whole Allied line. Soissons fell; Montdidier and Noyon were threatened. The trees of Compiègne reverberated like stringed instruments to the percussion of the guns. When Teilhard returned to action, his unit was in full retreat. It was mid-July before the Zouaves could collect themselves sufficiently to stage a minor counterattack.

The battle took place in a cornfield near the forest of Villers-Cotterêts. From the second day of fighting, Pierre helped drag the wounded out of what seemed to him the worst ground he had walked through in the war. Shells fell thick as hailstones, and abandoned tanks sank into the corn like burning ships. Low-flying airplanes riddled the field until it bloomed with corpses.

Since his induction in late 1914, Teilhard, who had conducted himself with sufficient gallantry to merit the Médaille Militaire, had at the same time worked to construct a viable personal philosophy to serve as a bulwark against his primitive fears. Suddenly, though, in that chaotic field, his intellectual armor fell apart. As he wrote to Marguerite, the field near Villers-Cotterêts seemed to have taken on a "supernatural" aspect. Running to and from the aid post, he felt that he was moving incessantly across a threshold "where that which is before death is in the process of passing into it. . . ." Throughout a full day and a half, he and two stretcher-bearers were pinned behind a tank by enemy fire, unable to reach a dying rifleman. "For the first time since the beginning of the war," he confessed, "I really considered the possibility that it might be *my* turn to die."

It took four days to conclude the operation successfully. And that August of 1918 the tide of battle turned a final time. The Allies, rejuvenated by the arrival of fresh American troops, pressed forward everywhere. On November 11, when Pierre's regiment was in the Vosges, the Armistice was signed. Still he continued to live on in the darkness of his forest-fighting days. Even the celebration on Armistice night full of tears, songs, and toasting with officers of his regiment seemed quite unreal to him; and when, in the wee hours of the morning, he returned to the local rectory to go to bed, he struggled hopelessly to fit a key, which seemed suddenly to have turned to rubber, into the lock. Finally, in some humiliation, he crawled onto the straw of a neighboring barn and fell asleep.

The advance toward Strasbourg became a victory march. In about another month Teilhard felt sufficiently healed in his mind to rejoice in the thought that the whole thing really had ended at last. That Christmas he returned to Paris for his brother Joseph's wedding. Though his parents were still mourning for Olivier, for all the others everything seemed impossibly gay again. Before the fashionable church of St.-Philippe-du-Roule, cold sunlight sparkled on the military decorations of the men and brightened the cheeks of the girls. Only Marguerite did not respond to the new gaiety. On New Year's Eve, when she said goodbye to Pierre near St.-Germain-des-Prés, they parted in such confusion that they even forgot to exchange New Year's greetings.

His patience with his cousin was invincible. "In spite of your 'ups and downs,'" Teilhard wrote her, "I feel that you are making progress. . . . I only pray . . . that (as I feel God has stabilized this year the deepest part of your life) He may allow a little of this stability to show in the visible side of your existence." Then he enclosed another pile of essays.

Meanwhile, the censors of his province, who were still examining his essays, began to feel uncomfortable again. While most of them refused to take him seriously, a few took him more seriously than he would have liked. There was a new provincial, Louis Chauvin, a gentle and very old man, who, with the best will in the world, had considerable difficulty deciding what to do with his relentlessly scribbling scientist son. In February 1919, perhaps in the hope that he could stop the flood of documents by loading Teilhard down with academic work, he gave him his permission to return to Boule as soon as he was mustered out, and to continue his science courses where he had left off.

When Pierre went back to Paris late that winter, he found it cold and rain-whipped. Frenchmen still wore uniforms, and an enormous population of visiting Americans crowded the streets. Every day the silver-helmeted Garde Républicaine clattered across the Rue Royale toward the Place de la Concorde, escorting some new foreign dignitary. While in the Salle de l'Horloge of the Quai d'Orsay a weary Woodrow Wilson argued with Clemenceau and Lloyd George over the disposition of empires, people like Teilhard found themselves caught up soon in an unreal social whirl. In his new circle of friends Teilhard discovered an apostolate in which he

brought, among others, the young Max de Begouën (son of
the amateur speleologist of the Pyrenees) back to the religion
of his fathers.

Marguerite Teillard had been awaiting Teilhard's coming
almost breathlessly. Now, she was sure, these two dedicated
souls at last could begin their religious work together. In her
wider (though still rarefied) circle of friends, she now included one of the first Frenchwomen to earn a degree in
medicine, the aristocratic wife of the Comte Melchior de
Polignac, and Marguerite's old teacher Léontine Zanta. Marguerite hastened to bring her cousin and Mlle. Zanta together.

For Teilhard, being "taken up" by Léontine Zanta was a
special compliment. A journalist turned professional feminist,
Mlle. Zanta was (despite her considerable girth and her close
to fifty years) a woman of a certain charm. When Teilhard
first knew her, she was already prematurely white-haired; she
had great violet eyes, a direct manner, and was so indefatigable a literary hostess that the irreverent Abbé Bremond
dubbed her "Hypatia." Among the portraits of Pascal and
Erasmus in her apartment on the Avenue de Madrid a few
steps from the blossoming Bois, Teilhard felt expansive. It
was pleasant for him to find himself in a milieu where he
could talk with well-known religious writers as an equal, and
even chat with a minor secular celebrity such as the play-
wright Maurice Donnay. He soon became a fixture at Mlle.
Zanta's soirées.

Only one month after his arrival in Paris, Marguerite
Teillard-Chambon abruptly left the city, announcing that she
needed rest and would spend her vacation with friends. During her absence, Teilhard wrote his cousin faithfully. And always with the same sublime incomprehension. He expressed
the hope that the quiet of the countryside would restore her
"tormented soul." By contrast, he noted, the hours of his own
life seemed to pass almost too quickly. He was delighted with
his Holy Week visits to his new friend. "Conversation began
with the first dish," he said, and he and his hostess chatted

away long after the other "disciples" had left. Then they thumbed through a newly published book by Duhamel, in which both she and he were struck by the similarity of some of Duhamel's intuitions to those in Pierre's unpublished papers.

More than ever, Teilhard continued in that letter, he was confirmed in his feeling that a taste for some "Tangible Absolute was the sensitive spot" in the modern soul. It was an area he wanted to explore more deeply. But before he could even begin, he had to apply himself to acquiring the scientific credentials that would give him the authority to make his ideas heard. He had to return to the classroom. But for how long?

It was, he knew, too early to feel downcast. All that he hoped for still lay before him. "My present duty," he wrote to Marguerite, "is to find joy in the fact that it is by *this* road, rather than by any other, that the Divine Action enters my life. Pray for me . . . *now,* while the limitations of Providence are still laid upon me."

# CHAPTER
# FIVE

*Praise to You, harsh Matter . . . dangerous
Matter . . . which one day will be dissolved with us
and carry us into the Heart of Reality . . .*
*Battering us and dressing our wounds . . .
struggling before You yield to us . . . destroying and
building, smashing and liberating . . .*
*Seed of our souls, Hand of God . . .*
*I bless You.*

This Shelleyesque "Hymn to Matter," which Teilhard wrote
while he was on retreat in Jersey in August 1919, was his formal declaration that he had at last made peace with the disturbing idea of the unreliability of physical reality. Though
for most people of that time, the Great War had thoroughly
discredited the nineteenth-century dream of progress, for
Teilhard it had done the opposite. He had just seen the material world threatened on the most appalling scale—cities
turned to rubble, fields to mud, villages to ugly scars—and,
though he had not himself carried a weapon in war, he had
seen death sweeping close to him time and time again. Two
of his five brothers had perished. Two other brothers carried
marks of the holocaust on their bodies. His teacher Boussac
had perished at Verdun. Yet, from that struggle—in which
thirty million had been killed or wounded—he had emerged
safe in his fragile flesh.

His summer trip to Jersey gave Teilhard a chance to renew

old friendships. The owlish Belgian Pierre Charles (already a theology teacher to the Jesuits at Louvain) was visiting the island; Auguste Valensin, his old comrade from Aix, now resident professor of philosophy at the theologate, had been eagerly awaiting his arrival.

Since they had had time to sit and talk again at any length, Teilhard and Valensin had turned psychologically in opposed directions. Teilhard came from the war physically sound, optimistic, and bearing his new-found trust in life before him like a banner. Valensin, in the manner of more traditional clerical asceticism, had become more and more of a pessimist in all that regarded "the things of this world." This outlook was not surprising. For him, the past ten years had been a constant struggle for life against diabetes and a cancerous tumor in his chest. While still quite ill, he had also been forced to battle for his intellectual integrity against the massed legions of Roman theologians of the Holy Office, as they ripped apart, revised, and finally refused the article "Divine Immanence" which he had written for the *Dictionary of Apologetics* edited by his confrere Adhémar d'Alès. In the same period, he had seen innumerable promising young thinkers knocked from their professional chairs for nonconformism on fine points of philosophy. He had watched the brilliant Rousselot so cruelly whipped into the outlands of the spirit that he poured his frustrated energy into a patriotic mystique and left for the front devoutly willing the bullet that took him at Les Éparges.*

When Teilhard arrived on Jersey, therefore, happy, full of new ideas and the delicious excitement of the daily progress of crossing new intellectual frontiers, he seemed like a wind off the sea to Valensin. As the theologian read his friend's brilliant, scattershot wartime essays, he felt his spirits rise. He immediately reproduced three copies of the "Hymn to Mat-

* "Rousselot est au feu, en première ligne. Il est parti avec une rêve: recevoir une balle dans le front . . ." (20-XI-14). Auguste Valensin, *Textes et Documents Inédits* (Paris: Aubier-Montaigne, 1961), p. 105.

ter," and several other war papers, for his old teacher Maurice
Blondel. Walking by day along the cliffs above the sea caves,
sitting at night before Valensin's study window, where the
salty air already had begun turning sharp with autumn, the
two friends talked incessantly. And when the Jersey theologian went off to winter in the kinder climate of Aix, he took
the duplicates of Teilhard's essays with him.

Teilhard came back to Paris in October to clear up the
work he had to cover to gain his required degrees in botany,
zoology, and geology before coming to paleontology. He soon
discovered that in the twelve-month interval since the Armistice the city had become a ferment of new ideas and life-
styles. It was what journalists were calling "the era of love
and gasoline." Fashionable young men and slim, short-skirted
girls with the figures of windblown angels parked their His-
pano-Suizas on the sidewalks of the Boulevard St.-Germain.
The once-staid quarter where Marguerite's school was located
had turned into a meeting place for painters and poets, where
the conversation was sometimes so brilliant that Jean Girau-
doux was moved to speculate that the war of 1914–18 might
have been "born out of the Germans' insensate desire to get
to Montparnasse." The political order too was in full flux.
Rightist and leftist extremists carrying red flags and led by an
aged Anatole France marched to the Place de l'Alma to
demand pensions.

In church circles, neo-Thomist aestheticism was the rage,
and the blond-bearded, clerical-mannered Jacques Maritain
was its prophet. His house at Meudon-Val-Fleury outside of
Paris drew an extraordinary assortment of visitors. Passing
Roman clerics mixed with celebrated Parisian artists such as
Julien Green, Mauriac, Cocteau, Rouault, and two men who
were currently reported to have had visions of the Blessed
Virgin—Paul Claudel and Max Jacobs. ("The fact," one contemporary has said, "that Max saw her on the subway is beside the point.")

Teilhard, who had been a spectator before the graceful

wonder that was Paris in 1912, was now a wondering onlooker before the festival of "Paris Après-Guerre." He lived now with the Jesuits on the Rue du Regard, commuted to classes in the Sorbonne and the Institut Catholique, and worked on his thesis at the museum. Somehow he also found time to work at clarifying the new way of regarding reality that had begun to concretize for him during the war.

Equipped as he now was with the tools of his profession, he began the task of stating his religious intuitions in scientif-ically acceptable terms. Since the Aristotelian "body-soul," "spirit-matter" distinction still did not make sense to him, he wrote new essays arguing for the action of one single person-alizing Process of the world. Though this process, he felt, had only reached its fullness in man, he now felt he could detect graduating "promises" of it through all the varieties of sensi-tive life, right back to the dumb matter which brought it forth.

Even the specimens on Teilhard's worktable seemed to confirm the instinctive appreciation of the fundamental Unity of Creation he had worked out in the war. Geology showed him an earth crushed and bent into strange mountain shapes, where the breathtaking chain of the Alps formed part of a single two-looped girdle of mountains that passed around the earth, even jutting up beneath the waters of the Pacific. Botany showed him, beyond the ancestors of man, an endless series of vegetable causes (whose links were often imper-ceptible because they were inevitably too fragile and too few at the time of this transformation) that led back to a simple chemical world. Zoology showed him a single line of human antecedents that moved backward fifty million years to such protomonkeys as the pocket-sized, big-eyed, long-legged tar-sier, whose splintered fossil bones he had first seen when he was cataloguing fossils for his 1913 Quercy paper.

The web of nature, as he saw it, was a tangled one, and full of hopeless knots. But at the same time, it was supple, almost always moving, blindly driving toward a breakthrough into

Consciousness. The instantaneous appearance of an "Adam" (or a "Peter" or a "Paul") without antecedents (and without presupposing for their existence an earth resulting from a vast sidereal activity) was unthinkable. Even if, as Teilhard did, one posited the existence of a being who at one time set the whole primordial mass into motion—a "Deity" whose omnipotence theologians had always limited by moral laws in declaring he could not sin, and by the laws of geometry in declaring he could not make a square circle—there seemed no reason why he should not also be, in some way, bound by the laws of physics.

In paper after paper, Teilhard worked out his ideas, mourning his Church's unwillingness to incorporate what science had discovered into its understanding of the world, criticizing the psychological "geocentricity" to which she clung psychologically four hundred years after she had ceased to support it astronomically, and rebuking those religious thinkers who recognized nothing new under the sun since "instantaneous creation."

With the death of Pius X at the beginning of World War I, the violent *intégrisme* had died down temporarily. Now it began to reassert itself. Though Benedict XV, the pope since 1914, was a relatively open-minded man, he too was old; and his government of the Church, like that of his predecessors, was falling more and more under the influence of a Curia which had barely changed personnel since the time of Pius X.

In a growing explosion of what critics called the "White Terror," the old Roman mistrust of "novelties" was turning to hysteria. A whole new dictionary of heresies—"ontologism," "semiontologism," "Kantianism," "semi-Kantianism" —sprouted up from nowhere. That spring Pius's Secretary of State, Rafael Merry del Val, began to exert such strong pressure on the superiors of religious orders and the rectors of Catholic universities to take a closer look at the orthodoxy of the philosophical leanings of their personnel that even the great Cardinal Mercier of Belgium saw his beloved university at Louvain accused of something called "scientism," and himself drawn into a struggle to keep the theory of evolution from being officially condemned by the Church.

Nor was it now only dogma that the Romans scrutinized. Since Leo XIII had issued his letter of approval of the thought of Thomas Aquinas, that philosophy had with each passing year acquired more of an "official" status. Right philosophizing came to be regarded as a prerequisite to right believing, and by the end of Benedict's reign, Roman seminarians vied with one another in parroting the textbooks of that "glory of the Neopolitan clergy," the Canon Sanseverino, and in quoting the man who had come to be regarded as the authentic teaching voice of Italianate Thomism, Réginald Garrigou-Lagrange of the Roman Academy of St. Thomas. "There were at that time in the Church four transcendentals: the One, the True, the Good, and the Opportune," the historian Pie Duployé has written. "And the last of these governed all the rest."

Though Garrigou had lived in the Holy City only since 1910, he was so convincing a polemicist that only one year after his arrival in Rome he had already been able to bring d'Alès to his knees with a demand for the revision of that year's edition of the *Dictionary*. Ten years later he had become more Roman than the Romans and, from a spare French cleric, had grown to a figure of nearer Aquinian girth. Many of the Catholic teachers now, particularly in his own country, walked softly to avoid being fixed in the glitter of his pince-nez, or arousing the bellow which (in unhappy analogy to that of his thirteenth-century master) could sound across Europe.

That year, the Jesuits came in for their own share of the trouble. Merry del Val succeeded in encouraging the Jesuit General Vladimir Ledochowski (a tough little Polish aristocrat with a military haircut, who had spent his boyhood in the court of the Austrian emperor and understood the usage of power) to set up a new, stricter board of censors in the So-

ciety for the purpose of examining the writings of its individual members and keeping a close eye on the "intellectual
tendencies" of the teachers in its seminaries. By summer,
Ledochowski had officially condemned "Rousselotism" and
forbidden his subjects to read or teach most of the propositions contained in the dead Jesuit's short essay "Les Yeux de
la Foi." The Curial clique, however, was not impressed; and
toward summer's end Garrigou engineered the publication of
an article in a Paris devotional magazine which asked that
Ledochowski be deposed on the ground that he had violated
the Company's constitutions by not pressing with sufficient
urgency that his subjects teach "a real distinction between *essence* and *existence* in creation."

In the ensuing reaction, most of Teilhard's more illustrious
friends found their professional security threatened. Valensin,
who scrupulously continued to mail out enormous quantities
of his own neo-Thomist manuscripts for correction, was permanently removed from his chair at Jersey and packed off to
Lyon to act as a substitute literature teacher at the university.
Pierre Charles, who from his chair in Louvain had been trying
to work out a synthesis between the antinominalism of St.
Thomas and the psychology of Duns Scotus, was indirectly
threatened with the loss of his professorship and fell "silent as
a tomb." The Scripture scholar Joseph Huby balanced carefully on the edge of his own chair and waited.

Unlike his confreres who had moved directly from their
studies to teaching posts in seminaries of the Order, Teilhard,
as an aspiring scientist, had had to begin all over as a university student in the secular disciplines he decided to pursue.
He had no students he could influence, no followers he might
mislead. All he could do was try to clarify his private vision
and encourage those with whose ideas he agreed.

In the summer of 1920 Teilhard went to see Charles and
the other adventurous intellectuals on the staff of the journal
*Revue des Questions Scientifiques* in Louvain. The visit was a
sobering one. Until he saw it with his own eyes, he had not

realized how much the avant-garde were suffering, how hard (while bending over backward to maintain a perfect loyalty to the Church) they tried to obey the dictates of their consciences in facing up to the questions that the new data provided by the scientific world imposed on them. "What we are witnessing, today," Teilhard wrote after Ledochowski's condemnation of Rousselotism, "is nothing more or less than a declaration of war by one kind of mentality on another. . . . Stifled at one point, we assert ourselves at another. . . . We serve the Church by forcing her hand."

By that time Teilhard had more or less completed his university studies. Still, he was bitterly aware of his own impotence to help his friends. During his August retreat at Hastings, however, he contrived an interview with the official Jesuit Visitor from Rome, a cheerful, youngish man with a reassuringly eager manner, who listened carefully, and left Teilhard convinced he was properly impressed by the seriousness of the situation. A little more relieved, Teilhard then joined Smith-Woodward on a sentimental journey to the Piltdown site at Lewes. But ever since the Wizard had died in 1917 ("of septic teeth," said a contemporary report, "while observing the effects of phosphorescent anti-Zeppelin bullets") persistent searches of the pit and the surrounding area had yielded nothing to researchers. This trip, too, was in vain.

When Teilhard thought of returning to Paris in the fall of 1920, he knew it would mean entering a whole new world. On the recommendation of the geologist Emmanuel de Margerie, he had been appointed to the chair of geology at the Institut Catholique left empty by the death of Boussac, and from that moment he knew that, like his friends, he would have a following of sorts. Then, with the publication of his thesis, he would mount the academic escalator from which France raises her power elite; and everything he did or said or wrote would be scrutinized by his superiors as closely as were the work and publications of the other Jesuits he had tried to help. It was a critical moment; and Valensin, knowing the almost naïve abandon with which Teilhard behaved characteristically, as well as the unfriendly eyes that watched out for those who might be thought of as speaking for the Church, could only stand despairingly aside and watch.

# CHAPTER
# SIX

Teilhard began lecturing at the Institut Catholique with a burning sense of mission. Although at first he had only two students, he was eager to take up even in a small way the battle of his friends. "You understand," he wrote triumphantly to Valensin soon after he returned to Paris, "how I have worked to secure this post. . . . I consider it my duty not to let a platform here escape me."

To some extent, his reputation had already spread. His prewar study of the Quercy fossils was considered a key paper in French paleontological research; and since demobilization, he had been writing regularly for *Études* and other learned periodicals and speaking on technical matters before learned societies. He also gave regular talks to groups of young Catholic engineers organized by Père Henri Pupey-Girard. In 1920, the same year he was made a Chevalier of the Legion of Honor for his war service and elected president of the French Geological Society, he sent his finished doctoral thesis, "Mammals of the French Lower Eocene and Their Strata," to the printer. That fall he also made the acquaintance of Édouard Le Roy, the pious mathematician with the forked patriarch's beard who had just replaced Bergson in the chair of philosophy of the Collège de France.

A man whose intensely personal piety made him distrustful of the Church's imposition of any one philosophical system in religious matters, Édouard Le Roy had long ago taken his place among the Church's devoutly loyal but anti-Thomist *maquis*. As early as 1907, in his book *Dogme et Critique*, he had suggested that the semantic formulations of Church doctrine should be thought of primarily as verbal tools, no more absolute in themselves than the semantic representations which science used to express its experience of reality. "All classical proofs aside," he once insisted, "the true affirmation of God is to be found in autonomous, independent, irreducible *moral* reality—and this is perhaps the fundamental one."

Every Wednesday evening, Teilhard would stop at Professor Le Roy's apartment for discussions which he often said, "did me as much good as prayer." In his turn, Le Roy found Teilhard's inquiring and poetic spirit an intellectual catalyst. In just three months the two men became so close it was sometimes difficult to say where the thought of one ended and that of the other began.

In December 1921 Teilhard's thesis was published in the *Annales Scientifiques*. The paper examined a collection of fossils of small animals unearthed near Rheims and in other places in the Sparnacian limestone deposits of the Paris basin, and compared them with earlier, less advanced fossils from the Thanetian sandbeds on the basin's rim. Teilhard used the minute differences in cranial structure and tooth formation in the bones of the two sets of animals to demonstrate that the Thanetian beds were a place of passage from one evolutionary phase to another, and at the same time to show that these animals seemed to have evolved in a way parallel to the fauna which the American geologists Gregory and Matthews had described in the "Tiffany" hydrocarbon beds along the rim of the Mississippi basin. In one stroke, then, his paper not only filled what up to that time had been a blank page in the history of evolution in France; it gave implicit support to Albert Gaudry's theory that, given exactly the same conditions, life everywhere tends to develop the same way.

On March 22, 1922, in the long-windowed amphitheater of the Sorbonne, Teilhard gave his *viva voce* defense of his thesis before a panel of impressively bearded professors and an overflowing audience. For him, it was not the traumatic event it had been for other candidates. Ever since his thesis was published several months earlier, it had received the enthusiastic approbation of most of his judges. It was even then being considered for a special award by the Geological Society.

One thing, only, gave the jury pause. In those days of open warfare between science and religion, Teilhard, as a "believer" who had taken up a scientific discipline, was naturally a bit suspect. Could he, other scientists wondered, really be as open-minded in evaluating all phenomena as a good researcher must be? A half hour's questioning convinced them that he could. The session ended with the president of the jury commending him for the "clarity of his spirit and his professional gifts," and awarding him with the highest honors.

If ever Pierre was convinced of the invincibility of truth, it was after that confrontation at the Sorbonne. But his very overconfidence was soon to lead him into great difficulties. Since he had bound himself to a religious organization to which he promised a quasi-military obedience, he was never entirely his own man. Only two weeks after the Sorbonne session, one Père Joseph Subtil, superior of the Jesuit scholasticate at Enghien, invited him to come to Belgium to talk about evolution to the student priests of the school.

Teilhard accepted the invitation, prepared, as always, to follow the questioning wherever it might lead. When, inevitably, his talk turned into an exploration of how, in the light of recently established scientific data about early man, churchmen were to consider the Genesis description of the Fall and the Tridentine doctrine of Original Sin, Teilhard speculated freely. After the lecture, two Enghien teachers, an orientalist named Antoine Malvy and a theologian, Louis Riedinger, continued to interrogate him. Finally they asked him if he would assemble his ideas on the subject in a written essay and leave it with them at the seminary for further study.

Essentially what the fathers were requesting was a theological opinion which was not per se within Teilhard's academic competence. However, he cheerfully complied with the request without making concessions to any religious scruples they might have about the subject.

He began by positing a priori the scientific impossibility of the existence of a historical Adam, or a Terrestrial Paradise (in the traditional meaning of the words) where the catastrophes of evil and death had been momentarily suspended. In their places, he offered three other possible explanations of the Genesis story, identifying the one he found most persuasive. He called his paper "Three Possible Representations of 'Original Sin.'"[1]

Fundamentally, the essay merely put a sharper focus on the concept of the universality of evil with which Teilhard had been wrestling all along. Unlike current theologians who were carefully dodging the "Eden" question with the premise that it was an event that took place so long ago that it left no physical traces, Teilhard took the position that Original Sin was a phenomenon that was invisible precisely because it was too large and too evident.

Returning to his old theory of Unity and Multiplicity, he maintained that because Matter always has a tendency to disorganize and return to its primitive chaotic state, the Creative Force had no choice but to enter into battle with disintegration from the moment It began creating. Because of the fragility of Matter, because of its inevitable tendency toward disintegration, sickness and death were necessary accompaniments of Life from the moment it existed on the planet. Later, when a world of reflective beings appeared, a new fragility came with it—this time in the moral order. In other words, "man sinned." The Fall of Adam described by Genesis, therefore, could, Teilhard suggested, be considered a shorthand description of all the human infidelity and cruelty man saw about him and within him, as well as an explanation of the presence of death and pain—sin's portents in the subhuman world. In his Epistle to the Romans, St. Paul had spoken of a world that "groans and travails even until now."* Was it not possible then, Teilhard asked, that when he composed this passage the first century Jew (writing more truly than he knew) could be suggesting that human sinfulness, together with pain, loss, and death, which had first preceded and then accompanied it, were the necessary shadow, the distorted mirror image of the Redemption itself?

Teilhard left Enghien in a cheerful frame of mind. But within two weeks, he began to feel uncomfortable about the whole affair. "As I advised Père Riedinger," he wrote to Valensin, "my paper represents only the first draft of a group of possible solutions, none of which are complete in their present form . . ." More theological research on the subject was absolutely necessary. Still, Teilhard complained, "Experience convinces me more and more each day that a cataclysmic representation of a 'Fall' bars the way to Christianity for many religiously inclined people who might otherwise embrace it."

It is remarkable that the priest, busy as he was with scientific projects, could find the time for so much philosophical speculation. Besides his work in Paris, he accepted an invitation from Louis Dollo, the director of the Brussels Museum, to undertake an investigation of the fossil mammals of the Belgium Lower Eocene, similar to the one he had done with French mammals. At that time he was also in charge of most of the Paris Museum's work of classifying fossils that were arriving, sometimes in thirty-crate lots, from the collection of the Jesuit explorer-priest Émile Licent.

Since 1919 Teilhard had been patiently sorting out the carelessly labeled specimens from Licent's museum at the Jesuit Collège des Hautes Études at Tientsin on the northern coast of China. Almost from the beginning of their mutal involvement, Licent had been urging Teilhard to come to Tientsin himself to help work out a sequence of China fossil vertebrates. To Licent's disappointment, Teilhard was never

* 8:22.

seriously tempted. Paris, he felt, was still the only place where he could fulfill his real vocation—that of assisting in the reconstructing of Christian doctrinal thinking so that it would better accord with the new scientific discoveries.

By May 1922 he had begun to wonder seriously how long his Paris platform would support him. As he wrote Valensin, he had begun to feel that he was "living a little *dans le feu. . . .*" He said he felt sure that he was following the path that was marked out for him. But his situation was wearisome in the extreme. At every moment, he wrote in a subsequent letter, he felt constrained to keep on building high enough within himself the "fire" of his sense of mission so as not to be devoured by the other "fire" of criticism directed at him from without.

By early 1922 Valensin was safely out of theology and on the Faculty of Letters of the University of Lyon. He soon became so popular a teacher that his audiences often crowded out of the classroom into the hallway and onto the flight of stairs beyond, and even made off with chairs to assure themselves of seats at future classes. But Teilhard's star was definitely falling. He spent the summer in a feverish round of activity, giving conferences, preaching retreats, visiting Belgium, and visiting in Lyon and Auvergne. He also traveled to the Pyrenees, to the Ariège to visit his young friends Max de Begouën and his wife and to see the bison caves on their property.

In the autumn Teilhard returned to Paris. As its wet, gray twilight fell, his spirit darkened too. He was now openly embroiled in controversy with his old adversaries the "moderate evolutionists," and was repeatedly accused of daring to design a "biological philosophy" that was at odds with the accepted Aristotelian-Thomist one. Unhappily, there seemed no way he could restore himself to the good graces of his superiors without denying those ideas without which, he wrote, "I could neither feed my thought nor maintain my faith." While his cousin Marguerite (for whom he had so little time since his return to Paris) announced she was planning to leave her post at Notre Dame de Sion "for reasons of health," to rest awhile with friends in Italy, Teilhard continued with his lectures at the Institut Catholique and cut down on his outside activities. Most of his free time was spent at the museum, cleaning and classifying old bones.

On October 6 he capitulated to his fate. He wrote Licent suggesting that he might be willing to go to China after all, but very briefly, and inquiring what such a commitment might entail. He was sure that the rector of the Institut Catholique would hold his chair for him; China was virgin territory for scientific research; and (he kept reassuring himself) if he gave the uproar time to pass, he could return to fulfill "his vocation" with even greater authority.

Licent, whose legendary temper had already discouraged many men from coming to assist him, was delighted. When he replied in December, he gave Teilhard the choice of anything from a six-month to a two-year stay. While wrestling with the choice, Teilhard gave a few more scientific conferences, and wrote for a philosophical journal what he insisted was a "persistent but nonaggressive" repetition of his views on evolution.[2]

The time had come for him to leave the field of battle for a while. But no matter how much he tried to rationalize his departure, he was aware that once he had removed himself from Paris, the prestige for which he had worked so hard was in danger of slipping from his grasp. Sometimes, as winter deepened in the city, his distress reached such a pitch that he faced the possibility that he might not even find a way to solve his difficulties. "Interiorly," he wrote Valensin in late December, "I am forced to choose between two opposing ideas: the one, the rather 'brutal' thought that nothing in life really matters except God; the other, an ever-sharpening awareness of how heavy-handed, narrow-minded, and weak is the modern Church. Sometimes, I find myself thinking, 'I want to be dissolved'† in order to escape this inner tearing."

† "Cupio dissolvi." Philippians 1:23.

# CHAPTER
# SEVEN

On April 10, 1923, Teilhard left Marseille for Tientsin, crossing many of the same seas he had sailed as a wide-eyed student missionary on his way to Egypt eighteen years before. But this time the voyage was a joyless one. The savage silhouettes of Sinai, the smooth iridescence of the Indian Ocean, the eye-aching blues and greens of Malaya, all the alien faces that thronged the ports of call threw him into a kind of vertigo. Never, he wrote to Mlle. Zanta and others, had the immensity and variety of the human mass seemed so overwhelming to him. It was, he said, "like going around the edges of a problem endlessly without ever getting to the core of it."

At a Saigon stopover, he visited the places where his brother Albéric had walked on shore leave at the turn of the century, and where a Teilhard d'Eyry had once been a consular official. At Shanghai, he knelt at his sister Françoise's grave, near her red-brick missionary convent in the French Concession. At Nanking, he took the "Blue Express," notorious for having been pillaged by bandits two weeks earlier, north along the coastline toward his destination.

As the train ground on, a monotonous landscape of patterned wheat fields, worked by coolies pulling plows, was succeeded by fields of green millet, and finally erupted into the sugar-loaf clusters of the Shantung mountain range. At every step, hordes of half-naked Chinese crying a cacophony of previously unimagined sounds moved toward the track, hawking trays of flyblown foodstuffs and exhibiting their misery. In his passage through that seemingly endless land that looked to him to be scarcely advanced from the Neolithic, Teilhard wrote to Abbé Breuil, he felt suddenly deprived of any "moral foothold . . . ," plunged into a world where the spirit as much as the body lay naked to all the winds of the earth.

Teilhard's arrival in China coincided with one of the most frenetic periods of its political history. After the fall of the Manchu dynasty in 1911, Sun Yat-sen's republican revolution for "nationalism, democracy, and people's livelihood" had succeeded briefly, then collapsed. That summer of 1923 the deposed President Sun was only a refugee on a gunboat off Canton, and the country had once more degenerated into a cluster of decentralized local turfs governed by *tuchuns*—military governors or warlords.

The *tuchuns*, each of whom commanded his own army, were a colorful, repellent, and even sometimes comic crew. Chang Tso-lin, a small, delicately built creature with exquisite hands and given to unpredictable black rages, was master of Manchuria. Wu P'ei-fu, a hard-drinking Sunday poet, was the lord of the provinces of Shantung and Honan. Liu Wen-hui was tyrant of Szechuan. East of Hopei were the wandering armies of "the Christian general" Feng Yu-hsiang, a six-and-a-half-foot giant who had first studied in Moscow, then embraced Protestant Christianity, baptized his soldiers with a fire hose, and marched them to the beat of "Onward, Christian Soldiers."

The behavior of the *tuchuns* was frequently indistinguishable from that of minor bandits who worked subdivisions of their fiefs. Local people were expected to provide for the occupying armies' needs without compensation. Poor farmers were bled for protection money—sometimes up to fifty years in advance. The average peasant, who cultivated a plot of land barely large enough to bury himself and his family, was completely at the mercy of the bandit—to say nothing of flood, famine, disease, landlords, and the *compradores*.

As the Blue Express moved up the hills to the great northern plains, the landscape grew steadily drier and less life-supporting. Vast stretches of pale green land spread out on each side of the track; high gray-blue or yellow hills, which had been stripped of foliage for firewood before China had a recorded history, jutted up like giant silt banks. The red earth and granite of the land were blanketed with yellow sandstone loess blown in from the Gobi. Depressed as he already was, Teilhard entered that wasteland feeling something even stronger than the stranger's usual unease.

His arrival at Tientsin did little to restore his spirits. A drab checkerboard of foreign commercial concessions, entered through fields of grave mounds, the city fronted on a harbor so muddy that for most of the year ships of any size were forced to anchor several miles out to sea and send launches through a bobbing slum of junks to conduct their business under the protection of their various navies. In the foreign quarter there were warehouses, factories, and heavy Victorian-style buildings, but little cultural or intellectual life. A kind of "sirocco" blew the fine yellow dust from the Gobi through the streets—"hot and melancholy," Teilhard noted, "dry enough to curl the pages of a book."

At the Jesuit *collège* on Race Course Road, Licent, his new collaborator, was waiting. Standing expressionless by his desk, with his powerful body encased in a long black *shang*, his eyes behind his glasses asquint from sinus trouble, Licent looked as formidable as any warlord Teilhard might have encountered on the journey north. Though the priests had corresponded extensively, they had only met once, in Paris in 1914 when Licent had come home, a rough missionary, awkward in society, to beg financial help. In Tientsin, however, he was in his element. He had built the *collège* museum to his own design and stocked it with fossils from the wildest parts of North China. He roamed the deserts there incessantly, sometimes covering two thousand miles a year, armed to the teeth, with only guards and coolies for company while a network of missionary friends kept him advised as to the security of the areas he wished to visit. Back at his museum, he watched over his collection with a redoubtable jealousy, in a building surrounded with barbed wire like a fort, whose windows he barricaded by night before lying down to sleep with a pistol near his hand.

Immediately upon arriving in Tientsin, Teilhard was sent by Licent off to study his collection, both the plaster casts of fossils he had already seen in France, and newer, uncast specimens. Teilhard turned to the task mechanically, still unable to reconcile himself to his situation. The apparently arrested civilization around him argued powerfully with his faith in social evolution, and the tempo of its life compared badly with the dynamism of the Europe he had left.

On the few dependent Chinese who clustered hungrily about the mission school—inquisitive, perverse, and cunning—he projected his distress. He wrote they seemed as "primitive as 'redskins' or Australian aborigines," and (what was more incredible to him) lived, as far as he could see, "in a spirit of complete utilitarianism, without any kind of idealism or hope."

What was not apparent to him at that moment was the fact that, due to the unequal meeting of East and West in China, a movement toward the future was already stirring. The nearby city of Peking was one of the centers of the new nationalist thought which had been born out of the encouragement of Western missionaries and the reaction to the intrusion of Western business interests and which was further nourished by the work of Chinese students returned from studies abroad. At just about this time, the first general dissemination of Chinese printed matter in the vernacular took place in Peking. There were several learned societies in the city, both foreign and Chinese, and some twenty institutions which laid claim to university status—three of which were probably as good as many in the West.

A sixteen-square-mile gold-roofed, red-walled city full of *hutungs* (small side streets), abandoned palaces, temples, and parks, so lovely that they seemed to have been dreamed there, Peking in 1923 was still one of the most beautiful capitals on earth. On one side of the Imperial Park was the Chinese Peita University, from which, in 1919, had come the twelve professors who met in the attic of a Shanghai convent school to lay the foundations for Chinese Communism, and where, for a while, one of the sublibrarians had been a young Cantonese named Mao Tse-tung. On the other side of the Peita, was the opulent, blue-tiled, Rockefeller-funded Peking Union Medical College—a research and teaching hospital which the magnanimous "Mr. Jr." had equipped with the finest facilities to be found anywhere in the world. Its anatomy department enjoyed access to an enviably large collection of cadavers culled from the mournful harvest of diseased or starved-to-death Chinese that the local police swept up daily from the streets. In the foothills to the northwest was the Protestant Yenching University, and in the center of Peking the Catholic Fujen University. Among the foreign scientific enterprises scattered through the town, one of the most active was the American Museum of Natural History's mission to Central Asia, led by the swashbuckling Roy Chapman Andrews.

In early June of 1923 Teilhard went to Peking to read a paper on Licent's latest discoveries before a meeting of the Chinese Geological Society. The visit was a revelation to him. In one single night he made contact with almost all of the city's small but active scientific community. He was introduced to the mineralogist Amadeus Grabau, the blunt, eccentric old man with the great bull's head, who had almost singlehandedly established the mineralogy department of the Peita. He met the slight, sandy-haired Davidson Black, head of the anatomy department at the Peking Union Medical

College. He talked with Roy Chapman Andrews, W. D. Matthews, and Walter Granger of the American Museum team, and with J. Gunnar Andersson, a Swedish explorer who had already made his reputation exploring the South Pole. Teilhard was surprised and delighted to find the Western-educated Chinese from the Chinese Geological Survey, Wong Wen-hao and V. K. Ting, Pei Wen-chung and C. C. Young, as easy to talk to as his own compatriots had been. By the time he was due to return from Peking to Tientsin, Teilhard was absolutely euphoric. He had never dreamed that here at the other end of the world he would find such brilliant intellectual companionship.

A few days later, dressed in work khakis, carrying saddles, weapons, and empty crates, Teilhard followed Licent out of Tientsin on his first Asian expedition. They boarded an antique train for the "Blue City," a rough village behind crenelated walls at the edge of the Mongol steppes, where they purchased letters of passage from the local madarin, then went on to Pao-t'ou to pick up mules, servants, and military escort. The goal of the journey was the Sjara Osso Gol, a deep gorge in the Ordos Desert whose sides rose up to a fantastic height on each side of a muddy little stream. Since access to this area was temporarily barred by the obstructionism of the leader of six hundred local brigands, who had recently announced his intention to round up all the "foreign devils" in the area and put their heads on fence posts, Licent turned his caravan north to Mongolia awhile, until things should settle down.

For weeks the party jogged across the powdery earth of Mongolia. The deeper it penetrated, the more spectral the landscape became. For days at a time, its sameness was unbroken except for an occasional scruff of trees surrounding a lamasery inhabited by monks in red or yellow robes, or, from time to time, the silhouettes of long-haired, big-booted Mongol horsemen, who followed the caravan with hostile eyes. That immersion into the Chinese landmass, more bleakly

mineral than the landscape of Auvergne, returned to Teilhard
a sense of physical and psychological well-being cradling him
in the "Materia Matrix" and the "Mother Earth" he never
ceased to love. Once more, as in his war years, when he was
often without the materials for saying Mass, he began to greet
the sunrise by offering to God as his priestly sacrifice the
Burning Bread of the material world and of his own unhappy
situation. He put the offering into words in a long essay-
prayer he called "The Mass on the World."[1]

After circling two hundred miles across Mongolia, Licent
turned his expedition south. At Ningsia, at the foot of the
Ala-shan mountains, below the bandit's turf to the east, he
stopped for three days to dig in a ravine eroded deep into the
red clay earth where an ancient lake once lay. Then he followed the line of the Great Wall of China toward Sjara Osso
Gol, his original goal.

While Teilhard stayed relatively silent, Licent chattered on
incessantly, emptying his rifle at pests and game, keeping
track of the distance covered by counting the revolutions of
the wheels of the cart he walked beside. The countryside was
fairly familiar to him. He knew the local farmers, said Mass
for them under the open sky using tabular earth mounds for
altars, and on the feast of the Assumption of the Virgin,
carried the Eucharist in procession behind brilliantly dressed
Mongol horsemen bearing savage banners and beating gongs.
When necessary, he even acted as amateur doctor. His medical techniques were makeshift and probably only fifty per
cent effective (gun grease, his sunburn remedy, probably
worked best) but they were certainly better than those locally
in use. During the digging at Sjara Osso Gol, Licent three
times interrupted his work to visit a farmer who had been
shot in the leg by a renegade soldier. He cleaned the wound
of the sand which the sick man's neighbors had poured in it
to seal it, berated the man's wife for her unwillingness to
make a bandage of a piece of cloth she had been desperately

hoarding and showed a clear annoyance at the villagers' "distrust of European surgery."

When, however, after four days of his ministrations, the unhappy Mongol died, leaving the woman bereft of both her husband and her drapery, the neighbors' mood turned ugly. Licent refused to be intimidated. He simply finished his dig and moved the expedition out.

After another month of prospecting in the upper Shensi, he and Teilhard set their tents, crates, and mules on large rafts on the north-flowing Hwang Ho and headed easily down river to Pao-t'ou. The returns from the adventure were enormous. In the fifty-foot excavation near Ningsia they had unearthed several hearths full of cooked bones of gazelles, woolly rhinoceroses, and ostriches, as well as chipped flints similar to those found in the Cro-Magnon caves of Europe; from the fauna deposits of the walls of the Sjara Osso Gol they brought back a large cache of fossilized bones and giant deer antlers which had been broken to use as tools; and from northern Shansi they obtained an extensive collection of quartzite cutting blades. When the finds had been examined, in his first real burst of enthusiasm since he had come to China Teilhard wrote the Abbé Breuil how delighted he was at the results of the expedition. Judging from the environmental evidence, "Man," he exulted, "was surely here!"

Although he had hoped to return to France as early as August 1923, Teilhard's superiors made it clear they they preferred him to prolong his stay in China. Pained and nervous though he was, he obeyed.

Tientsin in the winter of 1923–24 was drab, "colder and gloomier," he wrote, "to the heart than to the senses." The February dust storms burned the eye and made some of the foreign ladies go about in face veils like pioneer motorists, and the short daylight hours ruled out any possibility of social life. Teilhard worked late in the museum, classifying the new fossils and sending reports back to France.

To counteract his growing boredom, Teilhard began making more frequent visits to Peking. Among its brilliant intellectual company he could momentarily forget his problems. Then, when he returned to Race Course Road, he would distract himself by working on the Shensi fossils. He also plunged into a new clarification of his view of Reality that he called "My Universe."[2]

Meanwhile, back in Europe, a new pope had come to power. His name was Achille Ratti and he had ruled as Pius XI since 1922. But unfortunately for Teilhard, under his aegis the conservative factions of the Curia were as aggressive as ever. In December 1923 a biblical manual by the Sulpician Auguste Brassac, which had been used in French seminaries for a decade, unaccountably was placed on the Index for having taken what the Holy Office felt was "too flexible" an attitude toward the literal interpretation of Scripture. On the following August 27 a papal *motu proprio* was issued, admonishing Scripture scholars to remember St. Paul's warning that "knowledge puffs up . . ." and that "if anyone thinks he knows anything, he has not yet known as he ought to know."* In May 1924, a Holy Office decree on biblical studies invoked the admonitions of three dead popes against the "dangerous" spirit of inquiry, suddenly stalking the Catholic world. Things looked even less promising now for Teilhard. Though he had never laid specific claim to facility in Scripture criticism, in the early part of 1924 his friends in Europe wrote him three letters in as many days urging him to look to his own security. He professed to be unmoved by all the warnings. "People like us," he wrote to the mineralogist Abbé Gaudefroy, "are like Old Testament prophets . . . awaiting the same Messiah they did." For this belief, he continued, he was quite willing to die—"even if it means a death in the desert."

But the time of the desert was still to come. That summer Teilhard's permission for a brief return to Paris came at last.

* I Corinthians 8:1, 2.

By October 1924 he was back in France. The familiar wet
Parisian autumn seemed fresh and cool and welcoming. The
Seine tumbled gray-green under an opalescent sky; the Jardin
des Plantes was a glory of dahlias, daisies, and carnations, glittering in the uncertain light. Boule greeted him with his usual
gruff heartiness, and assigned him to supervise the theses of
two doctoral students at the museum. From the windows of
the old third-floor workroom where he had once prepared his
classes for the Institut, Teilhard watched mothers planting
brightly scrubbed children on the hired donkeys and ponies
that ambled up and down a path along the far side of the
building.

Memories of the China exile shook away lightly as the yellow dust out of his baggage. It was unbelievably good to be
home again. A young admirer, Henri de Lubac, stopped by
his apartment from time to time, bringing along another
Jesuit student, Gaston Fessard, to talk or to use his type-
writer. All day long, old friends—Paul Rivet, the Roger
Vaufreys, Paul Vaillant-Couturier, and Ida Treat—came by
his room at the museum to visit. Boule stood about, sucking
at his pipe and watching the uncrating of the new China fossils, while he growled from time to time that "before long,
the Father's bones will land us in the street." Some of
Teilhard's evenings were taken up by discussions with religiously concerned lay friends, who, during his absence, had
evolved the mutual loyalty of an embattled enclave. They
greeted him with the greatest possible enthusiasm. The happy
round of teas, lectures, and soirées seemed about to begin
again.

But suddenly one morning just before the start of the academic year, that whole bright world collapsed. In the mailbox
at the Rue du Vieux-Colombier, Teilhard found a letter from
Père Costa at Lyon, informing him that the paper on three
possible interpretations of the Fall that he had written for the
theologians at Enghien two years earlier had somehow found
its way to Rome. The censors there were horrified. Teilhard

was ordered to come down to the provincialate at once to sign a formal promise that never again would he write or say "anything contrary to the Church's 'traditional' position on Original Sin."

He turned the paper over in his hand. If it meant all that it seemed to, he stood reprimanded for his "irresponsible speculations" about a possible rapprochement between science and religion, and was ordered to put a pledge of future silence on the subject into writing. Such a reprimand, he knew too well, could mean a demand that he acknowledge the literal existence of a historic Adam and Eve, a serpent, a forbidden fruit —everything.

The night that he received the letter, he sat down and wrote to Auguste Valensin in Lyon, explaining his problem and asking for counsel. He knew too well the delicacy of his position. "I'll have to act with great prudence," he wrote, "to avoid being faced with an ultimatum with which I cannot loyally comply. . . . Unless I hear something to the contrary, I will arrive in Lyon Thursday, the twentieth of November, to stay twenty-four hours. Before seeing Monsieur Costa, I would like to talk to you alone."

# CHAPTER
# EIGHT

"Though other religious orders may surpass us in fastings, night-watching, and other severities of food and raiment," the Spanish soldier-saint Ignatius Loyola wrote in the sixteenth century, "*our* brothers must take precedence in true and perfect obedience—in the voluntary renouncement of private judgment."

Over the centuries, other Jesuit generals somewhat softened their founder's directive; and the accumulating constitutions of the Society eventually made provision that, in order that this obedience be exacted "in as mild and paternal a spirit as possible," a subordinate Jesuit might make "discreet remonstrances" to a superior when he felt his compliance might entail "danger of sin."

With this in mind, Teilhard had determined to try to compose an alternative version of the formula sent to Lyon—one to which he could in good conscience put his signature. He hoped to come up with a statement which would simultaneously reassure the old men of Rome, and protect him from compromising his freedom of scientific inquiry. It would be a neat trick if he could do it but, he hoped, not an impossible one.

It was dusk on November 20 when he arrived at Lyon, that ancient fog-bound clothmakers' city at the confluence of the Saône and the Rhone. Valensin was waiting for him. Once he reached his friend's study, Teilhard discussed his problem far into the night. Eventually he hit upon a substitute declaration he thought might serve. In it, he repeated his contention that his Enghien paper was only a demonstration of the possibility of reconciling the doctrine of Original Sin with scientific data, and offered his formal promise that henceforth he would limit such speculation to conversations with "professionals."

The next morning there was a nip of snow in the air, and the sky was dark with clouds. The two priests sank their chins into their coat collars and left the Rue Jarente together, turning the corner toward the Place Ampère, where the Lyon provincial's apartment was. The street they walked through was a narrow one, lined with shops uniformly gray and bourgeois. But underneath its colorless exterior, Lyon was anything but ordinary. For centuries it had been a fortress of religious intellectuals, a place of nightmares and bright visions, where mystical sects sprang up like weeds and God and the Devil lived side by side.

Before they turned the corner, if either Teilhard or Valensin had bothered to look behind him, he would have seen, across the Saône, the brooding mountain of Fourvière and the Old City with its ruins of a Roman amphitheater where early Christian martyrs had died, its clusters of convents and monasteries including the Jesuit scholasticate, its ancient churches, and most prominently, the recently rebuilt basilica of Our Lady, Queen of Martyrs, its exterior covered with a growth of fabulous stone beasts and birds and its golden Virgin leaning over the city in an attitude of benediction.

It took only a few minutes to reach the provincial's quarters. Costa de Beauregard had been pacing nervously. A dark, fine-boned man with a heavily clerical air, he was progressive enough to admire Maurice Blondel, but his adventurous mind was counterbalanced by so fastidious a temperment that he could not even suffer the use of blunt language in his presence. Now, elbows on the desk, eyes on his lightly touching fingertips, he sat and listened to Teilhard in troubled silence. Adventurous thinkers always made him a bit uncomfortable. He knew how effective the young priest had been as a force for re-establishing the intellectual respectability of the Order in Paris; he also knew that it was his responsibility to make his subject change his views. When the petitioner had finished offering his counterproposition to the Roman one, Costa only sighed. The best he could do, he said, was to send the substitute formula to the Jesuit headquarters in Rome and see what happened. Teilhard agreed to the proposal.

Though nothing had been settled by the encounter, when the interview was over Teilhard, to Valensin's surprise, seemed in an almost cheerful mood. He talked optimistically all the way to Perrache station, where they then sat together waiting for the Paris train. Finally, just as the first flakes of that winter's snow clouded the windows of his compartment, Teilhard smiled encouragingly at his old friend and continued waving until he was out of sight.

In the months that followed, he pressed on with his academic work. He revealed himself now quite openly as evolutionist. He put the finishing touches to a pointed argument to those "limited evolutionists" who contended that the paucity of fossil "missing links" in the animal series proved that evolution acted "only within established phyla."[1] In February 1925 he wrote a second paper urging scholars to use the conclusions reached by the more specialized sciences to construct a "systematics of life" as a new and separate discipline. In late spring he finished the key essay, "Hominization."[2]

This time Teilhard chastised the *scientific* establishment for classifying the human animal by physical characteristics alone—making him, therefore, only one small species in the order of primates. Man's capacity for growth and conquest, for transforming his environment until it seemed to exist only in reference to him, was entirely out of proportion to the small disparity between his morphology and that of his nearest animal relatives. Lower life forms had evolved tools out of their own bodies (hooves for running, wings for flying, fins for swimming); proto-man alone had learned to make tools quite apart from himself—tools that he could use and leave and use again. Once the hominid animal became *homo faber*, Teilhard believed, his brain became continually more self-aware until it crossed the threshhold into Reflectivity. Finally a uniquely human quality appeared—the tendency of man to identify consciously with the others of his species and to cooperate in common work. To this phenomenon Édouard Le Roy had given the name "conspiracy."

As the human "conspiracy" intensified, Teilhard maintained, so did humanity's control over its world. In the Neolithic age, man began to identify with different tribes and life-styles. Eventually, with the establishment of libraries and educational systems, man attained a true "race memory." At the time of the industrial revolution, when man's tool-making capacity was immensely enlarged, another leap occurred. Communications between minds great distances apart became almost instantaneous; and distant corners of the earth began to recognize their relationship to other parts. It was as though humanity was in the process of becoming one single organism with a single nervous system, tightening its hold upon the planet.

Some years earlier, the geologist Eduard Suess had added the concept of a "biosphere," or earth-skin made up of living things, to the older description of the planet as one made up of a hard mineral "lithosphere," wrapped around a denser and ultimately fluid "barysphere." In his turn (and in a leap from science to philosophy), Teilhard posited above Suess's biosphere the existence of an even more significant covering of the earth—its "thinking skin." For this, he invented a new name, the "noosphere."

It had taken unimaginably long, Teilhard knew, for the evolutionary *élan* to force dumb matter toward even the dimmest kind of reflective life.* Even working with his shorter, 1920s yardstick, he could see that, compared to other animal species, man was very young as a phenomenon of na-

---

* According to recent findings, it took uncounted eons before our earth was circling our sun, millions of years more to produce the most primitive living matter, and billions more for increasingly complex life mechanisms to evolve a creature which even resembles man as we know him.

ture. Man had, as yet, barely time to explore his own capacity. Writing in 1924, Teilhard did not dream of cybernetics. But he did see with an astonishingly accurate eye a whole new choice of possibilities opening in the human zone of creation. Though still very fresh and young, and therefore still too often childish in his behavior, man was standing on a threshold from which he could make undreamed-of progress toward individual and group achievement.

By the time spring came, Teilhard was standing in an avalanche of papers of his own making. As roneotypes of his essays were quietly distributed, read, and discussed, his celebrity grew. At Easter, during a field trip with Breuil, he stopped in to visit with Hastings theologate, where he found himself mobbed by the student priests (among them young de Lubac, who since his days on Jersey had been a member of a private group of students which dedicated its free time to study of the work of more advanced Jesuit thinkers such as Teilhard and Joseph Huby and which their companions ironically referred to as "La Pensée"). The young theologians of Hastings questioned Teilhard so eagerly that, as he wrote home joyfully to his family, "they keep me talking up to six hours a day!"

By hindsight, however, it is difficult to conceive of any way he could have spent that year that would have been more prejudicial to his cause in Rome. During the months since he had sent off his revised signatory formula, a Holy Office *monitum*[3] had condemned the idea that there would even be any such thing as change or growth in philosophy. By the time he came home from England, a bloc of conservative French bishops were so disturbed by Teilhard's influence that they complained to the Holy Office, which, in turn, put pressure on the Jesuits. The scientist's fate was sealed.

It had never required much to make the Jesuit general, Vladimir Ledochowski, take action against a troublesome subordinate. He shared with his friend the authoritarian Pius XI a temperamental distrust of democracy and a dedication to the extension of the Church's temporal as well as spiritual authority. In his years in office, Ledochowski always gave generously of his personnel to implement his pontiff's plans for reconciling the Vatican with all governments which were not "socialist."† With soldierly dedication, he poured out his resources to build and staff the new Roman educational institutions that were to help Pius realize his Renaissance dream of being a great builder-pope. In the light of the goals Ledochowski proposed for the Order, Teilhard's behavior was incomprehensible, and the notorious Enghien paper "De Peccato Originali" complete and quite subversive nonsense.

By the time the linden trees were green along the Tiber, the general wrote Costa his decision. This time he was determined there should be no misunderstanding. Teilhard, he ordered, was to bow to the demands of the letter of the past autumn, leave his post at the Institut Catholique, and, as soon as he could decently do so, betake himself from France.

On May 15 Costa recalled Teilhard to Lyon and relayed the general's orders. Teilhard was flabbergasted. For the first time in his life he was faced by a dilemma he could not cope with. "Oh, my friend," he wrote frantically to Valensin, "help me! . . . If I show defiance I will betray my fundamental faith in the fact that everything that happens to me is animated by God. . . . I'll compromise the religious value of my ideas. . . . I'll be accused of pride, estrangement from the Church, who knows what else! . . ."

But if he did not hold fast to his position, might not that act be worse? "Which," he cried, "is the more sacred of my vocations—the one I followed as a boy of eighteen? or my real vocation, which I discovered when I was a man? . . . How can I obey this order without making myself the victim of the very formalism I've always stood against? . . . Tell me, my

† One of the earliest and most passionate defenses of the compatibility between Catholicism and Fascism in Italy appeared in the Vatican-propagandist Jesuit publication *Civiltà Cattolica*. Again, it was a Jesuit, Father Tacchi-Venturi, whom Pius appointed Mussolini's adviser on Church affairs and liaison with the Vatican.

friend, that it would not be wrong to yield to the orders of my superiors!"

Outside his ecclesiastical world, nearly all of Teilhard's friends urged resistance. To Boule, the uproar was only further proof that no one could be a "believer" and scientist at once. Other, more flexible friends hurried to advise him. "Leave the Society," they urged. "Become a secular priest. Find a friendly bishop to protect you. . . ." "Vous êtes mal marié," growled the short-fused Abbé Breuil whenever the subject of Teilhard's attachment to the Jesuits came up. "Divorcez-la!"

If Teilhard really considered resigning from the Jesuits at that time, he could have done so only fleetingly. He knew too well what consequences, social and professional, had befallen other Jesuits who became secular priests.‡ Furthermore, he had been bred in the aristocratic tradition that insisted that when one gave one's word, one kept it—whatever the cost.

Depending, therefore, on the influence of sympathetic people more highly placed in the Church than he was, Teilhard waited, hoping against hope for help. Pères Mollat of Paris and Costa of Lyon visited Rome, and, presumably, pleaded his case for him. Msgr. Baudrillart, rector of the Institut Catholique, applied every pressure he could command to hold on to his promising professor. But to the men of Borgo Santo Spirito, such an uproar over the fate of one Jesuit out of twenty thousand seemed highly disproportionate. In the next months matters went from bad to worse. By June 1925 Rome was not only demanding that Teilhard give up his place in Paris; it was asking that he sign the November set of "propositions" including a statement of belief in the literal truth of the Book of Genesis—Adam, Eve, forbidden fruit, and all. To top it off, Ledochowski sent his spiritual son a personal letter, reminding him of how much "useless work" the simple possession of the "Deposit of Faith" spared the Catholic intellectual.

‡ E.g., Henri Bremond.

Just as Valensin had known he would, Teilhard had snapped the trap down on himself. There was nothing he could do but yield entirely or leave. After considerable deliberation, Valensin decided that Teilhard's best course was to consider the physical action of signing the document as a gesture of fidelity rather than a symbol of intellectual assent, and sign it. Fundamentally, he argued all the Society asked for was obedience. Heaven would judge the rest.

At that time it was the custom among the Jesuits to spend eight consecutive days a year in solitude, either at a retreat house or at some other unfamiliar place, examining their souls in the light of the points of "The Spiritual Exercises of St. Ignatius." Following a carefully regulated system of prayer and self-examination during which they exposed themselves to often-violent alternations of psychological consolation and desolation, retreatants were supposed to stimulate within themselves a complete abandonment to the Divine Will, as represented to them either by the "Exercises" or by their retreat masters. Since Teilhard had planned to make his 1925 retreat at the Jesuit *collège* of St. Étienne near Lyon sometime in July, he decided to put off his final decision about signing the proposition until then. Valensin immediately offered to come up and join him.

The same week that the notorious Scopes "Monkey Trial" took place across the sea in Tennessee,* Père Teilhard's battle between his conscience and the majestic stupidity of his superiors took place in near silence behind closed gothic doors. The result of his plunge into the "Exercises" was that, long before the retreat was over, he had put his signature to

---

* In that shirt-sleeved struggle between Clarence Darrow and William Jennings Bryan over a teacher's right to teach evolution in the public schools in a tiny town in the American Protestant Bible Belt, as the court refused one scientific technical expert after another the right to testify, Darrow finally called on Bryan himself to speak as an "expert witness" on the Bible. He so confused the old man with questions about the seven days of Creation and the Flood that Bryan lost his self-possession entirely. Bryan died soon afterward. Still, Darrow lost the case, and the law against teaching evolution in Tennessee's public schools remained on the books until 1967.

every single proposition Rome demanded—even though, as he wrote Édouard Le Roy, he had not changed his ideas or his sense of mission in the slightest. In some obscure way, he convinced himself that by making this soul-crushing act of submission he would win God's approval and help in spreading his "gospel of research" at a later time. The thought gave him a kind of peace.

But not a sturdy peace. In the next eight months in Paris, Teilhard's worry about his prospects continued to plague him. He finished his classes at the Institut Catholique and completed a new sheaf of scientific papers. His extracurricular lectures to student groups were still crowded to the doors. It was ironic, he remarked to Valensin, that the closer his hour of departure came, the more firmly established he found himself in a position to exert a salutary influence on the thinking people near him. Sometimes, even his extraordinarily practiced patience failed him. "I stand condemned," he once remarked to Paul Rivet, "by dolts and ignoramuses!"

On April 5, 1926, Teilhard boarded the steamship *Ankor* for the Far East—now, in every sense, an exile, uncertain as to whether he would see his native land again. He made only one friend on that sad voyage, Henry de Monfreid, a lean man with a pencil-line moustache and a level, light-eyed gaze, whose smile caught his one morning as he glanced up from a deck chair. They had, however, little time to talk. The stranger debarked at Djibouti; the *Ankor* proceeded on toward the Indian Ocean and to China.

As the days passed, Teilhard worked painfully on another essay, which he hoped would make his scientific views more palatable to his superiors.[4] Determined though he was to find some way back to Paris, when he faced the situation squarely, he knew that his only real hope for recall lay in the contract he had made with Boule, which demanded that from time to time he come back home to classify finds he had made in China and publish his conclusions. No matter what they felt about him personally, Teilhard felt, his superiors would have to honor that commitment, for appearances' sake, at least.

One month out of port, Pierre wrote his parents from the Red Sea. The weather had been mild. The nights were windless, with the ocean smooth and bright as milk. By day the water turned a brilliant blue, full of medusas and flying fish. "This morning," he wrote on May 2, "I witnessed a classic spectacle. A great blue fish, more than a meter long, pursued a flying fish through the water. Despite all its maneuvering, the unlucky creature was caught and eaten before it covered fifty meters. Then a gull appeared, skimming the water. Within minutes, not a morsel of the prey remained."

# II

# THE
# CHINA
# YEARS

# CHAPTER
# NINE

When he returned to China in June of 1926, Teilhard found it in an even greater state of confusion than when he left. The death of Sun Yat-sen in March 1925, at the very moment he seemed about to reassume control of the government, had left a dangerous vacuum behind it. During the next few months student activists staged demonstrations, and in the spring of 1926 violent uprisings seriously threatened foreign interests in the treaty ports.

By summer the Kuomintang party, led jointly by Sun's disciple Wang Ching-wei and the chief of the military academy of Whampoa, Chiang Kai-shek, declared itself to be the successor of Sun's party and set up a new "national government" in Canton. Real power, however, remained where it had always been—with the warlords. Adrift within itself, the Kuomintang received both rightists and Communists under its banner, gratefully accepting the military advice of such well-known Comintern agents as Mikhail Borodin, Vasili Blücher (Galen), and later the Indian M. N. Roy, and receiving financial backing from bankers or *compradores*. On the one hand, it encouraged the Communists in its ranks to keep trying to introduce unions among the peasant workers; on the other, it stubbornly refused them the right to organize a separate branch within the party.

That fateful year there were in China at least five million men under arms. Some lived under strict military discipline;

others were simple mercenaries, roaming the countryside in disorganized bands, looting, living off the land, changing allegiance from one day to the next. From nearby Manchuria, the *tuchun* Chang Tso-lin had just raced into Peking with the Japanese invaders hot on his heels and driven out that year's governor as far as Kalgan. A man who until then had never been put off by what he regarded as the "adolescent squabbling of the natives," Licent almost immediately on Teilhard's return to China assembled an expedition and started west toward Kansu province and the beginning of what had once been the "Old Silk Road."

By that time the country was such a tinderbox that even Licent could not cope with it. At the Wei River, five hundred miles southwest of Tientsin, his expedition ran into a Feng regiment which refused him leave to proceed farther. Since his guards and muleteers had been paid in advance, Licent simply turned east into Shensi province, where he could collect fossils and Teilhard could make notes on the Chinese Quaternary.

When he came back at last to Tientsin, Teilhard visited his friends in Peking much more frequently, still enchanted by the cosmopolitan company he discovered there. Still in great part under Western domination, Peking in the twenties remained one of the few authentic "ostrich islands" left in a shrinking world. Most of the Westerners lived around the Legation Quarter—a rectangle of tree-lined avenues, of chancelleries, customhouses, post offices, hospitals, and social clubs with assertive European façades and stiffly posed uniformed guards, and, protected on three sides ever since the Boxer uprising by the cleared ground of the glacis that cut straight through the city's middle. In and around Peking could be found human curiosities to suit any taste at all: proper diplomatic personnel, businessmen, scientists, missionaries, adventurers, remittance men, and even a clutch of rejects from their own cultures who had made a new world of their own far from the prying eyes of conventional societies. All the

Westerners to some degree acted out a kind of fantasy. They could live in Peking for as little as sixty dollars a month, in what today seems incredible luxury. In winter they rented refurbished Chinese palaces in the city and in summer lived at the seashore or in empty temples in the countryside, where they could keep strings of Mongolian ponies to ride in polo matches. Their world was one of entertainment and of gossip, of bowling games in Ming pavilions, of steeplechasing paper hunts, of an incessant indoor round of lunches, bridge, and cocktail parties, and of miraculous feasts which their Chinese "boys," in collaboration with those of their neighbors, could produce at an hour's notice, and at which a guest was often secretly surprised to find himself eating with his own monogrammed silver.

They created a society that an observer from later decades would find bewildering if not irritating. But to the contemporary visitor (particularly to one who, like Teilhard, enjoyed bizarre people and who had all the innocence and complacency of his time) the very insouciance of the Western Pekingese in the face of ever-present danger, what Teilhard was amused to call their "cynical serenity," only added to their charm.

In October 1926 Teilhard attended a Peking meeting of the Geological Society called to fete the touring Crown Prince* and Princess of Sweden. At that meeting the geologist Gunnar Andersson formally announced the discovery of two human-looking molars which he and Otto Zdansky had turned up at Choukoutien, near the "land of the demon foxes" outside Peking. There followed a series of parties at the Scandinavian Embassy, where the Prince and Princess stood like a pair of Vincennes figurines, greeting the guests at the top of a marble staircase, and then joined them to dance to the music of a military band and toast with the rose-scented wine served by white-robed, gold-sashed Chinese ser-

---

* As King Gustaf VI Adolf, he continued to be a dedicated hobbyist in anthropology and archeology until his death.

vants. From Peking the royal couple continued on to Tientsin. There, as the first snow of the season tumbled down,
Teilhard took them on a tour of Licent's museum.

The next month, Teilhard returned to Peking, where, despite the general political unrest, a Pan-Pacific Geologic Conference had convened. Among the scientists from New Zea-
land, Australia, Holland, France, and America as well as
China, he wrote, he discovered a new sense of being less the
citizen of one nation than a citizen of the earth. Still, his
awareness that the China assignment was an exile meant to
destroy all traces of his influence in Europe pained him
deeply, though he assured himself that, for the moment anyway, his time was better spent in China gathering uncommon
experience. As he wrote a friend, "I feel my roots are in Paris,
and I will not pull them up." Besides, he was never really at
his ease in Asia. He could not penetrate her mystery and he
knew it. He was painfully conscious of standing between two
worlds in China—one dead, and another waiting to be born—
like a half-dead tree he saw once near a pagoda at the end of a
flooded mandarinal road. The tree's branches were bare and
wizened at the top, while fresh green shoots pushed upward
from below. Once, when he contemplated that tree, he wrote
a friend, he wondered what it was that caused China's "creative power" to peak so often, then collapse again. Since it did
not occur to him to examine the question economically and
politically, he contented himself with wondering if there
might be some weakness in "the Chinese will" which made it
impossible for it to complete or conserve what it had built.
Perhaps, he wrote, the mystery could be solved only by young,
Western-influenced China, but not until another century had
passed.

The answer to his question was much closer than he
guessed. At that very moment the birth pangs of a new nation
were already well along. In April 1927 Chiang Kai-shek led
his armies northward to unite the whole nation under a single
flag. In Shanghai, Chinese workers and students (with Chou

En-lai, a former instructor at Whampoa, among them) staged a take-over of all major installations in the city in preparation for his arrival.

To the astonishment of the Réds, however, after leading his army to within twenty-seven miles of the city, Chiang suddenly stopped short, sent in his troops alone, and started north to establish a new capital at Nanking. Soon afterward he issued a document expelling from the ranks of his party the very people who had accomplished the Shanghai coup, and sent out by night members of the "Green Gang" and other Shanghai mobs in autos mounted with machine guns to liquidate the leftists in his party.

Some of them (including the widow of Dr. Sun) escaped to Hankow, where they set up a Nationalist government of their own. Meanwhile, in Nanking, Chiang became a Methodist, married into the Soong banking family, made friendly overtures to the West, and imported German advisers to improve his army. As the last blood of the April massacre sank into the red and yellow earth, so disappeared the Russian Comintern's old dream of taking over the Kuomintang and— for the moment—the Chinese revolution.

From the relative security of their concessions, the Europeans watched the civil war with apprehension. All year long, the tug-of-war between the rival governments continued. But in the north, where Teilhard was, things remained quiet. He had no trouble finishing his scientific work in Tientsin and finding time to begin writing "a little book of piety" which he hoped would restore his superiors' confidence in his good faith. He wrote it, he said, "as prayerfully and uncontentiously as possible." He called it *Le Milieu Divin*.

Though, since February 1927 the exile knew that at Father Ledochowski's order Msgr. Baudrillart had removed his name from the list of teachers at the Institut Catholique, hoping against hope as always, he thought if he could have the chance to plead his case once more, he still might bring about a reversal of the decision. Time after time he wrote to Rome and Lyon, asking for a brief home leave, reminding his superiors of his contract with Boule, and begging to be allowed to alternate between France and China for the next few years, perhaps with the provision that he spend eighteen months in Asia gathering data, then six months in Paris publishing what he found. His appointment as a "traveling" priest without a Paris post, he hoped, would simultaneously allay the fears in Rome and put him in a position where he would have scientific input from the East and the West at once. Though, as he wrote Valensin, he now occasionally questioned his own sincerity in staying in the Society, he still felt quite unable to break with it. He could not go back on his pledged word. To Professor Le Roy he wrote, "It's as you said it was in 1925. I still have just one choice: to be a perfect religious, or to be excommunicate."

While he waited for an answer to his letters, Teilhard finished his "little book of piety." He knew that no one could fault its fundamental orthodoxy. Try though he might, however, he could not change the fact that the perspective of the book could only have been that of his warmly earth-loving eyes. Its attitude also made plain that at that time many of the superfluous trappings of early twentieth-century Catholicism had become meaningless to him. The real focus of his life was "Christ—the same yesterday, now, and forever," and although he recognized gradations in the sanctity of things, a complete separation between the "sacred" and the "profane" was inconceivable to him.

Dedicated "to those who love the world," *Le Milieu Divin* espoused the notion that material Reality was the necessary medium through which man reached God. Teilhard defined the human spirit not as an insubstantial specter but as the sum and essence of all the vitality and consistency of the body—as "Matter at its most incendiary stage." To those who had eyes to see it, the world was an entity shot through within and without by the Divine Presence, "like a crystal impregnated by light," and man, at every moment, was acted on, from every side, by all the energies of the earth. When he worked effectively and conscientiously toward some unselfish end, man touched the "Holy," furthered by his self-achievement, and laid his life and work as an imperishable stone in that "New Jerusalem" which, through evolution, God had been slowly building up from the beginning of time. When man suffered, everything that he endured—up to and including the last, worst evil, death—only cast him back into the Hands of that Fierce Love which propelled creation forward in the beginning.

After months of considering Teilhard's proposal, his superiors at last capitulated. In great relief and with the manuscript of the *Milieu* in his suitcase, Teilhard set out for France from Shanghai on August 27, 1927.

But long before his ship docked in Marseille, he saw his old imprudences catch up with him again. A series of lectures by his friend Professor Le Roy, which not only espoused the very evolutionary views which had caused his exile in the first place but gave Teilhard full credit for his contributions to them, was reprinted in a Paris journal.[1] Very soon a rumor was circulating that the formidable Garrigou-Lagrange himself (now a consultor of the Holy Office as well as head of the Pontifical Academy of St. Thomas) was urgently pressing that Le Roy's "attack on all philosophy" be condemned outright.

At first some of his old friends in Louvain received Teilhard's "little book of piety" with enthusiasm, and there was even talk of publishing it in the Musée Lessianum, the press directed by the Jesuits of the scholasticate. But complications soon arose. Even his friend Père Charles suggested that the book would need considerable revision before presentation to a general public. Where Teilhard had meant *The Divine Milieu* to be a simple exposition of how one could love God *through* the world, there was always the possibility that others might interpret it as irreligious, if not actually pagan.

As the examination and reworking of the book prolonged

themselves, Teilhard began to lose his patience. In the lectures that he gave to student groups he began to refer quite openly to the themes he had outlined in the *Milieu*. To Père Charles, to Henri Dopp, to Joseph Maréchal, to all his friends in Belgium, it almost seemed that he was deliberately seeking a confrontation that would bring a discussion of his position in the Order out into the open.

On June 28, 1928, the confrontation came. Teilhard was then in Paris, this time staring across a desk into the face of his major superior in the country, the Jesuit French assistant, Norbert de Boynes. De Boynes at once made clear he had not come to talk about the book. He came explaining as plainly as he could that the Society of Jesus, rather than having been founded to produce a band of "religious pioneers," was conceived first and foremost to be the pope's First Legion and Old Guard. To his troublesome subordinate he offered a bleak ultimatum. Either Teilhard would agree then, there, and irrevocably to confine his work to strictly scientific subjects, or he would find himself relegated to some minor missionary outpost where not only would he be unable to promulgate his ideas, he would even be denied the opportunity to continue with his scientific work.

For Teilhard the whole thing finally came down to two questions. If his ideas were not to be utilized toward Christianizing a secularized world, how could he be of any service to the Church and the Society? More importantly, if his natural gift for synthesizing science and religion was to be suppressed, how was he to justify his existence even to himself? His arguments seemed to drop like bits of lead. "This man Le Roy," de Boynes inquired calmly as he closed the conversation, "is he *really* a Christian?"

From that morning through a summer of geological prospecting with friends, Teilhard's mind turned on just one thing: return to China away from the artificial constraints, the troubled eyes that followed him, and his own continuous awareness of the impossible position in which he stood. In

Lyon, where he visited occasionally, he sought the warmth of Valensin's friendship as well as that of a group of admiring theology students of Montée Fourvière, including de Lubac and Fessard. But Paris, the only place he felt that he could really be of service, was a desert.

On November 5 Teilhard left Marseille again, accompanied by the geologist Pierre Lamare, planning to break the trip briefly at Djibouti in French Somaliland to do some field work. He had arranged to stay with the mysterious Henry de Monfreid, the traveler he had encountered briefly on the *Ankor* bound for China two years earlier and since had seen once or twice at Boule's museum.

Long ago—and not perhaps without a certain childish pique—Teilhard had watched his family's pride in Albéric. Since then he had always cherished a helpless admiration for adventurers. De Monfreid was the adventurer *par excellence.* A gentleman of Auteuil who painted with water colors, wrote novels and outrageous memoirs, and made a hobby of paleontology when he was in Paris, he became in Somaliland the Moslem trader Abd el-Haj, blockade-runner, companion of slavers, and dealer in everything from pearls and firearms to aphrodisiacs and drugs. He had a fine house at Obock, a little factory and electric power plant across the border in Ethiopia, and a plantation rich with coffee and orange trees farther west in Ethiopia on the Harar plateau. Sliding like a blown leaf along the coral coastline in his dhow, de Monfreid was the bane of the lives of the French colonial authorities, who called him (as did many of his friends) "the Pirate."

The reunion with de Monfreid brought Teilhard a new kind of delight. After a lifetime of accepting his constraints with patience, he found in the Ethiopian adventure his first full taste of freedom. De Monfreid sailed out to meet him and Lamare. Then, while Lamare, taken with a sudden illness, rested in Djibouti, de Monfreid set out with Teilhard in his little boat across the bay to the Obock house with the long windows open to the four winds. After twelve days under

the house arrest the colonial government habitually reserved
for de Monfreid's visitors, Teilhard and his friend simply gave
up waiting for official permission and slipped across the border into Ethiopia.

For over a month the Europeans, with their tall, handsome
Danakil bearers trotting single file and carrying weapons in
one hand, made their way into the interior. After exploring
the rocky desert, they made a second trip to the bushland of
the Harar plateau. There bananas and eucalyptus trees and
mimosa grew in Eden-like profusion, and the rich earth fed
the multicolored birds, the antelopes, and the natives with
khat-blackened teeth with equal generosity. Baboons galloped
in tribes through the bush, entirely indifferent to the intruders' curiosity, while "our friends, the monkeys," Teilhard
noted, skittered through the branches overhead.

On Christmas Eve, Teilhard went with de Monfreid to a
Capuchin chapel to say midnight Mass. The room was small;
it smelled of earth; its open windows admitted the fragrant,
even breathing of the bush. The Danakils leaned their faces
on their weapons with candlelight reflected in their eyes, and
watched in fascination as Teilhard plied his magic over an
altar covered with a zebra skin.

When the Mass ended, de Monfreid galloped off into the
dark. The next day Teilhard set out with his bearers to
explore the pre-Neolithic world of the Errer Valley farther
south, where an ancient frescoed cave was said to be, as well
as the geology of the area around the Fontale volcano, two
thirds of the way from Diredawa to Addis Ababa. The primitive living conditions, the simple meals, even the occasional
battles with nests of giant wasps hanging at cave mouths that
often left his face a pudding of lumps and his bearers quite
bemused at his determination did not dissuade him from his
work. For the first time in his life, he felt completely free. He
woke at dawn quite automatically with the animals and birds;
at dusk he fell exhausted upon the ground into a dreamless
sleep. Health and a second youth seemed to be rising in his

body like a sap. When he bent at a stream to drink, the face he saw seemed almost unfamiliar—alive with energy, brown as an Arab's under his turban, its profile eagle-sharp. "If only my superior," he wryly wrote to his Parisian friends, "could see me now!"

In late January, when he finally left Djibouti, Teilhard used his shipboard hours to write "Le Sens Humain,"[2] and he immediately sent copies to Valensin and Père de Lubac. It was his first completely outspoken denunciation of the Roman Church's failure to respond to the aspirations of the modern world. Everywhere he looked, he wrote, he saw a humanity straining to move forward, to grow and conquer, crying for some Absolute in which it could achieve itself. Religion, he declared, must break out of the factious world of "verbal theologizing, quantitative sacramentarianism, and oversubtle devotional practicing," and ally itself with this forward thrust of mankind. "The time has come," he concluded, "for us to save Christ from the clerics, in order to save the World."

# CHAPTER
# TEN

By the time Teilhard reached Tientsin in early March of 1929, the Hankow government had collapsed. Chiang Kai-shek had moved his army farther north, united most of coastal China, taken Peking, and returned to his new and gaudy capital of Nanking at the mouth of the Yangtze.

The orderly regime at the *collège* on Race Course Road was just the same. But Teilhard now saw its peace and measured pace with different eyes. "The things that I believe in now," he wrote to Gaudefroy, "are very few: first, Christ; then, the world. . . ." If he continued to bow to ecclesiastical and Jesuit etiquette, he did so now for "new and higher reasons"—the most important of them being that "If I were to desert the place that Life has assigned to me, I would betray the World."

Teilhard's relationship with Licent also underwent a subtle shift. He had always differed with his colleague as to the form foreign research should take in China, but now the difference seemed irreconcilable. Like Boule, Licent saw the work of museums such as the one in Tientsin as French outposts on foreign soil. Teilhard's conviction was that scientific knowledge belonged to all mankind. At that very moment, in fact, at Choukoutien, forty miles southwest of Peking, on the site where Gunnar Andersson had found the fossil tooth, an international effort was in progress that was to become one of the most significant investigations into human origins to be mounted in this century.

Ever since the formal announcement of Andersson's discovery in 1926, the world of paleontology had waited breathlessly for further news. When the Swedes had pulled up stakes and left, the project was taken over by the Chinese Geological Survey under the chairmanship of the Belgian-trained Chinese geologist Wong Wen-hao and the "honorary directorship" of Davidson Black of the Peking Union Medical College. Since then, ten humanoid teeth, innumerable pieces of extinct animal bones, and the crushed skull of what seemed to be a human adolescent had been unearthed. For more than three years Black had been nagging Teilhard to join the group as "honorary adviser on vertebrate paleontology." And that spring of 1929, entirely over Licent's objections, he formally accepted a commission to work at least part of the time at Peking.

When Teilhard in April 1929 made his first trip since the Survey take-over to the dig at Choukoutien, he was astonished at the progress that had been made there. What in 1926 had been only a ditch twelve feet long and seventeen feet deep had turned by 1929 into the enterprise of slowly stripping away an entire hillside. Since the local people had always been coal miners or limestone quarry workers, experienced labor was easily obtainable, and that year the golden earth worked by blue-coated coolies was completely sectioned off in squares outlined in whitewash. The hardest rocks were broken by blasting, and a pulley system lowered the debris sixty feet to the ground, where pieces were labeled, wrapped, and shipped to Peking.

For Teilhard, a position with the Survey meant having a perfect scientific work with which to occupy himself while he worked out his philosophical description of the growing "Personalization" of the material world. He wrote about it in a paper requested by the Apostolic Delegation to Peking, a

copy of which he sent back to his little group of admirers in
the theologate at Fourvière.[1]

That fall, the yield at Choukoutien had not been really
startling. Pei Wen-chung, the young Chinese who was in
charge of working the site, kept the dig going long after the
coming of the Chinese season of the "great cold," its scheduled closing date. By December, when the ground was definitely too hard to work, Pei paid off his laborers and dismissed
them. Then, before shutting everything down, he carried a
torch to the cave identified as Locality I to take some final
measurements.

Pei passed his yardstick over the limestone roof. Suddenly
it scraped an odd protrusion. Carefully chiseling away at it, he
pried the piece out, cleaned it lightly, and examined it with
some astonishment. What he found, embedded in a piece of
travertine, was a good-sized section of animal cranium too
large to be anthropoid. Could it be related to the teeth the
Swedes had found? Aware of the possible value of the piece,
Pei wrapped it in soiled laundry so as not to attract the attention of any bandits who might be in the neighborhood and
carried it back to Davidson Black in the city.

By the time Pei arrived at the PUMC the following day, it
was nearly dusk. But by the standard of Black, whose habit it
was to do most of his work at night, it was barely noon.
When he saw what Pei had brought him, he could hardly
contain his excitement.

Up to that time, Black's career had been a seemingly un-
directed one. He had studied medicine in Canada and paleontology in England, taught literature at America's North-
western University, and come to the PUMC anatomy department in 1919. In 1922 he made a dogged fund-raising
trip through Europe giving lectures to get money for the work
at Choukoutien, with a replica of the Swedes' Sinanthropus
tooth dangling from his watch chain. A dreamer by temperament, he was often compared by his lively, bridge-playing
wife, Adena, to the spellbound, sleepwalking Mr. Toad in

*The Wind in the Willows*—a creature living in a happy dream "quite useless for practical purposes," forever following a chimera that was always just beyond his grasp.

Up to that night in 1929, Black's evenings at the PUMC had been routine. He was glad to be interrupted by the crowd of rather disreputable young men who habitually turned up at the lab to drink beer and giggle over his anatomy books and his curious private collection of human parts; or, as dawn approached, to be telephoned by Roy Andrews with an invitation to join him for a dish of scrambled eggs in one of the all-night dancing parlors near the Ch'ien-men Gate. But that night, with Pei's fossil in his hand, Black saw his lifetime dream turn into reality. After his peppery little secretary, Olga Hempel, called in to say goodnight, he locked his laboratory against intruders and, while the dark gathered against his windows, began to cut the fossil from its matrix with dental tools.

As the hours wore on, Black watched breathlessly as the faceless skullpiece emerged from the cleaned pieces on his worktable. The bone in his hand had come from an incredible being—a creature with the morphology of a Neanderthal and the cranial capacity of the smaller Pithecanthropus. He had been (Teilhard wrote Gaudefroy a bit precipitously after he examined it some days later) "as typical a link between man and the apes as one could wish for." He was ugly and inconsiderable; his small eyes would have peered warily from under a troublesome weight of brow; his nose and chin (if they were ever found) would be only an expressionless muzzle. He must have been somewhat hairy, naked, and quite probably a cannibal. But whatever else he may have been, he was in many ways the far-away precursor of the Mandarin, a sketch for that being which would eventually be present-day man.

While Black worked on the cranium in one building, Teilhard and C. C. Young worked in the laboratory of the adjacent Lockhart Hall, coordinating the geological and animal materials that were found beside the fossil in the caves. Christmas was coming, and on Morrison and Hata-men streets the market stalls proffered the indigenous red- or white-berried mistletoe the Chinese called "heavenly bamboo" and evergreen trees carted from the forests of southern Jehol.

As feasts of fowl and oysters followed one another in the various legations and the Peking Hotel, and the Chinese Salvation Army caroled relentlessly outside their headquarters, Teilhard kept Christmas, sometimes in the company of Black and his family and sometimes with the eccentric Grabau, whose little house at the end of a dusty lane near the Peita remained a mecca for the Peking scientists when their work was done. At the American embassy, a young military attaché, William A. Worton, became a special friend.

When Teilhard returned to Tientsin after Christmas, he was a full week late. Stuttering with rage, Licent denounced him for "going over to the Chinese," called him a "coolie," and made other accusations of the kind (Teilhard wrote to a friend) "to which 'in the world' one answers with a blow." Still, however unseemly the old explorer's language might have been, his accusation hit the mark. Interiorly, Teilhard had already migrated to Peking. There lived his closest friends and comrades, and there was the only scientific work that truly interested him.

After the face-down with Licent, Teilhard spent the greater part of his time in Peking. Because there was not then a Jesuit house in the city, he boarded with the Lazarists in their sprawling convent full of priceless gifts a Chinese emperor had sent to the representatives of Louis XVI, near the Forbidden City and the icebox-gothic Catholic cathedral before which Chinese merchants hawked objects *artis pietatis*. The residence had real advantages. It was close to Teilhard's laboratory at the PUMC; and he could come and go very much as he pleased. So long as he was ready to pay the Chinese doorkeeper for his trouble in letting him in at night, he could keep his own hours. He had easy access to friends—Sven Hedin, Black, Andrews, and the whimsical PUMC parasitologist Rhineholt Höppeli, whom he joined over long liquid lunches at the Hôtel du Nord—to formal dinners with members of the diplomatic community, and to the camaraderie of other, often rowdy, passing scientist-adventurers.

For the tireless hostesses of the foreign community, whose dinner-party equations were often exercises in higher mathematics, Teilhard's arrival was a providence. Though there was always a surplus of "extra men" in Peking (White Russian exiles, European and American businessmen, younger sons from wealthy families who received a small check monthly just to stay away from home, and who, if they found no legitimate business to support them, almost inevitably ended up in the opium trade), the Jesuit scientist was a different kind of being altogether. After he emerged from his interior crisis of 1928, all his old shyness and inner constriction seemed to have melted away. Physically he was little changed from the lean, aristocratic wanderer who had impressed Henry de Monfreid, smiling up from a ship's deck chair four years earlier—"that great devil of a priest, clear as crystal, about whom there was nothing clerical, unctuous, turgid, or shady" —but he now had a new grace and ease. Silhouetted in a moon door in impeccably tailored clerical black, walking, both hands extended in greeting, through the ambiguous shadows of a wintry Chinese garden, his face like old wood on which the lines were prematurely etched, his bright Voltairean glance turning to a sunburst smile at the sight of an old friend or a sympathetic lady, he was a man of extraordinary charm. Further—for some of his new friends at least— he carried with him a mysterious aura of secret sorrow and a legend of persecution by his Church that made him irresistible.

Though Teilhard had not, at first, much facility in English, he reserved a special affection for that small circle whom he called "my Americans." To his European eye, they seemed endearingly easy, friendly, and generous, ungrudgingly appreciative of his skill, and opulently equipped with all the technical facilities imaginable for pursuing scientific work. He remarked to Gaudefroy that he regretted he could find no "priestly apostolate" in Peking; but he did have a group of devoted friends on whom he tried to be a salutary influence. To Roy Chapman Andrews, he was "the French savant"; to George Barbour, "one of those few human beings" he had ever met who had "the power to think beyound the rest"; to Mrs. Lucile Swan, an American sculptress who went to China in 1929, "one of the most fascinating men I ever met."

Before her death in 1965 Mrs. Swan recalled her meeting with Teilhard at one of Grabau's evening parties. While on a round-the-world trip in flight from unhappy memories of her past life, she had come to Peking. Behind her, she left visions of a stormy and finally broken marriage. An ample, vigorous woman with crinkly hair, a warm smile, and a Bohemian disdain for the frivolities of fashion, she was hardly a stunning ornament at the old geologist's table. But she was that relatively rare commodity in Peking, the unattached, respectable female.

As Mrs. Swan later remembered it, she was seated next to Père Teilhard at the table. Her conversation with the tall, handsome stranger with the clingingly accented English began with her inquiring "what kind of 'ologist'" he was. Teilhard laughed, explaining his scientific credentials and his association with the Geological Survey. He said he was a priest, and surprised her by going on to say that, for him, science was a support rather than a contradiction for the probability of the existence of a God. To Mrs. Swan's amazement, as she sat in the dusk sipping Rhine wine at a Manchurian table at the world's end, looking into those warm and probing eyes, she found herself speculating about the meaning of her existence as she had never dreamt it possible for her to do with a total stranger until then.

"My stay in Peking gave me many things," she concluded

in later years, "a new interest in my work, friends I could expose my troubles to with confidence, and most of all—from Pierre's conversations alone—the conviction that I needed to find a relationship with a Higher Power in my life. . . . Though I never returned to any Church (it always seemed to me Pierre was trying to start a religion of his own), after a few weeks of seeing him daily, I, too, began to feel a confidence in what he called 'the primacy of the spiritual.' . . . I was almost forty, but for the first time in years I felt young and full of hope again. I decided to prolong my stay in China."

# CHAPTER
# ELEVEN

The early months of 1930, Teilhard wrote the Abbé Gaude-froy, slipped like sand between his fingers. Peking in the deep of winter was a place of such lovely irreality that everything beyond its great red walls dimmed in the minds of its visitors. The city was deep in snow that year, and beyond the low, curved roofs, the Western Hills shone pearly against a sky of incredible blue. Through lanes scarred with tracks of rick-shaws and barrows the Chinese, wearing heavy sheepskin or fur-collared, padded cotton coats and sometimes three-cor-nered hats like Renaissance Venetians, pattered soundlessly along. Vendors hawked hot chestnuts and fragrant sweet po-tatoes on the corners. Europeans skated on the frozen moat around the walls of the Forbidden City and on the flooded tennis court of the International Club. From time to time an eager student could be found there, skating on the glassy ice the shape of the Chinese characters he was trying to commit to memory.

Peking's inimitable conglomerate of whines, chatter and chants, gongs, bells, and clappers—its sweet smells simulta-neously spicy and nauseous—by now were quite familiar to Teilhard. In the stinging clarity of that winter air, he worked with remarkable facility. In just four months he finished his contributions to the monograph Black was writing about the Sinanthropus, drew up outlines for several papers of his own on the geology of the Chinese Tertiary and Quaternary, and continued to make notes for new religio-scientific essays.

Mrs. Swan had settled down in an abandoned temple on a *hutung* in the west of the Tartar City, where she allowed herself to be flamboyantly courted by a Swedish trader several years her junior. She gave sculpturing lessons to the ladies of the Western community, but every afternoon reserved teatime for Père Teilhard. Day after day, sometimes for her alone, sometimes for groups of other women friends, he came to her austerely furnished, pillared parlor and articulated his philosophical ideas over nut cookies and toast with jam.

Pressures to join the Peking social round that year were heavy, and messengers bearing chit books of invitations came daily to Teilhard's Lazarist convent gate. The discovery of the Sinanthropus had, in fact, endowed all the scientists of Choukoutien with unexpected glamour, and provided the other Westerners with as much excitement as if one of their neighbors had turned up a giant emerald under the bricks of his courtyard. One hostess even circulated the story that when her Chinese "boy" had called to drop a note into the door slot of one of the scientists' houses, he had seen it whisked away by a hairy hand, heard a simian gallop back and forth across the courtyard, then saw the reply poked through the slot by the same improbable hand.

That April, just as Roy Chapman Andrews finished preparations for his museum team's last expedition into the Gobi, Teilhard was returning from a field trip to Manchuria. Despite the fact that Teilhard did not then and never would know one word of Chinese, because of his official connections with the Chinese Geological Survey and because his reputation had already pricked the interest of the museum's head back in New York, J. P. Morgan's nephew the quirkily pious Henry Fairfield Osborn,* Andrews asked Teilhard to come along. The next week, wearing the expedition's regulation

---

* At about that time Osborn was unsuccessfully campaigning to have a statue of "Saint" Louis Pasteur erected in Riverside Church, rather than a commemorative panel in the relief commemorating all great human thinkers.

caps with ear flaps and heavily lined coats, the team piled into cars and headed out into the desert.

For most of the early summer they prowled the yellow dunes and gray crags of the Gobi, carrying water with them as they went. The venture was enormously successful. On the rim of a dried-up lake more than 2½ million years old, researchers came upon bones of fifteen great shovel-toothed mastodons, sunk eons ago in primeval quicksand. Fifty miles to the west of that lake, in an escarpment possibly 36 million years older, they found a huge câche of bones of monstrous animals including giant pigs and that claw-footed animal, something between a rhinoceros and a horse, that is still on display in the museum's fourth-floor Hall of Mammals. When the party returned to Peking to crate their haul, the expedition members were surprised to find they had some ninety cases of fossil material to ship back to the States.

While Andrews prepared for a triumphant return to America, Teilhard looked forward to his trip to France that fall with considerably less enthusiasm. His father's health was failing, and Sarcenat, he knew, would be full of gloom. In Paris, where Marguerite Teillard-Chambon (writing under the pen name Claude Aragonnès) continued to build her reputation after the publication of her prize-winning but neurasthenic novel *La Loi du Faible,*[1] the story of a beautiful and brilliant woman who sacrifices herself to the blind, egocentric cousin she had loved since adolescence, he foresaw wearing social obligations. Then, too, there was the bitter fact that the tension between him and Rome had not eased at all. The diocesan censor of Malines had already refused permission for the publication in the *Revue des Questions Scientifiques* of a little essay he had written on transformism, and the censors of his own Order were now demanding a second revision of his beloved *Milieu Divin.*

Teilhard's home visit from September to December 1930 was, therefore, necessarily a short one. The only purely carefree memories it left him with related to his conferences with the automobile maker André Citroën, who the year before had invited him through diplomatic channels in China to join his projected expedition across Asia.

The Citroën crossing, which was to begin in early 1931, was a long-cherished dream of the company's second-in-command, Georges-Marie Haardt, a high-strung, dandyish fellow who had participated in two earlier such crossings in the Sahara and in Alaska. The Asia trip, however, was to be Haardt's personal moment of glory—the longest continuous, scientifically documented motor transit in history, in which some thirty to fifty travelers, including technicians, military men, artists, doctors, photographers, journalists, and scientists, would travel in fifteen Citroën C-6 halftracks eight thousand miles from the Mediterranean to the China Sea. Despite civil strife in Russia and in Asia, despite incredible physical obstacles (torrential rivers, perpendicular mountains, and the alternately hot or glacial Gobi), Haardt dreamed about the trip, as one commentator has said, "like a paralytic going to Lourdes."

On his way back to China, Teilhard stopped in America on expedition business with people from the National Geographic Society in Washington who planned to come along on the trip. While in New York, he dropped by the Museum of Natural History for several days to enjoy a bit of clubmanship with Fairfield Osborn. From there, he crossed the continent by train, pausing only once in Chicago to visit Henry Field, and sailed from the West Coast. Since he traveled only in the company of the privileged and comfortable, Teilhard passed through the nation sheltered from the sights and shocks of the Depression. He never saw the desperate sharecroppers or the long lines of the hungry unemployed. And, unlike Duhamel, who visited America a short time earlier and was appalled at its "vulgarity," Teilhard was awed at its size, abundance, and resilience.

Sailing out of San Francisco Bay, he took time to explore the new kind of "soul" that he believed he sensed in America. In a lyrical essay that he called "The Spirit of the Earth," he examined the "conspiracy" of individuals from every class and background he believed he had just seen engaged in a great effort to raise mankind to a new, higher stage. America's vast resources and her apparently boundless energy reminded him that the possibilities still open to the human race were much too large to be absorbed by "the old individual and national groupings which up to now have served the architects of the Earth. . . ." "We try to build 'a great house' bigger," he wrote, "and always to the same design as our familiar dwelling place." But now, he felt, the old structural designs no longer worked. Mankind could not remain divided if it was to open itself to its own highest possibilities. "The Age of Nations is now over," he announced triumphantly. "The time has come for men to shake off their ancient prejudices and turn together to building the earth."[2]

When Teilhard came back to Tientsin in the early spring of 1931, preparations for the Citroën expedition had been completed. The party was divided into two groups: one, under the command of Haardt and Louis Audoin-Dubreuil, set out eastward from Beirut; the other, to which Teilhard belonged, was under a young naval lieutenant named Victor Point, and traveled west from Peking. The two arms of the expedition were to meet in midsummer at the ancient fortified city of Kashgar in the mountains of Sinkiang; then both groups would return together to Peking.

On a chilly April morning, in a halo of dust and a "whirr like the sound of low-flying airplanes,"[3] Haardt's trucks and tractors rolled toward the old Damascus Road out of Beirut. Though Soviet complaints had already caused them to decide to reroute their expedition to avoid all Russian territory, once they began clattering merrily through the deserts of Syria and Persia and the rougher land of Afghanistan, they ran into other diplomatic problems. At the Khyber Pass they were surprised to be confronted by embarrassed British representatives, edgy at the prospect of this mechanized troop of starry-eyed adventurers rattling through an outland full of tribes which even they had difficulty keeping peaceful. The British suggested to Haardt that the route which would probably provoke the least tribal upset was by the Gilgit Road, which, unfortunately, meant crossing the Himalayas, the Karakoram mountain range, and the Hindu Kush.

The change in plans demanded that the expedition dismantle its machines and carry the parts over the treacherous mountains on horseback, but Haardt's determination to reach his rendezvous point was unshaken. For sixty-five days his team climbed the north Indian mountains, forded raging torrents or ferried their trucks across with block and tackle, lashed their cars to sheer cliffsides, and slid on horseback through the virgin snows of the roof of the world. At last, on September 16, they rolled wearily down to a valley of vineyards, melon fields, and flower gardens, and the Chinese city of Kashgar.

The natives there, unhappily, were far from friendly. After accusing the travelers of everything from being a French expedition sent to unseat the government of Sinkiang to being a belligerent foreign mechanized unit advancing on Peking, two hundred Chinese soldiers "escorted" them northeast for six days more to the city of Aksu, from where they were summarily refused permission to proceed.

Meanwhile, on the other side of the continent, Point's arm of the expedition had its own share of trouble. Beyond Kalgan, the Gobi grew consistently drier and more impassible. Hoarding their water, the members of the expedition scratched their way across deceptive seas of loess with weird granite outcroppings and dead-end ravines, moving on relentlessly in the face of blinding sandstorms, incessant mechanical failure, and (in Kansu province) a bloody Chinese civil war.

It is difficult to analyze the nature of the determination that held them to their course. For the most part, they seemed driven on by nerve alone. But for Teilhard, who had written that "the greatest recompense of research lies in arriving at the point where reality appears in its deepest and most virginal state," the crossing was a genuine religious pilgrimage.

The climax of the journey came for him with the descent into the rarely visited Turfan basin—a fertile hollow five hundred feet below sea level, where the glittering little Tarim River rushed with tremendous force through the wild poplars into the Lop Nor—the heart, as Teilhard saw it, of "one of the most sacred and mysterious" geologic regions of Upper Asia. On two sides of the valley, the shining pile of the Tien Shan range rose to breathtaking heights. These mountains, whose ancient, finely worn upthrusts of rock bore calcite elements dating back to the Primary era, were among the oldest in China. And in deposits washed down into the basin, he believed, a careful researcher might find sediment dating back millions of years, and be able to decipher many of the geologic movements which created the morphology of Upper Asia.

But Turfan was just as hostile to Point's group as Aksu had been to Haardt's. A few days after their arrival, a delegation from the group was summoned north to Urumchi to talk to the local "governor," one Marshal King.

King's reception of the travelers was decidedly a cool one. A few days after their visit, the governor's ambassador, a little man bobbing politely in a long scholar's gown and derby hat, came in to explain. The marshal, he protested, was engaged in his own war. He had almost no mechanized equipment, and since the Frenchmen had so much, he thought it would be a nice gesture on their part if they would turn their cars and wireless over to him and finish their trip on horseback. If they did, arrangements could, of course, be made to let them leave at once.

After a surreptitious wireless conversation with Haardt, then still on the other side of the Tien Shan, Point promised the governor that the Citroën company would send him the automobiles via Moscow. Cautiously the marshal gave Point,

Teilhard, and a few others permission to make the six-hundred-mile trip along the southern rim of the Tien Shan to bring Haardt to Urumchi.

After the reunion, there was nothing left to do but stop and wait for the arrival of their ransom. The marshal "entertained" them at exasperating length with lunches, dinner dances, and the company of an exotically robed Mongol princess, whom they met one day sitting outside a primitive tent, crooning a song of Mistinguett's. The princess was as anxious to get away from Sinkiang as they were. Still, it was not until November that a dusty Citroën functionary appeared on the Urumchi road with three sedans and several crates of radio equipment. Visas were delivered all around, and the party started eastward toward Peking.

At high noon on February 12, 1932, Haardt led his expedition onto the grounds of the French legation in the Foreign Quarter.

Finally, the receptions, the military honors, the plaudits, of the press—all the glory he had dreamed of for so long—were his. But his triumph was short-lived. Three weeks to the day after entering Peking, Haardt was felled by a violent pulmonary attack and died in Hong Kong. Back in France, a few months later, the irrepressibly romantic Victor Point died, too, a suicide over the infidelity of a pretty actress who had been his mistress.

Teilhard settled back in Peking with a sharp feeling of disappointment over the missed opportunities for serious geological investigation of the terrain that he had crossed, the long weeks wasted as a prisoner at Urumchi, and the unhappy anticlimax of the expedition. But this was only the beginning. Waiting for him in Peking had been a letter from his brother Joseph telling him that his father had died that New Year's Eve while he was in the Gobi. Another letter, from his cousin Marguerite, had advised him that the Holy Office in Rome not only had put several of the early works of his friend Édouard Le Roy on the Index of Forbidden Books but had demanded an immediate public retraction of the ideas espoused therein.

After rushing off a letter of consolation to his mother, Teilhard wrote an explosive one to Le Roy. "You must know, my dear friend," he said, "how much I, too, feel this last blow! . . . The people who condemn you are simply incapable of recognizing anything as true unless they hear it in the vocabulary they learned when they were schoolboys. . . . If this sort of thing keeps up, I feel I well may die in the arms of the World, rather than in those of the Church!"

When he did go back to France reluctantly that autumn, he found the psychological climate hopelessly oppressive. Despite Valensin's continuing intervention in his behalf, his new Jesuit provincial, Christophe de Bonneville, had set his face against Teilhard. Professor Le Roy, following the same logic he had urged on the young priest during his own crisis of obedience in 1925, had already signed a recantation of his works, adding (for what it was worth) that he could not make head or tail out of the condemnation. In October the Oratorian biblical scholar Lucien Laberthonnière, long a whipping boy of the conservative Catholic press, died piously but "in a crisis of melancholy and without a sou." At the same time, Teilhard learned that an unretouched early copy of his *Milieu Divin* had been spirited off to Rome, where it was being icily examined. For one awful moment it seemed entirely possible that the whole body of his work might be condemned, just as the work of Pierre Rousselot had been condemned ten years before.

Though he stayed in Europe barely four months on this trip, the waiting time seemed endless. He visited the American sculptress Malvina Hoffman, a pupil of Rodin's who had just exhibited a collection of one hundred of her figures of ethnic types at the Trocadéro Museum before shipping them to Chicago's Field Museum for its Hall of Man. Evening after evening he sat before the crackling fire in her salon while shadows leapt across the walls; there he chatted with the

Abbé Breuil, the African explorer Marcel Griaule, and the folklorist Henri Rivière, or listened pensively while Ernest Schelling played Chopin. He managed to lecture twice on the Peking Man before de Lubac and the other admiring young Jesuits at Fourvière. But most of the time he was worried and defensive. All he could think of was how to get back most quickly to his China refuge.

When he finally did return in March 1933, it seemed he brought his bad luck with him. Peking, which up to then was very little touched by the upheaval attendant on the slow coming together of a new nation, now faced an ugly and more tangible uncertainty—this time precipitated by Japan's incursion. Though that nation's "privileged status" in China had been recognized by the treaty that ended the Russo-Japanese War in 1905, on September 18, 1931, while Teilhard was in Urumchi, an armed clash between Chinese and Japanese at Mukden had brought Japanese military units pouring into Manchuria. In three months the Imperial army had taken the whole province and constituted a puppet empire there, to which it had since added Jehol and parts of Inner Mongolia for the boy emperor Pu Yi. Even in Peking Teilhard could see how Japanese influence had grown. A pitiless reality was descending on the dreamland of Cathay.

At the Survey, work continued despite the uncertainty of the political situation. That summer Teilhard joined Black and his co-workers on a brief trip which he described as having moved "through rivers of beer and ice cream," to a geological conference in Washington, D.C. There he first met a young German geologist named Helmut de Terra, whom Black was encouraging to make a study of the Himalayas to add to the Survey's own research on the geological setting for the beginning of life in Asia.

In Peking in October the Survey team came upon a new windfall of treasures at Choukoutien. A younger cave near the top of the hill yielded a third cranium in good condition, some pierced sea shells, worked stones, and the remains of ostriches and elephants. Throughout the fall and winter Teilhard worked on the environmental material from the caves, describing it in itself and with reference to the bones. The flow of Japanese scientists and visitors to Lockhart Hall was now unceasing. Tensions increased on every side.

Still, for Teilhard those problems were only small annoyance compared to his personal distress. Alone in his convent room at night, he lived and relived the dismal events of his 1932 visit to France. Near Christmas he wrote another essay expressing his exasperation over his Church's continued projection of so static and irrelevant an image of herself to modern man.[4] Dwelling as he did in "the heart of the Church as well as in the court of the Gentiles," the Jesuit knew too well what both sides felt, and he mourned his imposed impotence to do anything to bring them together. This obsession continued to disturb his sleep and nag his waking mind all through the winter of 1933 and into the spring of 1934.

# CHAPTER
# TWELVE

By early 1934 the luck that despite everything had sustained
the Geological Survey suddenly ran out. In February its Chinese director, Wong Wen-hao, had suffered a skull fracture in
an automobile accident and was hospitalized for several
months. On March 15 Davidson Black died at his desk of a
heart attack.

Black had just returned from the patients' wing of the
PUMC, after having shown some signs of cardiac trouble. To
his doctors, who continued to advise bed rest, he replied that
resting was the most difficult work he knew. Early that evening he went to his lab, apparently in good spirits. At 7:00
P.M. his assistant Dr. Paul Stevenson dropped by, chatted
with him for a quarter hour, and then left. When Stevenson
returned a little later, he found his colleague's slight, green-
suited body crumpled on the floor beside his worktable
covered with maps and books and his samples of the Sin-
anthropi. Stevenson telephoned for help. Shortly thereafter,
friends carried Black into the "cold room" of the pathology
department and gently laid him in its desolation of cadavers.

As Black was a professed agnostic, his passing was Teilhard's first close witness of the death of an unbelieving friend.
When, in the company of Olga Hempel, who brought a
bunch of roses to the bier, he went to view the body, she was
astonished at the vehemence of his grief. "This cannot be the
end for him!" she heard him murmur. "He has done so very

much! . . . Somehow he must be continued!" The stoic acceptance of Black's passing by his relatives and his acquaintances quite horrified Teilhard. "I looked at Davey's poor body in the icehouse," he wrote to Lucile Swan, "and swore upon it to myself that I would find the meaning for such apparent waste. . . . It cannot end in total obliteration!"

Only the pressure of unfinished work and the urgency of projects to be closed down helped to keep Teilhard steady at the time. The Rockefeller Foundation gave him a free hand in taking over some of the plans Black had laid out for the year. Most pressing was the problem of the imminent arrival from America of the geologist George Barbour. Like de Terra, Barbour had been approached by Black in Washington the previous summer with the suggestion that he undertake a study of the conditions that would be hospitable to the start of life along the Yangtze to enlarge the Survey's work in the Hwang Ho district. The night Black died, Barbour had sailed as far as Honolulu. Though he received a cablegram advising him of the event, he decided to continue on to China. After serving as a pallbearer at Black's Anglican burial service in the PUMC auditorium, Teilhard rushed down to Shanghai with "Eddy" Bien and C. C. Young to meet him.

The Survey team left Nanking in mid-April and turned inland toward Hankow on a steamer packed with Nationalist soldiers who, ignoring the Japanese incursion in the north, had set out to join Chiang's Third Extermination Campaign against the Communists in Kwangsi province. The Survey vessel moved slowly through the shallow brown waters, afloat with ghostlike junks and broken here and there by the vertical hill-islands jutting out of the mist, like the impossible shapes in classical Chinese paintings. By early June it had passed the terraced foggy city of Chungking and, at Barbour's urging, penetrated deep into the Red Basin of Szechuan.

"This river trip," Teilhard reported in a letter to Mrs. Swan, "has been deeply satisfying from a geological point of

view. . . ." But, he admitted, he often found the voyage trying. The blow of Black's passing had bruised him deeply. He
felt suddenly helpless before the new obstreperousness that
once-docile Chinese companions like Young began to demonstrate. And (though perhaps he did not realize it himself) he
was becoming increasingly uncomfortable over the growing
demands that Mrs. Swan was making on his attention.

Teilhard's friendship with Mrs. Swan had put him in a curious position. Though he had always made the most of his
social and scientific liberty in Peking, he did so without ever
pretending to relax, even in the slightest degree, his long-leash
tie to the Society of Jesus and his priestly vows. Against this
attitude Lucile began to argue. In one sense, she did have
reason to feel possessive. In the years since she had known
Teilhard, she had been secretary, mother, sister, friend, and
(as he habitually assured her) "Inspiration" to him. Each day
he visited her house for tea, and picnicked with her and her
friends on weekends under the trees near the great round,
open-air Altar of Heaven. He read her all his papers, which
she typed up, and even sometimes translated into rough English; then she oversaw their printing in little orange-covered
booklets the Alsatian Henri Vetch turned out so cheaply
from his Librairie Française on the busy ground floor of the
Hôtel du Pékin.

In exchange for her assistance, Teilhard paid her the
quaint, old-fashioned compliments of a troubadour. In the
letters that he wrote her from field trips, he named her his
"Compass Point," his "Light," the "Active Seed" that
brought him the "Tide of Life." He never had the aspect or
the outlook of a monk, as she imagined one; and his gallantry
was of a kind that she had never known before. Further, she
had grown up in the Protestant tradition in which celibacy for
clergymen was the exception rather than the rule. Therefore,
and despite the fact she had never been divorced from her
painter husband, institutionalized, perhaps permanently, with
a nervous ailment, she saw no reason why her relationship

with the handsome Frenchman might not progress beyond what up to that point had been only a deep mutual sympathy.

On his side, Teilhard's situation was unique for a man with a genuine calling to the priesthood. His long exile left him with a deep sense of deprivation of most kinds of human warmth. But more important, he was perfectly aware that if he ever was to finish what he saw as his life's work, he needed some encouragement and help. Ever since, at the age of thirty, he had discovered the exhilaration that the uncritical admiration of women friends brought him, he had begun, perhaps unconsciously, to establish semisentimental relationships with them—though always on a completely nonphysical plane. His wartime paper "L'Éternel Féminin,"[1] written for his cousin Marguerite, was, as a matter of fact, a celebration of the advantages of nonphysical but "passionate" friendship between the sexes. Now, sixteen years later, he had behind him ample experience of how far a bit of gallantry and Gallic charm could go to win the friendship or the help he often needed from the ladies that he knew.

By 1934 Mrs. Swan had replaced his cousin Marguerite as his closest female confidante. At first, when he saw the light that flooded her face at his entrance into her garden, he was only pleased. Later, when he began to recognize something else, a distinct uneasiness stole over him. In February 1934 he decided to examine this new problem in an essay which he called "The Evolution of Chastity."[2]

To this day, that paper stands as a first-class curiosity of Teilhardiana. Though to a casual reader, it may seem an embarrassingly inept piece of special pleading, when viewed in the context of the author's psychological makeup, his seminary unbringing, and the evaluation of "the place of woman" accepted by both sexes at the time, it emerges as the logical extension of Teilhard's lifelong tendency to "volatilize" (try to extract some sort of indestructible spiritual reality from) undependable Matter.

From as early as Teilhard could remember, the "things of this world"—that bright, mysterious material conglomerate whose sweetness so delighted him—had always turned to ashes in his hands. Very long ago, he had decided that the only way he could preserve it in his own life was to draw out of it (just as he imagined God did) that part of it which could not pass away.

Like "L'Éternel Féminin," "L'Évolution de la Chasteté" is a highly subjective document. Deliberately or not, it was conceived mostly as an answer to questions that reoccurred constantly in Teilhard's personal life. Though genuinely attracted to women all his life, he was a Roman priest who took his vows seriously. He, therefore, had to find some interpretation of those vows that would square with his psychology. The "Feminine," as he had experienced it in his mother, his sister Guiguite, and his lady admirers, he always had interpreted as a kind of "force," meant to lead him beyond himself to higher things. In the essay "L'Évolution de la Chasteté," a document primarily written from the male celibate's point of view, he advanced the theory that the primary contribution of "woman" to human evolution lay not in any effort she might make to help "build the earth," nor in any consoling physical exchange she might have to offer to a man, nor even in the part she played in the propagation of the species. Her role was to be a "Beatrice" who beckoned men beyond themselves to God. Whenever encountered, Teilhard declared, the "Feminine" was an "intoxicating liquor . . . ," "a troubling perfume . . . ," "the most formidable of all the Energies in Nature." But, for that very reason, it was something to be "used" and "tamed."

Whenever, Teilhard warned in that essay, a celibate who had risen to a plateau above the life of the senses stopped to consider any one particular woman as a final goal, he thereby "short-circuited" the energy that could drive him on to God and, in the process, demeaned the high humanity he had achieved at such great cost. Ultimately, Teilhard felt, "woman" was less a mirror for showing a man to himself than a crystal disseminating the Brightness of the Divine. When, in the course of time, he concluded, and following the ascetic perceptions already instinctive in most religions on the question of celibacy, the resources that lay waiting untapped in sublimated, nonphysical engagements between men and women would be universally appreciated, and a new and higher stage of evolution would be reached. "Mankind," he announced, "for the second time, will have discovered Fire!"

In the little parlor or the garden courtyard of the plain-spoken Lucile Swan, under the ambiguous smile of her old servant Wong, interrupted by the frolicking of her mongrel puppy Tung-shi, the whole exalted business simply sounded silly. Time and time again in conversations with Teilhard, she tried to raise the problem of her relationship with him. But whenever she did, he changed the subject so gently yet so firmly that her only recourse was to challenge his attitude in notes she sent him across town. Patiently he explained and re-explained his position. "The fundamental bearing of my life," he wrote, "has always been to prove that the love of God justifies and exalts, rather than destroys, earthly powers of knowing and loving. . . . I dream," he told her more than once, "of going to God under the pressures of the strongest and most violent currents of the earth!"

Teilhard meant what he said about wanting to reach God through matter, but he meant it exactly *as* he said it. To Lucile, however, who continued to play the role of the romantic female, his reasoning was purest nonsense. She objected; he replied to her letters; his answers confused her even more. "For the very reason that you are such a treasure to me, dear Lucile," he wrote in one long note, "I ask you not to build too much of your life on me. . . . Remember, whatever sweetness I force myself not to give you, I do in order to be worthy of you."

Finally, in complete frustration, Lucile went off in July of 1934 to a "dude ranch" near Kalgan where some Swedish friends had stocked Mongolian ponies, to think her problem through. At their last meeting before her departure, she told Teilhard she was at an emotional crossroads and thought it might perhaps be best to end her friendship with him then and there. She stayed away over a month, spending most of her time talking her troubles over with a woman friend through the steam of the ranch's sauna bath.

But in reality she had no choice at all. Lucile had already lived through too much agitation to want to see a new drama begin. It was the strain left by a series of scenes in New York with her husband before their separation that sent her to Peking in the first place. Such a situation, she determined, must not be repeated. Even a phantom romance with one of the most attractive men she had ever met was better than nothing —at least for the moment. In any case, when she came back to her house in Peking that autumn, she declared she was willing to accept Teilhard's friendship on whatever terms he made.

Meanwhile, thinking that he might have hit on some new insights in his "Chastity" paper, the Jesuit shipped copies of it off to his old friend Père Valensin in Lyon. Valensin shot the essay back at once, in exasperation, writing him in no uncertain terms that as far as that particular aspect of human experience was concerned, Teilhard had not the faintest idea what he was talking about. He also added a new, more strongly worded warning against the indiscriminate dissemination of such dilettante essays, which could only prove worrisome to ecclesiastical censors.

By the time the letter arrived, Teilhard seemed almost to have forgotten all about his "Chastity" paper. He had just finished a new one, "Comment Je Crois"[3]—a painfully serious probing of the genesis and quality of his religious faith, which had been requested of him by a Toulousian friend, Msgr. Bruno de Solages.* Still insisting that the way to God was

---

* Teilhard and Solages had first met in the summer of 1928 at one of the *Semaines d'apologétiques*, the "intellectual retreats," then held under the direction of Maurice Vaussard at Juilly.

*through* and not *outside* of matter, he again proclaimed himself as irredeemably a "child of the earth" as "one of the children of heaven." So tightly was Teilhard's religion bound with science in his "God-in-the-world" Weltanschauung that he even insisted: "If by some interior regression I should lose my faith in Christ or in a Personal God or Spirit, I would continue to believe quite helplessly in the World."

On New Year's Eve of 1934 Mrs. Swan gave a party for a few close friends. Wearing a Bavarian peasant costume, she served vodka to her guests, her parlor full of greens and candles, her broad face alight with happiness. The next night, she and Teilhard dined alone. The wine or Teilhard's evident pleasure in her company emboldened her to bring up once again what she regarded as their mutual problem. When Teilhard blithely told her of his crowded travel calendar for the rest of the year—his plans to go to Kwangsi to explore some curious limestone caves he had heard about, then home to Paris, and then on to the Himalayas with Helmut de Terra —the conversation lagged. The evening ended on a perceptible note of strain.

In February 1935 Teilhard came back to Peking from the field. Now it was Lucile's turn to announce her departure. She had decided, she said, to go home to America for a while to exhibit her sculpture and visit her aged parents.

A few days after she sailed, she was relieved to receive a letter from Teilhard expressing his sadness at the void she had left behind her. Thereafter, she had a letter almost daily, telling her in detail how often he stopped at the top of her street to stare at her empty house, and how in her absence, even "the pink charms of the Peking spring make me a little ill."

Needless to say, Teilhard survived. That spring was busier than usual for him. Among the Tientsin Jesuits he found a new disciple—one Maurice Trassaert, a young science and mathematics teacher from the Collège des Hautes Études who visited him often in Peking and worked with him on a paper comparing his collection of the extinct herbivores of

Shansi with Licent's. In March a balding, bespectacled, brilliant anatomist named Franz Weidenreich, who had fled to America from Germany at the first flare-up of Nazi anti-Semitism, arrived at the laboratory, commissioned by the Rockefeller Foundation to be permanent successor to Davidson Black. At the same time, the Abbé Breuil again arrived in Peking† for a month's stay, and by the middle of May, with Weidenreich properly established in the Cenozoic laboratory, Teilhard joined Breuil on the Trans-Siberian back to France.

This time, when he arrived in Paris, Teilhard went straight to the residence attached to the intellectual Jesuit journal *Études* on the elegant little Rue Monsieur. The warmth of the welcome he received there surprised and overwhelmed him. Besides his old friends from Jersey—the biblical scholar Joseph Huby, the essayist Henri du Passage, the devotional writer Paul Doncœur, and the aging Adhémar d'Alès—he found living in the house men from a new generation of younger Jesuits who had been his admirers and correspondents when they were completing theology studies at Fourvière. In their school years (together with Père de Lubac) they had, on their own initiative, continued "La Pensée," the study group they all worked in at Hastings, until complaints of "elitism" by their fellow students at Fourvière had caused the Lyon provincial to disband them. But the formal end of their group neither extinguished their mutual affection nor erased the memory of their intellectual adventures. Among "La Pensée" alumni were the political writer Gaston Fessard and, more important to Teilhard, *Études'* new director, the subtle, stubborn, deeply spiritual René d'Ouince.

Once settled in with the community of *Études*, Teilhard—for the first time in more years than he cared to remember—felt entirely at home. He particularly rejoiced in the protection of d'Ouince, who made it clear from the time of his arrival

† At Davidson Black's invitation, Breuil had made his first visit to Peking in 1931, while Teilhard was away on the Citroën expedition.

that he intended to do all he could to guard Teilhard as much
from his own carelessness as from misunderstanding by his superiors. In his youthful enthusiasm, d'Ouince went even farther. He hoped Teilhard could aid him in his plans for
breathing new life into the journal and turning it into a vehicle for a dialogue between believers and nonbelievers in the
new political crisis into which France was, at that moment,
plunged.

If dialogue there was to be, it was bound to be a heated
one. In 1935 the barricades of ideological conflict were already standing high. The leaders of the republic, its mode of
action, its system of values were being put to question. The
franc had dropped to one-fifth its prewar value. Govern-
mental cabinet after cabinet fell—some after only one
month's tenure. Official corruption and financial scandals,
such as the Stavisky affair, drove the overtaxed and underpaid
middle class to near revolt. A year earlier, an angry mob of
100,000 demonstrators had moved into the shining square of
the Place de la Concorde in a riot violent enough to recall to
some French writers the protests that brought down the
Commune in 1871.

That summer of 1935 superpatriotic rightist organizations
—the royalist Camelots du Roi, the Cagoulards, a revived Action Française, and a semifascist Croix du Feu—were strutting
noisily through the streets, sometimes in uniform, sometimes
carrying banners and placards. At the same time, the partisans
of the left staged factory shutdowns and violent counter-
demonstrations. All over the nation, petty personal vendettas
masked themselves behind ideological enthusiasm which they
pressed with private rage. Even the new Popular Front, which
Léon Blum managed to weld between Communists and
Socialists, was falling rapidly apart.

For Teilhard, who in his boyhood had tried to keep his
counsel even during the noisy political discussions of his
brothers, it was distressing to find France in such a state. Except in conversations about theology with the men of *Études*

or with friends such as Père de Lubac, who came to Paris to discuss "Comment Je Crois" with him, and whose opinion he began to value more and more, he had to be constantly on guard to keep his political neutrality.

Even when he went home to Auvergne that summer, his visit was unusually short. But this was due far less to the acrimonius political climate of the place as it was to the fact that so much of all he had treasured and loved there was gone or passing away. While Teilhard was last in China his youngest brother, Victor, who ever since the war had fought for his life against the lung damage he had sustained from poison gas, had died. His invalid sister Guiguite, who for years had been president of a quaintly religio-military society called the Catholic Union of the Sick, was suffering bitterly from periodic attacks of paralysis, blindness, and inability to speak. At eighty-three, Teilhard's mother's health was poor. "Today," he wrote Mrs. Swan that August, "I am in the family house, on the mountain slope facing a wonderful landscape. . . . Externally, I am at peace. . . . But for several reasons—the imminence of my departure among them—I do not feel comfortable within. . . . I have the feeling that I am standing aside and looking at the child or young man who once used to be me. . . . And for my mother (if not for my sister) I *am* that young man."

In early September he set sail for India. At Eritrea he watched with weary disinvolvement as regiments of sweating young Italians boarded troopships bound for Ethiopia. It was not until October 2, when he arrived at Srinagar, that he began to feel enthusiasm for his work again.

The Kashmiri city was a lovely place—a frontier town at the foot of the Himalayas, crisscrossed with canals and houseboats, and set in an autumn blaze of walnut trees. Helmut de Terra was waiting with his chic, dark-haired wife Rhoda and baby daughter Noël. After a day's rest, the men set out for two weeks to study the pine-covered hills of the Sind valley and the nearby mountain passes, which still bore scars from caterpillar tracks Haardt's expedition had left behind in 1931. After traveling the Salt Range foothills of the lower Himalayas, they made a brief junket to Mohenjo Daro. They dug in the Sohan valley for paleolithic artifacts—scraping and cutting tools which Teilhard dated at the same age as the Sinanthropus. A corpulent, yet vulnerable-seeming man, de Terra found his philosophical conversations with Teilhard quite fascinating. For him, as for Teilhard, the trip ended on a real note of regret.

In December 1935 de Terra went home to America. At the invitation of the Dutchman Ralph von Koenigswald, who had recently made some stunning breakthroughs in paleontology in the Indies, Teilhard continued on to Java.

Sixty-five years earlier, the anatomist Eugène Dubois had found on a site near the Solo River the bones of a creature seemingly intermediate between man and the apes. He called his discovery *Pithecanthropus erectus*. Since 1931 von Koenigswald had unearthed a whole collection of Neanderthal skulls that seemed roughly at the same evolutionary stage as the Sinanthropus. For ten days, he and Teilhard trekked through the bush, sleeping in native huts, often employing the whole population of the little *kampangs* to help their digging. They sifted through the earth at a site where a stone industry, similar to the one Teilhard had just seen at the Narabada River, had recently been discovered. A few days later they stood on a cave floor littered with debris like that found in the fossil-bearing caves of Choukoutien. All the evidence they examined, they believed, pointed to the possibility that Java had been a crossroads for two currents of human development—one spreading southeast from India, and the other south from China.

For Teilhard, who had begun his trip from Auvergne questioning the value of further digging into the past, and wondering whether all this studying of monuments, bones, and ancient earth was only staring down into a bottomless grave,[4] the field trip was a psychological renewal. Before it ended, any doubt he may have entertained about his scientific work was momentarily allayed.

However, as his ship turned north toward Tientsin, his horizon darkened. There was still no formal declaration of war between China and Japan. But by December 1935 the invaders were well established on the mainland. Aware that Wong, Grabau, and many of the Survey members had taken much of the Sinanthropus materials to Nanking, Teilhard wondered how much material was left to work on in the Cenozoic lab.

Then, too, there was the standing problem of how to deal with Mrs. Swan. Since they had parted nearly a year earlier, Teilhard had done all he could to keep her from worrying about the future. He had asked her just to trust herself lovingly to Life the way he did and be still. "You object," he had written her from Paris that past summer, "that in defending celibacy, I am denying one of the fundamental laws of the universe. . . . I have already told you how hesitant I am about the idea. . . . Evidently, procreation will be necessary until the earth is full enough to reach a certain degree of interdependence and unity. But procreation is *not* the only object of love. . . . For the time being, let's not discuss too much."

For the remainder of his trip, they had not discussed the question at all. But now, with the China coast before him, Teilhard knew the hiatus would be over. The night before he docked at Shanghai, he sent belated Christmas greetings to the then-septuagenarian Léontine Zanta, thanking her for her fidelity to him over the years and for the warmth and understanding she had shown him since they first met in 1919. "If only all women were like you," he concluded the letter, "it would make the 'Conquest of Fire' much more easy!"

# CHAPTER
# THIRTEEN

On February 9, 1936, Teilhard's mother died of pleurisy. A week later, in a retreat at Tientsin, he wrote another essay on "spiritualization," which asserted that the apparently unfeeling universe in spite of all appearances must have at base a "heart and face."[1]

When he returned to Peking, he seemed tired and depressed, sharply conscious of the hollows in his bones and the bitter winds that blew through them. He spent much of his time with other priests, among whom he liberally, almost carelessly dispensed copies of his essays. At the urging of Bishop Constantini of the Propaganda, formerly Apostolic Delegate to Peking, he wrote a paper for the College of the Propaganda in Rome, again urging that the Church become the ally of evolving mankind.[2]

That August, while he was on a field trip to Shantung, news reached him that his sister Guiguite, too, was dead. After having passed her "marshal's baton" to the woman she commissioned her second-in-command, she was laid to rest near Clermont beside her parents, with the sad little flag of the Catholic Union of the Sick in her waxy hands.

Back in Peking the next month, Teilhard found himself depending more and more on the visits of young Trassaert, who continued to be fascinated by the new world of knowledge that the Cenozoic lab unlocked for him, and showed considerable skill in working there. Early in their friendship, Teilhard had decided that Trassaert's talents marked him for a career in paleontology and wrote persistently to his superiors in Europe recommending that Trassaert be called home to study for an advanced degree in that field.

The legation entertainments were proceeding with a hectic and autumnal brilliance now. At the Grand Hotel, the "Malalo" (the name Western Pekingese gave to tourists from the round-the-world cruise ship which brought them to China) still appeared, even though they came in smaller numbers. Mrs. Lucy Calhoun, an aged diplomat's widow with a hearing aid which had an unfortunate tendency to buzz uncontrollably, had turned her lovely temple residence into a hotel and now entertained the most motley crowd of visitors she had ever had to take into her house. A unilingual "Living Buddha" with a pock-marked, beaten-copper face, exiled by the still "nonbelligerent" Japanese from his monastery in Mongolia and blandly carrying a fortune in gold under his hat, presided over cocktail parties. The basso Chaliapin, with his failing voice, gave a concert for the Westerners when he passed through Peking, and stayed in the Hôtel du Pékin, where film stars such as Anna May Wong and Warner Oland (the movie "Charlie Chan") had brought momentary klieg-light glamour to the city.

In 1936 several anti-Western demonstrations had already shaken the treaty ports. Peking continued relatively quiet. But the feeling of uncertainty in the old city mounted day by day. In the hills outside Peking, bands of Red guerrillas, who had broken out of a Kuomintang encirclement in Kwangsi in 1934, then joined the Long March six thousand miles north to their new capital at Yenan in the dusty Shansi basin, raided Japanese installations near the Manchurian border and along the railroad line across the north. Within the city, the representatives of Japan grew continually more abrasive and proprietarial. The Westerners made a pretense of keeping up the old, insouciant life, but their gaiety was forced. Though no one mentioned it aloud, it was plain that the Legation reign was coming to an end.

And when it came, it did not come too prettily. For a quarter of a century, the commitments of the Boxer settlement had succeeded in preventing the commission of any real crime by an Oriental against an Occidental within the city limits. But one January morning in 1937 the body of Pamela Werner, the seventeen-year-old daughter of a British ex-consul, was found on the Tartar Wall, horribly mutilated, her chest cavity deftly hollowed out. The two Scotland Yard inspectors imported from Shanghai to find her killer never turned up a trace of him. Inevitably, though, in their investigations, they chipped away at the façade of propriety which the foreigners had built so carefully over the years and, as scandal after scandal broke into the open, the myth of Western moral superiority dissolved.

Like suddenly invaded nests of roaches, the denizens of the city's foreign subsociety scattered into the light. Drug addicts, heroin manufacturers, deviates, sensation-seekers, who had crowded the endless series of masquerade parties to seek their satisfactions in anonymity, the discreet patrons of the pleasure houses of delicate Chinese or White Russian girls near the Ch'ien-men Gate felt the shock of scrutiny upon them, froze a moment, and then hurried underground. There was a momentary loss of tolerance in the community for its numerous drug dealers. A free-love cult, presided over by a placid American dentist, which met regularly to perform its rites to musical accompaniment and which was attended by some of Peking's most prominent citizens, was suddenly universally deplored.

For weeks thereafter, the bangled doyennes of the Foreign Quarter tapped lacquered nails on the eternal bridge tables and discussed the crime. They knew the murderer might well have been a Japanese or Chinese, or even one of the medical students from the PUMC who until that time had been forced to work on their daily allotment of Chinese cadavers from the streets. But they also knew the crime could just as easily have been committed by some "dear friend" they had entertained the night before.

One month after the murder, Teilhard left China for America and Europe, this time bringing a cast of the Sinanthropus skull for the American Museum of Natural History in New York and a paper he was scheduled to read on the subject at a Carnegie-sponsored meeting in Philadelphia. Traveling with the young antique dealer William Drummond, Teilhard caught something of his companion's boyish playfulness and joined him in dropping bottles with "Help!" messages from portholes.

When he landed in Seattle, Teilhard was dismayed to find how much of a sensation news of the Werner murder had created in American newspapers. The Seattle immigration officers received him very warily. Drummond did not disturb them, but the Jesuit was anything but a reassuring sight. There he stood, a foreigner from then-notorious Peking, dressed in an improbable clerical costume, speaking with a strange accent, carrying a big black box containing a misshapen skull. He tried without success to explain himself. At last he sat down shivering in the open customs shed, sputtering useless French, while his friend argued in his defense.

Released near dawn, Teilhard proceeded east across America with only one stop, to visit Henry Field's museum in Chicago. By March he was in Philadelphia, staying with the de Terras, and preparing to discuss the Sinanthropus at the Academy of Science. Incredibly enough, he still seemed not to have accepted the fact that if he wished to survive as a Jesuit, he had to confine himself to science whenever he spoke in public. To a fascinated *New York Times* man, who apprehended him just as he was leaving the lecture hall, he delivered himself of another of his religio-scientific statements and compared pre-man's psychic breakthrough into Reflectivity to the change of state that happens to water at its boiling point. The article appeared in New York the next day. At

the Catholic college of Villanova, where he went to receive
the Mendel Medal, Teilhard said substantially the same
thing. More reporters rushed to Philadelphia to interview
him, and within the week he was notorious in both American
and Canadian newspapers as THE JESUIT WHO BELIEVES MAN
DESCENDED FROM THE APES. By the time he arrived at the
Jesuit Boston College, where he had been invited to be
similarly honored, he found his invitation had been with-
drawn.

By early May Teilhard was back in France. Reverberations
from what in clerical circles had come to be called the
"Villanova Incident" had long since reached Rome. There
was the expectable explosion. When Teilhard made his formal visit to Lyon, a new provincial, Joseph du Bouchet, informed him as stiffly as he could that he was ordered by his
major superiors to stop disseminating his outrageous ideas
and to sit still until his fate was decided.

Fortunately, at that juncture in his life, "sitting still" was
probably the best thing Père Teilhard could do. He had come
home to France that year a shadow of his former self. He was
fifty-six—overly thin, spreading just a little in the middle. His
color was poor and he suffered intermittently from fever. A
few days after his arrival in Paris, he was dispatched to the
Hôpital Pasteur for tests and treatment of what seemed to
be malaria.

To a man who so carefully clocked the passage of time and
his progressive diminution in it, the confinement came as a
real shock. To Mrs. Swan in China he wrote that he had
reached another turning point. If he went on writing essays
unacceptable to Church authorities, there was no chance at
all that he would reach a large audience in his lifetime. If, on
the other hand, he made a last attempt to summarize his
whole philosophy of man in a single book, soft-peddling its
more radical aspects or modifying their shock value by the use
of a more acceptable vocabulary, there was a possibility he

might be published. "Better to adjust," he told her, "than simply to react."

At the hospital, however, Teilhard found neither the peace nor the leisure to accomplish very much. Day after day a stream of agitated visitors came to see him, bringing with them more news of the political deterioration of Europe.

That summer the Spanish Civil War was in full and bloody explosion. Idealism on both sides had collapsed. Franco led his Moroccan armies back to Spain and began a blood bath in which Spaniard fought Spaniard with foreign weapons, while Kremlin-recruited volunteers clashed with Germans and Italians in rehearsal for a wider, more rewarding war.

In France, the split between supporters of the right and left grew deeper. Even though Léon Blum's Popular Front had finally succeeded in writing paid vacations and the forty-hour week into law over the protests of the conservatives, the leftist coalition Blum had built was pulling apart at the seams. People on whose cooperation he depended were now denouncing him for refusing to give formal French military support to the Spanish Republicans. To save the floundering economy, he proposed a bill to take France off the gold standard. The angry leftists joined the rightists in resisting him. By June of 1937 his power base was so eroded that he handed in his resignation.

One year before, from China, in the essay "Sauvons l'Humanité,"[3] Teilhard had offered his own solution to the present problems of mankind. To the exasperation of his friends from right and left, he took no stand but to call again for the formation of a "Human Front" in which men of all persuasions might unite to bring about human advancement.

Returning starry-eyed from a tourist trip to Russia, Ida Treat rebuked him for his lack of involvement. "I just can't understand your standing around with a holier-than-thou attitude," she said, "when the world is in the state it's in!" But Teilhard felt he could not do otherwise. The left, for all its

vigor, was too antipersonalistic, too materialistic, too obviously under Russian influence. The right, though it professed
to honor human values, stood solidly with Europe's vested interests. Besides, Teilhard knew, he had trouble enough trying
to be scientist, visionary, and cleric without venturing into
politics.

In point of fact, though, even then, his evolutionary
theories could be read as having a great deal more political import than he claimed for them. He had designed a "biological
philosophy," but he had also designed a teleological and
therefore a political one. In every essay that he wrote, he had
indicated that human history was the continuation on the
conscious level of the work of once-blind evolution. It followed then that the same "psychic energy" (or *élan vital*, in
Bergson's phrase) that in primeval times had drawn the first
particles of matter together and begun the movement upward
through repeated combination and complexifications, now
took the form of a yearning in man for his social betterment
—the very thing that lay behind the Spanish peasant's (or the
population of any underdeveloped country's) reach for bread
and land.

When, after less than a four-month stay in Paris, Teilhard
took the *D'Artagnan* back to China, his head was ringing
with the declarations of faith made by his friends in the
conflicting "isms" of the time. He wrote another essay—oddly
enough, the most daringly optimistic semiscientific piece that
he was to do in his long lifetime. He called it "Human Energy."[4]

In this paper (or, in a deeper sense, this protest) against
the painful political and social disintegration he saw around
him, Teilhard described how, in his opinion, the forces hidden in the earth must one day be deployed in the achievement of his hoped-for "Human Front." The processes he
outlined were partially the fruit of a long conversation with
Alexis Carrel, whom he had seen in New York City before his
voyage home. To this day, the ideas there recorded seem ec-

centric and disturbing; and, unless carefully understood, they evoke the shadow of a rather terrifying "Brave New World." For anyone who follows Teilhard's logic without faltering to the end, however, the conclusions are inevitable.

The means, the product, and the goal of evolution, he proclaimed as always, was man in a completed state. Ever since rational beings had begun to see themselves as a species superior to and unlike the rest, they unconsciously began the work of "spiritualizing," or civilizing, themselves. Millennia later (circa 1800), after the idea of "humanity" as a single whole became a common concept, individual human minds began to move consciously toward a common end.

Since the industrial revolution, population had been increasing geometrically (as compared with food supply, which increased arithmetically), and long-distance communications had become easier. Some people began to understand that their survival depended on their solidarity with others like themselves across the world. At first they acted on the thought from self-interest; then in the twentieth century the technological revolution began to change that dim perception into a generally accepted fact. Communication became practically instantaneous, and it became the conventional wisdom among economists that nations depended on one another for production and exchange of goods. Finally, through their newly acquired skill in the manipulation of genes and chromosomes, it even began to seem possible to biologists that they had the power to improve the race. For the first time in history, it seemed, humanity was about to take its destiny into its own hands.

Since, in comparison to other species, mankind was still comparatively young and new upon the earth, it was impossible to say how long it would take to turn these new perceptions into action and move to a higher, more united plane. But the movement would take place; of this he had no doubt. In the end of the process, when man had "achieved" himself and individuals worked together as one body for the growth and betterment of all of their parts, then, just as, long ago, when individual hominoids had undergone the first "crisis of Reflection," the single entity "mankind" would be ready for its last and most important crisis—its infolding on the Thing within it that was more "spiritual" and personal than it could be alone.

To a less intellectually presbyopic man than Teilhard was, the things then happening in Europe and in the Orient might have made the essay seem a mockery. During his months in Europe, war in the East had exploded with terrifying force. The Japanese army had taken most of North China; her air power ruled the skies and raked the ground, and the warlords scattered helplessly before it. Chiang Kai-shek had been kidnapped the previous Christmastime by Manchuria's defeated "Young Marshal," Chang Hsueh-liang, and held prisoner in Sian until he would agree to join the Reds in the north in the fight against Japan. For the moment, the Reds established themselves in an uneasy alliance with Chiang's troops in what came to be called the Eighth Route Army. On July 7, 1937, the Japanese had made Chiang's position irreversible. They crossed the Marco Polo Bridge and took Peking.

Teilhard, however, with his unshakably European outlook and his curious lack of interest in the politics of China, viewed the burning world around him with the detachment of an astronomer gazing at an exploding star. When his boat pulled into Hong Kong, there was a cholera epidemic raging in the city. In Shanghai, where it moored overnight, he and other passengers watched from the deck as fires, started by the bombs of inept Chinese Nationalist pilots aiming at Japanese installations, lit up a city in panic. It was at Shanghai that he finished writing "Human Energy."

The Peking he returned to some days later seemed another Mukden. Old Chinese houses had even been provided with false fronts to make them resemble their counterparts in Japan, and the familiar street odors of the city were now mixed with the smell of dried fish like Kobe or Yokahama.

Imperial soldiers, wearing surgical masks to protect themselves from the filth of the city, tramped the streets in phalanxes behind officers trailing long, curved swords, knocking coolies from their path with rifle butts, or crashed in trucks through the narrow *hutungs*, scattering rickshaws as they went. Geisha girls in brilliant kimonos stepped delicately across the roads. And even though Teilhard's Western friends remained ostensibly safe and uninvolved behind the Legation glacis, the psychological atmosphere in which they pursued their entertainments went from bad to worse.

Teilhard still tried to live in China just as he had always done. He worked in his laboratory until teatime, then went to visit Mrs. Swan. The autumn afternoons that year were warm enough to sit before a table in the courtyard, under the turning leaves of the ginkgo trees. Bright-colored kites, and pigeons with polytonic whistles attached to their tails, still sailed overhead. Sometimes, as the evening gathered in the garden, he would scratch the bark of one of the ancient trees and lecture on the life cycles of the insects that inhabited it. Sometimes, when the weather was fine, he took long walks with friends in the Imperial Park, where he stopped and talked about the breathtaking mutations the Chinese had bred into the goldfish with the diaphanous trailing fins or multicolored ribbon eyebrows that swam in the garden's "Ali Baba" jars.

But even this last period of pretended normalcy could not be long maintained. Quite soon after his return to China, Teilhard was summoned to Chabanel Hall, a language school the Jesuits had just finished building far to the north of the Tartar City. The Jesuit Visitor in China, one Father George Marin, a black-bearded, black-tempered American, trained in a Jesuit province in Canada, who had as completely authoritarian an outlook as Ledochowski, was then presiding over the new house. At the moment of their first meeting, the Visitor announced that he had decided Teilhard must renounce his "vagabond existence" with the Lazarists and move to the safety of the brotherhood at Chabanel.

As a raw autum turned into a bleak winter, the restrictions of life at the missionary school became more and more suffocating for Teilhard. He could not think with clarity; he felt that he was working in a vacuum. Since his moving into Chabanel, his projected book on man showed little progress. "I *think* I see *some* things more clearly," he wrote to Mrs. Swan back in the city, "but I desperately need an outside spark to illuminate the subject for me."

In that connection, he concluded, a trip into the field would be a godsend. At just that time, Helmut de Terra, with whom he had dug in India, was on a Carnegie-funded field trip and had invited him to join him. When he presented the project to Father Marin for his consideration, Teilhard did so with all the persuasiveness that he could muster. And in December, just as Japan was setting up her own "Provisional Government of Peking," he sailed from Tientsin for the warm blue waters of Swatow and Burma.

# CHAPTER
# FOURTEEN

It was May before Teilhard came back again to China. He was in time for Lucile's birthday, and he brought her a little ruby he had purchased in Mogok. From a tourist's point of view, the Burma expedition was idyllic. The gentle Buddhist world of brilliantly gowned people, of jungles full of animals along the Irrawaddy, of the desolate ochre soil veined with rubies and tourmalines farther north where he and his friends had prospected, of overnight stays in British "bungalows" among the hummingbirds and parakeets, of days spent with his hands pressed into "Mother Earth," and the sweat pouring into his eyes, had left him feeling physically better than he had in years.

But from a scientific point of view, the trip was only indifferently successful. Impossible terrain on the western mountain heights separating Burma from the Bay of Bengal, and rough traveling conditions in the Shan mountains had forced the expedition to write off many of its projects. Even visits to old Burmese cities, where Teilhard, in imitation of his friend von Koenigswald, had spent much of his time in apothecary shops searching, among the snakes and dried bat-wing remedies, for the "dragon's teeth," which sometimes turned out to have belonged to extinct anthropoid apes, had yielded nothing.

The best thing about the trip had been the company. A young Harvard anthropologist named Hallam Movius and his wife, assigned to the expedition, had been pleasant, eager workers. And despite a muted tension that was growing between the de Terras, Teilhard continued to find them fascinating. Though Helmut's feet were often crippled with blisters, and though inexplicable neck pains frequently incapacitated him for field work, Teilhard was touched by what he saw as the German's "anxious anticipation of the future and almost dolorous need for a philosophical principle on which to build his life."

Rhoda de Terra he admired for quite different reasons. A strong-willed, quick and self-sufficient woman, direct and matter-of-fact, she was, he thought, "remarkably intuitive in psychological matters." Further, to his astonishment, she seemed to function without any need to find an "ultimate justification for her existence." By the time the trip was over, Mrs. de Terra had become one of Teilhard's most faithful correspondents.

As he resettled in Peking in 1938, Teilhard had reason for being in better spirits than he had been in a long time. Even though he still lived at Chabanel under Father Marin's stifling surveillance, he now had news that led him to believe his next trip to Paris could be the one that brought him home for good. While still in Burma, he had received word that both the Institut de Paléontologie Humaine and the Laboratoire des Hautes Études in Paris were offering him important posts. Though he knew there was bound to be considerable pulling and hauling with his Roman superiors about accepting the appointments, he felt that this time they would have to let him have his way if only to save themselves embarrassment. Steeling himself for the upcoming battle, he wrote Mrs. de Terra from Peking that he was nervous about the struggle. "Still," he added, "it's an experience I feel I must go through."

That June among the newly arrived Jesuits at Tientsin Teilhard found himself a new and sturdy friend. He was Pierre Leroy, a light-haired Champagnois biologist whom

Teilhard had met twice in the past and always found extremely winning. Leroy had been called to China in the wake of an attempt on the part of the Jesuits of the Collège des Hautes Études to reorganize their school to meet the challenge of exploding Asian war. One of the first steps in their plan had been to absorb Licent's museum into a new science department built around a core of young and active priests such as Leroy, and make Émile Licent its "honorary director."

Seeing his life's work so undervalued, and himself reduced to nothing but a figurehead, the terrible-tempered Licent roared like a wounded behemoth. He left for Europe, vowing to appeal to the highest authorities in the Society either to restore him to his former place in Tientsin or remove him from China forever.

Leroy was a longtime admirer of Père Licent. He felt for his distress, but still could offer nothing more than words of comfort. A few weeks after the young priest's installation at Tientsin, Teilhard came up to visit. Sympathy between them was immediate.

In every way, Leroy turned out to be a better comrade for Teilhard than Trassaert was. Unlike Trassaert, Leroy, for all his surface grace and gaiety, was from the start acutely sensitive to the springs of anguish from which Teilhard's apparent "optimism" came. Under the hand of Father Marin ("le Monstre Marin"* to most of their whimsical French acquaintances), Teilhard's life was growing increasingly difficult. Time after time the superior lost his temper with Teilhard. He denounced him as a "communist, a pantheist, and an evolutionist." Naturally reluctant, as always, to prolong a scene, Teilhard always ended the confrontations as quickly and politely as he could, leading bewildered agnostic friends such as the spirited Mrs. Gowan to remark of him, "He was handsome; he was charming; he was brilliant. He was everything but brave."

* "The Marine Monster"—the biblical sea beast which swallowed Jonah.

Because of the distance of the Jesuit house from the city, Teilhard's relations with the other members of the Catholic missionary community were sharply curtailed by his residence there. In the frustration of the moment, he was doubly happy to have in Pierre Leroy a Jesuit friend with whom he could speak freely, sure of immediate comprehension. As often as Teilhard had once gone to Tientsin, Leroy now came to Peking to work with his new friend in Lockhart Hall.

That summer, Teilhard's deluge of letters to his European superiors on Trassaert's behalf had at last borne fruit. Trassaert was summoned home to Strasbourg to study for a degree in paleontology. In mid-September he, Teilhard, and Leroy left together for Japan, where they spent a few weeks as tourists. When Leroy returned to China, Trassaert went on to Europe, and Teilhard followed him home a few weeks later after a trip across America.

Once back in Paris and at *Études,* where he was surrounded by allies, Teilhard relaxed. D'Ouince was still superior of the house. Du Passage, Doncœur, Huby, Fessard, and the brilliant young historian and admirer of "La Pensée" Joseph Lecler were there. So was Yves de Montcheuil, a devout and fiery professor from the Institut Catholique, whom Teilhard had met at Fourvière some years earlier through Père de Lubac. So pleased was d'Ouince to have Teilhard with him again that, the very evening he arrived, the superior suggested to a visiting priest from the University of Nancy who was looking for speakers to address his youth group there that he invite Teilhard to speak. Delighted with the scientist's acceptance, the chaplain hurried off to print up his announcements.

But a few days later, when Teilhard made his ritual visit to Lyon to check in with a new provincial, Joseph du Bouchet, he was shocked to find that his reputation within the Society had dropped to a new low. Father Marin, it appeared, had a longer arm than Teilhard had imagined. His influence reached all the way to Rome, where his displeasure over what

he felt was Teilhard's "unclerical" conduct in China had
made a serious impression. After the usual Roman explosion
and the ensuing letter of correction, Père du Bouchet, an
Auvergnat as stubborn as Teilhard, had dug his heels into the
ground. Teilhard was stiffly warned to mend his ways. The
Nancy talk was now out of the question.

When Teilhard went home to Auvergne that Christmas,
he went in search of peace. On the flat, familiar plain of the
Limagne, near his brother Gabriel's house at Murol, everything was black and white with snow—the house so cold that
tracked-in ice lay unmelted in the hallways. Gabriel, who had
always been quick to sense the nuances of Pierre's state of
mind, was delicately solicitous, stealing into his freezing bedroom before dawn to relight the fire, bringing over his lively
blond nephew Olivier (son of their "Parisian" brother, Joseph) to join his own handsome twin boy and girl in entertaining him. "Gabriel," Teilhard was fond of saying "is the
real 'Jesuit' in the family. . . . I am just a spiritual adventurer."

Those short December afternoons, Teilhard walked along
the icy Allier, sorting out his thoughts to the accompaniment
of music from a far-off radio. When evening fell, he came back
to the farmhouse, huddling with the family around the fireplace in the grand salon, where Gabriel tried to cheer him by
recalling stories of autumn hunting visits in their childhood,
pointing out pieces of wood piled on the hearth which came
from this or that part of the estate. But Gabriel's solici-
tousness was all to no avail. Desolation lay like stone in
Teilhard's mind, and, when he returned to Paris, he even
semiseriously discussed with the Begouëns and Ida Treat for
the first time in his life the possibility of his leaving the
Jesuits for the secular priesthood.

While he was away, however, d'Ouince had not been idle.
In January 1939 he wrote the general in Rome again, rere-
questing permission for the Nancy talk and offering to take
personal responsibility for editing Teilhard's lecture. Quite

unexpectedly, the general agreed, and at the end of February Teilhard went south to the pink-brick city of Toulouse to speak at the local Institut Catholique. There he visited with its rector, his old friend Bruno de Solages, and spent hours in private conversation. The lecture went off without a hitch.

That March, *Études* published Teilhard's "La Mystique de la Science," an essay which reproposed, as an alternative to the various "isms" then abroad, a "mysticism" in which all "seekers" or researchers working in the sciences join their efforts for the betterment of man. The article was well received. But while Teilhard seemed just about to redeem himself a little and regain a small foothold in France, there loomed another fateful circumstance—one about which neither he nor any of his friends could do a thing.

For several months most of the Catholic world had known Pius XI was ill. His intimates hinted that in his last years he had been deeply troubled about the long-range effects of the political enterprises of his pontificate. Although at the beginning of his reign he had made an uneasy peace with the Italian and German dictators, and even signed concordats with them, as death approached he seemed to slip into dark moods —particularly when he spoke about the repression of the Catholic Church in Nazi Germany. As early as March 1937, when the embattled German bishops pleaded with him for an official statement, the pope issued "Mit Brennender Sorge," an almost word-for-word rendition of Cardinal Faulhaber's condemnation of Hitler's treatment of German Catholics, elaborated with a few historical passages by the ex-nuncio to Germany, Cardinal Eugenio Pacelli. He followed the encyclical by stronger ones condemning Communist Russia and persecution of the Church by an anticlerical government in Mexico.

When he had issued "Mit Brennender Sorge," the Builder-Pope was not repudiating the work of his long reign. But he was old and heartsick at the direction in which the world was going. In recent years, he had seen Mussolini introduce official anti-Semitism into Italy, and Hitler increase his restrictions on Catholic practice in the territories he controlled. Finally, in a gesture that boded ill for further compromise between the faithful and the dictators, Pius XI suddenly summoned the entire Italian episcopate to Rome. Before he could address them, his ailing body failed. On February 10, 1939, "that stiff-necked man," as Mussolini often called him, died.

By March 2 a papal conclave had elected Eugenio Pacelli pope. Pacelli, who took the name of Pius XII, had once been Ratti's hand-picked man. He was not, however, the heir of the grieving, dying pope who had called the Italian conclave but of the confident autocrat that Pius XI had been in his prime. Like many of his predecessors, he was an alumnus of the Holy Office. His Rome was that of Ledochowski and Garrigou-Lagrange, of aging and powerful cardinals such as Merry de Val's old colleague Nicola Canali, of Adeodato Piazza, of the young Giuseppe Pizzardo, and of the dour new chief of the Holy Office, Francesco Marchetti-Selvaggiani. As soon as news of the election reached Teilhard, any hope he might have entertained about a change in the Roman attitude toward him evaporated. Pushing his problems from his mind, he hurried off to England to attend a geological conference and visit his old friends, the prehistorians Dorothy Garrod and T. T. Paterson.

When he returned to Paris only a few weeks afterward, Teilhard was startled at the change of emotional climate there. Spain was finally capitulating to Franco; the Wehrmacht was entering Prague; and France seemed swept into the vertigo that accompanies a helpless drop into catastrophe. As a lovely harvest of chestnut blossoms and spring flowers nodded around the Louvre and the Luxembourg gardens, Teilhard watched an incredulous populace digging bomb shelters, walking along the boulevards in uniform, and, in cafés, gesticulating helplessly over their anisettes while they argued with one another about the certainty of doom to come.

Without warning, Teilhard found himself under attack from Rome again. The censors had discovered a paper called "The Spiritual Phenomenon,"[1] written two years earlier, which explicitly challenged the Aristotelian distinction between spirit and matter. It further implied that, since reflectivity existed fully and operatively in man, then "germs of consciousness," at least, necessarily existed in even the smallest particle of "brute matter." To the Holy Office and to Ledochowski, the paper made it plain that Teilhard's thinking was as unregenerate as ever.

Near Eastertime Norbert de Boynes, Teilhard's interrogator of 1928, turned up at *Études*. This time his distress was even greater. Though he had never really understood Teilhard's philosophy, he had, until then at least, always trusted his good will. This latest paper challenged even that. De Boynes arrived at the house on the Rue Monsieur expecting to find among the Jesuits living there a reaction similar to his own. To his surprise, most of them rallied around Teilhard with so passionate a solidarity that he was baffled.

The upshot of the visit was that one month later d'Ouince received a surprisingly sympathetic letter from the generalate. It gave Teilhard permission to go back to China briefly to complete his unfinished work and promised that on his return to France he would be allowed to write his philosophic essays, provided that d'Ouince edit them, and thus "erase the sad impression that his mimeographed notes produced."

Though the letter was a very minor victory, it was much more than either Teilhard or d'Ouince had hoped for. Only one more trip to China, and (Teilhard was convinced) he could return to Paris and with his superior's support make his position understood at last.

Just before the summer's heat set in, Teilhard departed for what he believed would be his last short exile. He went by ship via America, accompanied by the increasingly conservative Pierre Charles,† who was going to give a semester of lectures at Fordham University, and his cousin Marguerite Teillard-Chambon. After a few days in New York, he crossed to the West Coast to join Weidenreich and the geologist Charles Camp at a Pacific Science Congress. Then in late August, in the company of Mrs. Swan and several lady missionaries from Yenching University, he sailed again for China.

The crossing was an uneventful one. The sea was calm under a blue sky, and the voyage prolonged itself without incident. Teilhard and the ladies debarked at Kobe, from where they took a Japanese steamer to Taku on the China coast. Suddenly, for the first time in his years of exile, Teilhard himself was touched by one of the natural catastrophes that were always part of daily life for the Chinese. Taku had turned into a disaster area. The Hai Ho floods of 1939 had been cataclysmic, and all lines of transportation to Tientsin were completely out. "Too much water," the steamer captain warned. "You go back to Japan." There was no inn or hotel in the place, but the travelers refused to leave. Carefully hoarding the meager sandwiches he left them, they settled down for the night in acute embarrassment on the wooden floor of a two-room "club," built by some English businessmen. The next afternoon, as they waited despairingly on the dock in the sweltering heat, eating grapes Mrs. Swan had had the foresight to buy in Kobe, they rejoiced to see a vagrant Chinese boat, headed for Tientsin, materialize out of the mist.

The night that followed was even worse. Sick and malodorous refugees crowded the boat back-to-back; there was no room even to sit down. Though Teilhard had hoped to escape

† Since the mid-twenties, the once mischievous and imaginative Père Charles had turned his attention from philosophy to the safer ground of missiology. His work became so well thought of that from 1932 on he had been teaching several months a year at the Gregorian University in Rome.

from Father Marin's critical eye by boarding with the Jesuits at Tientsin when he passed the city this time, he found the school so crowded with flood refugees that he did not even stop. He pushed on to the ancient capital, and spent the night at the Hôtel du Pékin, where he hoped that a hot meal and a good bed would set him up for his encounter with Marin the next day.

The dreaded confrontation never came. On September 1, two days before Teilhard arrived in China, German troops had thundered into Poland, and France and England declared war. Though he admonished Teilhard that he was receiving him despite the fact that he was an "undesirable," Marin bowed to the inevitable and took Teilhard into Chabanel again.

Back in Europe, as Hitler threw the full weight of his Panzers against Poland, mobilization was declared in France. A large force sent into the Saar by the French General Gamelin quickly drove the German occupiers out; but the moment Poland fell, Gamelin rushed his forces back again behind the vaunted security of the Maginot Line. For France, the war ground to a halt. French and German soldiers peered at one another from their bunkers, while behind the lines civilian life went on much the same as ever.

Like many Europeans stranded in Peking, Teilhard was at a loss about what to do. Just two months earlier, his future had seemed so promising. Now he had a whole set of discouraging circumstances to deal with. If the war were to develop into a long and bloody struggle like the last one, what would become of his last chance to spread his message? Could it be, he wrote his brother Joseph, that he still had a duty to try to get back to France and do what he could in a war for which so few of his compatriots showed much enthusiasm? Rembering how "out of contact with the real movement of humanity" those men who had not known the crucible of the war of 1914–18 had been, he wondered if he should not make the effort to return. But could he, at his age and in his state of health, stand up to the trip? Still, if he simply waited where he was, how long would his exile last?

Since 1918, Teilhard had seen so much ideological conflict inside France that this so-far bloodless quarrel with Germany struck little fire in him. Perhaps, he prayed, the "war" would only be one more short parenthesis among the many that had always gathered between him and the fulfillment of his mission. With so little national pride or solidarity displayed among his compatriots at home, perhaps all would be over in a few months. Then, he told himself, he would be ready to spend his diminishing energies in the perhaps more united world that would come after.

# III

# THE
# WAR

# CHAPTER
# FIFTEEN

From the autumn of 1938 Teilhard had planned the outline of his magistral book on man, and he had worked on it in fits and starts. By the autumn of 1939 it was already mapped out clearly in his head. But, given its scope and complexity, the prospect of putting the whole thing down on paper gave him pause. To sit, almost without interruption, for as long as it might take, before a scratch pad in the neo-Chinese "monastery" of Chabanel, and to draw out nearly eighty thousand words that would reflect a complete and convincing statement of his vision of humanity with all its biological, sociological, and mystical aspects, in a way that would neither offend nor patronize nonbelievers, discouraged even him.

Still, now that the results of the conflict in Europe had temporarily removed so much other business from his mind, he knew that the long-postponed moment to produce his book had come.

It was, he told himself, the work he had been born for—the task of setting down in one long statement a religio-scientific philosophic system that would make as much sense to the ordinary educated man of the twentieth century as the *Summa* of Thomas Aquinas had to the scholar of the high Middle Ages. But, given the proliferation of technology and the huge harvest of scientific data over the last half century, the undertaking was an infinitely more complex task than it had been for Thomas, and one impossible to approach in the same way.

And there was also a new optic limitation. Unlike Aquinas
and most other philosophers who examined reality from without, Teilhard, who understood himself to be part of an evolving world, knew he must write about it from *within*. He could
not, therefore, hope to describe all of what was happening, or
predict its future development with precision. All he could do
was examine that movement in himself and describe its general drift as experimentally perceived.

He called his book *Le Phénomène Humain.*[1] The vision of
the work was fundamentally the same as the answer outlined
in "La Vie Cosmique" in 1916. He had already written two
other short adumbrations on that theme, both under the title
"Le Phénomène Humain," the first in 1928, the second in
1930. Now, however, with his ideas clarified and buttressed by
twenty-five years of field and laboratory work, he was ready to
explore the subject in depth.

Teilhard began his exposition, as always, by proposing as
the key to understanding evolution on the planet man himself.* He divided his manuscript into four parts: Prelife, Life,
Thought, and finally—the topic which had always haunted
him—Survival. Because he understood the universe as but a
single organism, he believed that all its properties, however
rarely they might manifest themselves completely, had to be
present to some degree at every level of the evolutionary scale.
This meant that psychic activity which manifests itself fully
in human thought must also prolong itself backward to the
point where the roots of matter "disappear from view."

Thus for Teilhard, all created reality had a "within" as well
as a "without," although, in the inorganic world, only "fleet-
ing hints" of it existed.

* Though, like many scientists of the day, Teilhard accepted the mathematical probability of other similarly evolved intelligences existing on other
planets, he confines his discussion in *The Phenomenon of Man* to the only
intelligent material life of which he was aware. However, since he believed
that, given the required conditions, *all* matter is capable of evolving toward
spirit, his theory is easily expandable to the point where it can embrace the
process of evolution throughout the universe.

There were, therefore, two kinds of energy at work in the world: a measurable force, observable in the interaction of various material units with one another, as in thermo-dynamic, kinetic, electomagnetic, and mechanical energy (to these he gave the name "tangential energy"); and a still-un-measured "radial" or psychic energy, the energy which drove all the elements of the world upward from their natural state of pure disorder until it finally appeared operatively in the human being with his thirst for self-achievement and attrac-tion toward a superior absolute. From whatever "corpuscle" (or grain) in the tiniest, simplest inert physical unit, all the way up the scale of evolution to that marvel of complexity, man, this increase in the "interiority" of things, Teilhard insisted, could always be seen as directly proportional to their complexity—that is, to the degree of their physical organi-zation of "centration" upon themselves.

Eons ago, whether after some quasi-Laplacian act of con-densation of existing gases, or in a sudden, as yet unexplained pulling-together of disparate material units into an exploding mass, the universe with all of its galaxies, stars, and planets was born. On the "privileged" planet earth, swinging at just the right distance and angle from its sun, atoms near the surface combined and recombined in a remarkable fashion, and eventually reached a "critical" state where completely new modes of being became possible.

Not only did the molecules of the earth's crust associate in the dead-end geometric arrangement of brute matter; they quickly evolved into the more intricate, open associations of the constituents of life. At this point their almost imper-ceptible "radial" energy flooded backward on itself and pushed them further upward on the scale of evolution. First as viruses, and later as single cells, the units came together with their molecules, combining and recombining, their ge-netic structure changing, all along the time scale, as different forms of life appeared. During this period, time after time, evolving life forms ran into barriers where, depending on their interior coding, they either remained forever fixed just as they were, in a fully functional condition, or as in the case of other sufficiently complex beings, under the pressure of their back-ward-flooding radial energy, reached on upward toward a higher state of awareness.

Once life appeared on earth, Teilhard declared, the "within" of living beings (however perishable and dependent upon their physical base they still might be) could, in some degree, properly be called their "souls." But, because the un-raveling stuff of the once-gathered universe was constantly groping for greater and greater awareness and sensitivity to stimuli, developing nonreflective species proliferated and com-plexified in apparently random play. The more complex the being became, the sharper its awareness grew, and the sharper its hunger for even greater awareness.

"No sooner had Life started," wrote Teilhard, "than it swarmed." It spread until it formed the earth-covering that Suess had called the "biosphere." At this point, the "psychic temperature" of the earth as a whole not only rose but accel-erated. For billions of years, living matter spread and strug-gled upward "radially," and flooded into increasingly con-scious aggregates, acting and reacting on themselves. All through that time, whole new series of complexities had, in a sense, been "bubbling up." And only very recently that blindly stirring matter had reached the last barrier before it, the threshold of intelligence.

In the world of living things, Teilhard explained, evolution had proceeded with the same headlong (and finally, with the appearance of animal life) bloody rush it had first demon-strated in the geological catastrophes of brute matter. It left an enormity of waste behind it. Not only did uncounted numbers of plant and animal species appear and disappear along the way, but entire worlds of life forms possessed the earth awhile and died out, leaving their unlikely bones in swamps and bogs.

It had taken millions of years and innumerable transformations before "soft, furry, playful, progeny-carrying animals with glimmers of personality" evolved among the chordates, and millions more before biped creatures in the primate group reached the barrier that separated awareness from true thought. One million or so years ago according to Teilhard (three million or more according to more recent estimates) in *one* group alone that energy, expanding in increasingly complex responses to stimuli, flooded inward on itself and moved toward true self-consciousness. Thus reflectivity dawned in a single privileged group. Without any violent upheaval, without seeming to be other than one animal among many but "dropping stone tools behind him all over the old world from North China to the Cape of Good Hope," man appeared.

However softly and unremarkably he came, once man took his place among the animals, evolution changed its course. A new kind of covering began to form over the earth, a covering of thought and of the works of thinking beings. Having reached this point, Teilhard was ready to explore his major preoccupation: the meaning of human existence and the question of survival.

The old anxiety about his own fragility that he first knew as a child at Sarcenat had never really left him. Since those long-ago days when he reached about his head to caress the iron banister post in Clermont, or those autumn afternoons when he walked through the woods at Murol jingling cartridge cases in his pockets or collecting stones, he had, of course, learned considerably more about the genesis of the apparently stable and inert elements he once clung to so desperately. He had opted for the religion of his mother, and thereby for a faith that implied the existence of "spirit"—the one element which could not provably be destroyed. Thereafter, he had spent his life wandering the earth, studying the evolution of animal bodies, examining their various forms and trying to understand the apparently irreversible movement toward increased consciousness.

The conclusions he came to resembled Bergson's—but only

to a certain point. For Bergson, evolution was a process by which things *diverged* into a multiplicity of forms. For Teilhard, it was a *convergent* process—a process of emergence from the darkness of unknowing into light. From the moment that reflection was achieved, the question of a goal appeared— a direction to be followed for those beings clambering upward from the dark.

Again Teilhard recalled the curious disproportion between true man's slight morphological divergence from his closest animal neighbors, and his enormous psychological distance from them. Unlike any other living species, man remembered things. He could wonder about the future; he could worry about the past. He could solve problems; he could use complicated tools. Even the ancient cave paintings he had done showed he knew, quite clearly, both hope and dread. Other animals, of course, were aware. It could be said that they *knew* things. But only man, with his sense of self-identity, knew that he knew them.

Just as, after life appeared, evolution had set out in a new direction, so after the "hominization of life," another new evolutionary process, human socialization, began. In an amazingly short space of time, man conquered the earth and covered it with a network of rapid communication. With the thickening and pressing together of the human population at the beginning of the Neolithic Age, a conscious kind of social and economic interdependence had begun. By the time the nineteenth-century Industrial Age arrived, goals, ideas, and hopes everywhere in the world had become more and more alike. A similarity of needs was forcing men to care for other men, as the price of caring for themselves.

Writing in 1940, Teilhard thought he could see signs of the rapid approach of human "planetization." Great waves (both malign and benevolent) of collectivism, or alliance for war, were just then sweeping the earth like storms. Advances in communications made it possible for individuals physically to cross the world in hours, or to send messages from one end of

it to the other in fractions of seconds. Along with the uproot-
ing of old ways of life and the destruction of cities and cultures which World War II brought with it, there came as a
by-product of man's fury new scientific achievement and cultural growth that reached to the remotest corners of the
globe. In 1940 even the nationalism of many smaller countries was already to some extent being submerged in the larger
split between the Axis nations and the Allies.

What, then, he asked himself, could one hope for when
the war came to an end? Since living space and life resources
were limited, and since the growth of human population
(however much controlled) was bound to continue, since
scientific progress and technology accelerated irreversibly, the
question arose for him: Where would the human voyage go
from there? Could an improved, growing, and ever more
closely associated mankind be expected to continue on the
earth for a long time, or would it be forced to colonize other
planets? And since human individuals would continue to increase at a geometric rate and man would change as he grew
older as a race, what were the phases that awaited this remarkable collectivity, if it was to achieve itself fully? Finally,
what would happen when the "psychic temperature" of the
human species reached its own critical barrier? Could anyone
really believe that at the end of all this agony, this waste, this
labor, the final "arrangement" of psyches that evolution built
across the millennia would simply be disintegration?

Teilhard was no dicer against doom as Pascal had been. For
his own psychological peace he had very early opted for what
he felt was reasoned optimism. And though other kinds of energetics always interested him, it was humanity and humanity's most powerful energy—love—in which he put his trust.

Sartre has said that "Hell is other people." Teilhard saw
nothing to exclude the possibility that they might be Paradise.
When "the human nuclei were pressed naked one against the
other," man (unlike the lower animals, which in crowded
conditions, generally run mad) could reflect on his condition

and control it. Men would, he believed, learn in time to care for one another as a whole, to protect and share with one another, and even be willing to sacrifice their individual interests for the great "self" of mankind, in the certainty that their mutual cooperation could only individualize them further. When this attitude became common, Teilhard held, the psychic temperature of the conscious world would reach a new incandescence. Men, individually and collectively, would naturally turn inward on themselves in search of union with a being more living and more conscious than they were themselves. And such a being could only be that mysterious force which lay at the heart of reality from the beginning—the point of incandescence and personal passage to which Teilhard gave the code name "Omega."†

Such union meant, of course, a collective detachment of the finally united psyches from the fragile physical bases that had brought them into being and supported their existence. Teilhard, the priest, was persuaded that such a progress had been at work since reflectivity appeared. All the time that evolution did its work on this side of death, a world of dematerialized psychological centers, he believed, had been collecting on its other side, in the wholly stable personal center which first began and then sustained creation. All through human history, it had been so, with psyches drifting, one by one, out of their bodies when physical death occurred. The only difference between these individual deaths and the general "death" at world's end lay in the fact that in the last great leap of consciousness, thinking centers would be shaken all together, from their physical supports into the one nonphysical and utterly stable center, where the other prema-

† In other essays, Teilhard makes clear that his "Point Omega" is the cosmic aspect of Christ, much referred to in the epistles of Saint Paul. This Christ is the same Jesus of Nazareth through whom God made Himself part of creation two thousand years ago, and who would finally possess creation at its maturation. It should be added that, since all the universe is but a single stuff, God would only have to enter the tangible universe at one time and in one place (or planet) to possess and Christify the whole of creation.

turely detached, isolated psyches long ago freed from their disintegrated physical bases were now waiting.

Thus Teilhard envisioned the end of the evolutionary process. To "theologians," he left the question of "the new Heaven and the new Earth" to be reconstructed, either from "the ashes of the world," or by some other means. Since the life span on the earth of certain vertebrates is very long (turtles, for example, go back 200 million years), man, he thought, who had lived on earth only a fraction of these years, was extremely young. It was fascinating to imagine all the possibilities he would develop in the time before him. In *The Phenomenon of Man* Teilhard was not even much concerned as to whether there would be a final bifurcation of the human stock, whereby some units of the thinking world would turn away from the force which had produced them, and deteriorate with disassociating matter; or whether all thinking beings of the universe would move together to their source. Whichever way this last leap went—toward total unity or only partial unity—Teilhard was certain that "the world will end in Ecstasy."‡

From autumn until spring, Teilhard worked steadily on his manuscript. But even with this task to occupy him, the restricted life at Chabanel continued to oppress him. Though he comported himself as a model religious, he was lonely and ill, eager to escape from his rice-paper prison. Friends who saw him that winter of 1939–40 remember the pain in his face as he sat in his rickshaw, bundled to the eyes, setting off in the gathering dusk from the Cenozoic lab for the long ride in the powdery snow through the Imperial City, past Coal Hill and the frozen paddy fields, to Chabanel. Only once, one February night when he acted as toastmaster for Grabau's birthday dinner, did he ask for permission to return home late. He tried to reconcile himself to exile as long as the conflict in Europe lasted. But once he saw his manuscript finished and

‡ From the Greek *ekstasis*, "standing outside."

no end to his exile yet in sight, he knew he had to find another occupation to keep him busy while he was in China.

The solution to his problem came that spring by way of Père Leroy. As the "phony war" in Europe, that awful state of things that was neither peace nor war, dragged on, the young priest had become more and more troubled about the fate of the collection in Licent's museum. A foreign treaty port containing many powerful European business concessions, Tienstsin had by then assumed the atmosphere of an armed camp. Barbed-wire barricades now separated the Westerners' section from the Chinese city, and the foreigners more and more often were stopped by Japanese soldiers for search or simple insult. To the Jesuits of Race Course Road, who were forced to accept more and more Chinese students who could not reach the schools of Shanghai and the south, the importance of preserving Licent's museum assumed diminishing importance. And by early spring of 1940, Leroy had little doubt that the collection was destined to be swallowed like an ill-made ark in the sea of continental war.

It was then that Teilhard suggested Leroy try to save it. Why not, he asked, look for a little money and, of course, the proper authorization, and ship the best of Licent's library and the fossil pieces off to then-peaceful Peking for safekeeping? There, even with a very small staff, a new scientific center of the sort that Black and Weidenreich had once proposed could be established.

Since the mechanically and chemically accumulating earth crust was inseparable, both in genesis and function, from the life mass that evolved from it, the best way to study living forms is to do so in connection with their particular environment. In the 1930s, the great plain of North China, still so little disturbed either by geological catastrophe or human intervention, was a marvelous laboratory for field workers to examine the evolution of both living and fossil vertebrates. With the creation of an Institute of Geo-Biology in which Teilhard would serve as geologist, Leroy as biologist, and perhaps another priest as botanist, Davidson Black's dream of describing the rise of vertebrates in China might, in a small way, be continued.

With a casual disregard for the fact that the country he proposed to study was in the midst of the most chaotic war it had ever suffered, he presented his idea to Père Leroy. Since life in China always seemed a bit unreal, Leroy was in no way startled by Teilhard's suggestion. A few days after listening to Teilhard's idea, he rushed down to Peking to ask the aid of his friend Ambassador Henri Cosme, who not only offered him the use of the officers' barracks of the French embassy (empty since the recall of the military to France the past September) for their new enterprise, but who arranged for them to have a gift of five thousand dollars from Foreign Ministry funds to get the project off the ground.

Thus, in a single stroke Teilhard's and Leroy's problems both were solved. The Tientsin superior, Père Charvet, was happy to say goodbye to Leroy, whom he feared would soon become "another Licent," and Chabanel's Père Marin was overjoyed to be relieved of the disturbing presence of Teilhard. A botanist was assigned to work with them, and a father minister appointed to see to the house. All that remained for Teilhard and Leroy to do was assemble the best specimens out of the enormous collection of fossils Licent had spent his life accumulating, and then to pack and ship them the eighty miles west to Peking.

Well into May, whenever the uncertain railroad to Tientsin was working, Teilhard continued to visit the *collège* to finish sorting out Licent's old collection. Commuting, though necessary, was wearing. Though winter had ended softly in Peking, in Tientsin, where the Hai Ho floods of the previous summer had filled the property on Race Course Road with water over three feet deep and reduced one of the exasperated priests to crossing the court in biretta and bathing suit, everything was still thick with mud. The museum gallery had been flooded and the fossils badly damaged. Licent never was a careful classifier, and now even the specimens he did mark had come unglued.

Even if it could be gone at with a peaceful mind, reassembling the fossils would have been a frustrating job. But, like most of the members of the foreign community, Leroy and Teilhard felt they spent that spring in China in suspended time. Japanese troops ravaged the countryside and even stomped through certain northern cities, making daily life uncertain. But in Europe Germany seemed to show a perplexing lack of interest in engaging the Western enemies who had declared war on her the previous September. Though in March Russia devoured Finland, life in France remained unchanged. The argument between mobilization and antimobilization factions within the country seemed more real than the German threat without. The government sent ten thousand footballs to amuse and exercise the soldiers on the Maginot Line. Ladies of means sent rosebushes to beautify the concrete bunkers. Generals imported private chefs and champagne to civilize the life there. But the boredom of the guardians of the Line was not to be assuaged. If rumors of an imminent German invasion flew one day, they were cancelled out the next by Hitler's announcement that, declaration of war or no, he had no quarrel with France, which he claimed had been dragged into the conflict on the heels of an English promise to aid Poland. When, on April 9, the Nazis invaded Denmark and attacked the Norwegian coast, it appeared to many hopeful Frenchmen that the greedy German eye was entirely turned toward the North Sea. As in a trance, French sentinels trained their telescopes on the east for signs of activity. But nothing moved at all.

Suddenly on the night of May 9, 1940, the whole earth shuddered. Spearheaded by heavy air attacks, the Wehrmacht smashed through Holland and Belgium in the direction of Liège and the Ardennes. The lines of France's resistance tore like paper under German steel. On June 4 the last of the bewildered British and the few French and Belgian troops they could take with them were evacuated from Dunkirk. Paris fell on June 14, and Philippe Pétain, the eighty-four-year-old hero of Verdun was called in to head a government. On June 17 Charles de Gaulle flew out of Bordeaux in a light plane, carrying with him the best of his country's honor. On June 21 France surrendered.

Within two weeks Germany had occupied all of France north of the Loire and her entire Atlantic coast. Marshal Pétain set up the capital of his new "Free Zone" at Vichy. Only the British, driven back across the Channel, now stood in the way of German conquest of the whole of Europe. Across the world, friendships, families, even religious houses, were torn in two. "See!" one Tientsin German Jesuit had exulted to a Dutch confrere when Holland fell. "This is what we Germans can do when we want to!"

Among the French in China, the shock and grief were terrible. Even Teilhard, who had been brought up not to show his feelings, often felt paralyzed with bewilderment. More than once in those last visits to Tientsin, Leroy had surprised him sitting idly before a fossil tray from the long chest that ran through the center of Licent's high-windowed gallery looking shockingly old and small, his glasses on his lap, rubbing tears from his cheeks with the back of his hand and murmuring softly to himself, "I don't understand; I just don't understand."

# CHAPTER
# SIXTEEN

On July 11, 1940, in crates as big as elephant cages, the shipment of Tientsin specimens arrived in Peking. They lumbered down the Rue Labrousse, frightening the Chinese police, sending the little White Russian photographer Vargosov scurrying for tripod and camera to record the event and almost toppling his enormous bathrobed roommate in the process.

By then, Teilhard and Leroy, a Tientsin botanist named Roi, and the father minister, Étienne Merveille, had been living at the Institute more than a month. The fifth member of the household was Rat d'Eau, a big brown Chesapeake retriever who had followed Leroy from Tientsin and who had the habit of collecting bits of brick from the corner of the barracks courtyard and parading before Teilhard with the fragments in his mouth.

During the first four months in Peking, the Jesuits spent most of their time uncrating and sorting out the specimens they had brought. Their new establishment was a most pleasant place to work—a Spartan, dark red building from which one had only to step into the street at any hour to chat with friends. Until the summer's heat set in and most of the foreign community left for the hills or the seashore, the priests could socialize with their neighbors during the long lunch breaks and visit them in the afternoon from five o'clock, when the day's work was done, until eight, when Père Merveille closed the door.

In June Teilhard had put what he hoped was the final polish on his "big book on man." The afternoon he finished it, he brought the manscript to Lucile Swan in her garden. As happy, perhaps, as he was to see the long labor finished, she immediately sat down to read it, looking (at Teilhard's suggestion) for its inspiration in the Gospel of John.

Lucile arranged for three clean copies of the manuscript to be typed and ready for examination. But in the days that followed her departure for vacation, Teilhard wondered for whose eyes? Père d'Ouince, who had promised to be the editor of his papers, was now captive in a German prisoner-of-war camp; the military situation made deliveries to Rome uncertain; and even if a copy of the book could somehow be gotten to the generalate in Italy, who, Teilhard wondered, would be there to speak on his behalf? To ensure the manuscript's survival in a neutral country until the war's end, Lucile, just before leaving, had suggested that Teilhard ask a sympathetic American diplomat named John Wiley, who was passing through Peking en route to Washington, to take a copy with him to Father Edmond Walsh of Georgetown, while Teilhard kept the other two copies temporarily in his desk.

By August the personnel of the new Institute of Geo-Biology had changed. Père Roi (who had never really felt at ease in Peking) left for Shanghai, and the gentle Étienne Merveille was replaced by the ascetic Paul Bornet. Teilhard and Leroy were left much on their own. Their days began to assume a common rhythm. They alternated as acolytes at each other's early morning Masses, breakfasted together, smoked and talked awhile, then finished the morning working on mongraphs about the Tientsin fossils. At noon they suffered silently through one of the inedible repasts of boiled beef that the unimaginative Bornet served three times a day, then separated for the afternoon, Leroy working on the endocrinology of earthworms in his laboratory and Teilhard mulling over new philosophical papers in his study. While other Europeans were away enjoying the fresh winds of the mountains or the sea breezes on their verandas at the ocean resort of Peitaho, they spent their free time walking together through the streets of a sticky city noisy with cicadas and as empty as Paris in August. Occasionally they made excursions to local monuments as far out as the Summer Palace—where once, forgetting the Chinese habit of writing even English from right to left, they stood baffled (like many other Latin-educated clerics) before a sign that read "SUB LAPICINUM," until the advertised vehicle arrived to take them back to town.

When, in late September, the vacationing Westerners came back to Peking, social life picked up again. The Cosmes, the Dorgets, the Raphaels, and the Jesuits' friends in the rapidly shrinking American colony once more began receiving. Each afternoon Teilhard and Leroy took their tea with Mrs. Swan, and on Sundays they went with some group to a picnic in the Western Hills. While Leroy sat on the grass and talked, or helped his hosts in serving, the tireless Teilhard climbed the hills like a mountain goat ("If I had tried to keep up with him" Leroy still sighs, "it would have killed me!"), chipping away at the rocks with his little hammer. More than once, when the bespectacled Paul Raphael (himself a mineralogist) went to fetch him back for lunch, he found Teilhard perched on a steep-grade hillside like some strange bird, staring intently at pebbles in his hand. One day, as Raphael commented on the depth of his concentration, he explained, smiling, "To me these stones are living things."

The picnic parties usually finished up at someone's house, most frequently in the parlor of Tillie Hoffman, a red-haired secretary from the American embassy (fondly called "Tillie the Toiler" by the community), who had the distinction of owning one of the of the few private pianos in Peking, whose gray Angora cat, curled in a green jade bowl, Teilhard would stroke while he listened to Leroy play his musical compositions for the assembly.

With the arrival of autumn, the French embassy, understaffed since the fall of France in June, received a complement of Vichy appointees, and mocking images of its old, graceful lifestyle reappeared. Soon the embassy was apparently conducting its business as usual. By day its typewriters clattered busily and its telephones jangled as though there were really something to say. In the evening, gentlemen in white tie and decorations still met occasionally to dance with clingingly gowned ladies and stroll across the parquet floors through the labyrinthine glass galleries. The social scene was animated now by visits to Peking of the new Shanghai consul, Roland de Margerie—nephew of Teilhard's old friend the geologist Emmanuel de Margerie—a cultivated, dashing man whom Teilhard described as "an aristocrat out of the eighteenth century somehow strayed into our own."

Like all the other actors in the new shadow-play French community, Teilhard and Leroy strained for any grain of sure information from outside. Each night at nine they made a ritual of sitting down in the long green salon of the Institute of Geo-Biology and turning on either the Voice of London or a sometimes audible broadcast out of San Francisco, to balance against the propaganda of the Domei or the German Transoceanic news agencies, which assaulted them all day.

The worst of it was trying to make sense out of the rebroadcast news from Vichy. The descriptions of life in postarmistice France were inconceivable. It was reported that French working people, weary after decades of political corruption, actually admired the vitality and unity of purpose of their conquerors; and in the first year of the armistice, one hundred thousand of them freely volunteered to go to work in factories in Germany. Recordings of Pétain's grandfatherly voice denouncing equally capitalism, liberalism, Marxism, and other "abstract systems of ideology," and urging patience and forbearance, in what Teilhard called "copybook maxims

for good children," were constantly played on the local radio.
Teilhard's letters home consisted mostly of variations on the
questions "Where are you? . . . How are you? . . . What is
really going on over there?" The nearest thing to a reply came
in a disturbing cryptic postcard Teilhard received via Switzerland from a French historian he knew. "It is terrible here,"
the note read. "All the bishops and cardinals are following
Vichy."

"We grow used to knowing nothing, foreseeing nothing
. . . ," Teilhard wrote to his cousin Marguerite as months
wore on. "We are practically prisoners ourselves. . . ." Finally, from the Apostolic Delegate, Bishop Zanin, whose ecclesiastical channels for information had remained open, he
received one piece of sad but certain news. His young friend
Maurice Trassaert, whose steadfastness had always troubled
him, had left the Jesuits. When war broke out, and the young
priest's father and brother were killed under a German-
bombed roof, his fragile "faith in man" was shattered. Trassaert joined the army, and was later reported to have married
his young secretary. All Teilhard could then be sure of was
that he was alive and safe, living in the Vichy Zone.

In that first winter of the war the nervous depression which
had troubled him since childhood descended on Teilhard
with a vengeance. Though, at the suggestion of Madame
Henri Cosme, he considered going on a lecture tour to South
America to raise money to maintain his little institution,
Rome quickly refused him. Sometimes his semipsychological
distress took him with a physical violence. He would wake at
night, covered with sweat after dreaming that his heart and
lungs had stopped, and feel for his pulse or cough into a
handkerchief for a sign of blood that never came. Nor did
morning drive the dark away. Sometimes, even when he was
in company, his eyes would lose their luster and he would
murmur, "Please excuse me. I don't feel well." Then Père
Leroy had only two choices: following him to comfort him,
or remaining where he was and pretending that nothing had

happened. Usually, in some embarrassment, he excused himself and left.

For six long months the two unexamined copies of *The Phenomenon* lay in Teilhard's desk drawer. By spring his agitation over them was quite unbearable. On March 6, 1941, concluding that anything was better than living with such uncertainty, he took one copy out, wrapped it carefully, and sent it off to Rome. "Now," he wrote the Abbé Breuil a few weeks later, "the die is truly cast."

Meanwhile, on the world scale, another storm seemed just about to break. In 1941 tension between Tokyo and Washington had been mounting. America seemed determined to resist further Japanese incursion in Asia. On the other hand, Japan could see no reason why—since the Europeans built Pacific empires—she, an Asian nation, could not do the same. That year the same America which a century earlier had forced entry into Japan's close world stood aghast at the spectacle of a new enemy with an alien Samurai mystique, which had at the same time acquired all the technical proficiency of the twentieth century.

The American colony in Peking was shrinking rapidly. The American President Lines had canceled its Orient run the year before, and women and children were departing by any other means they could find. Olga Hempel Gowan had sailed for home the previous December, to be replaced at Lockhart Hall by the tomboyish, chain-smoking, German-born Claire Herschfeld. When spring came, Mrs. Calhoun closed down her "hotel" and prepared to leave Peking. Robert, the younger of the Drummond brothers, wound up his affairs and set out to join the Red Cross in Chungking. Even Mrs. Swan, who had determinedly put off her packing until the last minute, saw she, too, must leave. An exasperated American diplomat friend kept scolding, " 'Swanny,' what in heaven's name are you still doing here? . . . Go home!"

Lucile tried to stretch her Indian Summer of the Imagination as long as possible. She had finished Weidenreich's commission to sculpture the probable appearance of the Peking man,* and even though she knew that the souvenirs of the magic city where she had lived for twelve years could not survive in the outside world, she laid them carefully away like party favors. Every moment left her she planned around Teilhard. On May 1, in the company of Bob Drummond, the German Eleanor Tafel, and the PUMC parasitologist Rhineholt Höppeli, she arranged a picnic amid the temples and flowering plum trees of the Western Hills to celebrate the Jesuit's sixtieth birthday. Miss Tafel brought a chocolate cake decorated with candles. Besides the small picnic group, Lucile invited a larger number of his friends to a cocktail party later at her house. Though Teilhard responded to it all with his habitual polite enthusiasm, the gathering had something of a valedictory about it.

August 8, 1941, was the date Lucile dreaded. It was then that the last suitable freighter was to leave from Chinwang-tao. At a party a week before, she met a Marine officer who offered to send some of his men to help her move her baggage. On the morning of her departure, Teilhard stopped by alone to see her. The moment he appeared she melted into tears. He gave her a goodbye letter to take with her, and a copy of the representation of the Sacred Heart of Jesus, like the one he kept on his desk in the Institute of Geo-Biology beside a picture of Galileo. Though he kept on insisting their separation was to be a short one, nothing he could do seemed able to raise her spirits.

Riding side by side with him along the glacis toward Ch'ien-men Gate and the railroad station, Lucile continued to weep openly. As the old friends stood on the train platform, Teilhard turned and smiled at her a final time. The years had marked their passage on his face, but his gray-green eyes were just the same as they had been at Grabau's dinner party. "God bless you, Lucile," he said. Then he turned to

* The Sinanthropus skull was in reality that of a female. The researchers at Peking called her "Nellie."

Mrs. Calhoun, who was leaving in the same party. Bowing gallantly over her notoriously recalcitrant hearing aid, he cried at the top of his lungs, "Goodbye, Mrs. Calhoun!" The old lady drew herself up grandly. "Really," she kept muttering as the train pulled from the station, "I'm not deaf, you know!"

The rest of the month Teilhard spent in the Institute alone with Père Bornet. In September 1941 a frazzled Leroy came back from Indochina, full of frightening news. That August, over the objections of the colonists but with Vichy's consent, Japanese troops had landed at Saigon and headed for new bases near the city.† Though Leroy was bursting to talk about his adventures, Teilhard was much too preoccupied with problems of his own to give him the attention he deserved. Having been refused permission to attend a World Congress of Religions that summer in New York at which both Maritain and Einstein were speaking, Teilhard had sent a paper[1]; now, when an invitation to attend the congress planned for 1942 arrived, he wrote to Rome again.

That fall and winter looked so bleak for Westerners in China that Dr. Houghton briefly thought of moving the entire PUMC staff and equipment to join the Kuomintang. When the move proved impracticable, he settled for ordering that the precious bones of the Sinanthropus be packed and hidden in the PUMC safe until they could be moved to safer ground. The medical school and its laboratories remained where they were, "ready," as the American State Department had advised it to be, "for all eventualities."

That fall Japanese-American relations took a drastic downturn. After making three attempts to hold together a quasi-moderate cabinet, the enigmatic Japanese premier, Prince Konoye, ceded power to General Hideki Tojo and the mili-

---

† When the Japanese made their first landing at Haiphong in July 1940, French troops put up a brief but vigorous resistance. Thereafter, from September to December, the Japanese-supported Thais busied themselves cutting their own slice from Cambodia.

tarists. On November 3 Tojo's special envoy Saburo Kurusu arrived in Washington with the new premier's proposals. They were in effect a call for war. America was to give up interfering with Japanese expansion, remove trade restrictions against her, recognize her conquests, and reopen trade negotiations—all under pain of military confrontation. The United States refused, but negotiations ostensibly continued.

Even after the Tojo take-over, Teilhard had continued writing contacts in America and Rome in the hope of finding a place for himself in the United States when the inevitable explosion came. Though answers from American scientists were welcoming, his Roman superiors remained adamantly silent.

Sunday, December 7 (Saturday, December 6, on the American side of the International Dateline), was a cold, bright day in Peking. Teilhard made his usual picnic trip with Leroy and other friends to the Western Hills. The company was gay and entertaining, but, feeling a bit dispirited, he excused himself early and went home.

Outside the Geo-Biological Institute, the Japanese parade ground was noisier than usual that night. But since that compound lay across the street and nearest to Father Bornet's quarters, the sounds of unusual activity were muffled in Teilhard's room.

After listening to the evening broadcast of the Voice of London, which discussed the next day's scheduled meeting between Kurusu and Hull, Teilhard and Leroy had said good night and gone to bed. The proceedings in Washington had a strange Kabuki air, and both men left the salon inexplicably distressed. On the way to his bedroom, Teilhard passed the corridor fronting on the moon-bright Chinese courtyard, and inside, undressed slowly and distractedly. Even without artificial light, a bomber's moon had reflected harshly on the frozen ground outside. The light was pale and white, uncomfortably reminiscent of the death's-head moonlight he had described standing in the battlefield of the Aisne valley so long ago.[2] His little room was cold—much colder than usual in Peking for a December night. While Teilhard finished his evening prayers, he felt his fingers tremble. He piled more charcoal balls into the pipe stove of his little room, crossed himself, drew thick cotton quilts up about his chin, and drifted off into a restless sleep.

# CHAPTER
# SEVENTEEN

Monday was Poney Burchard's banking day. That morning of December 8, as always when she went on early errands, she dressed quickly so as not to disturb her ailing husband, breakfasted alone, and quietly left the house. The weather was fine for the time of year, with the air bright and clear as glass, and a dry, powdery snow drifting slowly down. But crossing into Legation Street from the direction of the Russian compound, she suddenly felt an odd sense of unease. The streets she had passed by were almost empty. Only a few Japanese soldiers, triumphantly drunk on rice wine, staggered across the snow, stopping to point and laugh at her. When she reached the German bank, she found it closed; two brawny Japanese guards crossed rifles at the entrance. "You go home," they barked at her. "Bank closed. No money today."

Across the avenue she glimpsed the furtive figure of an antique dealer she knew. He crunched over the snow toward her. "They've done it," he announced breathlessly when he reached her side. "This morning, the Japanese bombed Pearl Harbor!"

Then, coming around the corner of Meiji Street, Mrs. Burchard sighted the lean, shuffling silhouette of Père Teilhard. He had also heard about the bombing. He could, however, add little to what she already knew. Early that morning, when he and Père Leroy had tried to enter Lockhart Hall, they found the whole PUMC complex cordoned off. Doctors and nurses were permitted to enter the hospital to minister to their patients. But no one else could pass.

After a brief exchange, Mrs. Burchard hurried away to try to borrow cash from friends. Teilhard returned to the Institute of Geo-Biology, where Leroy crouched alone before the radio fiddling distractedly with the dial. All frequencies were jammed by the blaring of the "Kimigayo," interspersed with announcements of the Japanese invasion of the Philippines and the take-over of Malaya.

They stared at each other in dismay. Now what could they expect? Would the rampaging Japanese still honor the commitments they had made to Vichy and leave the French in peace? What was to become of the Americans and British turned overnight into "enemy aliens"? Since they were scientists, they were bound to wonder as well, what might happen to the irreplaceable Sinanthropus bones which had been packed and hidden at the Rockefeller hospital. As far as either of them knew, the bones were still locked away in its safe,* whereas the environmental fossil material, which they had been working with, was in the lab at Lockhart Hall.

At almost the moment they were talking, at the American embassy the dismal surrender ritual was in progress. Since Ambassador Nelson Johnson was momentarily in Nanking, the chargé, Richard W. Buttrick, having burned his code keys and papers, officially surrendered the building to the Japanese commandant. Embassy personnel were rounded up, allowed

---

* Without their knowledge, Dr. Houghton had arranged with the U. S. Marine commandant, Colonel Ashurst, to send the fossils from the PUMC to the Museum of Natural History in New York. They were to be deposited with the luggage of a homebound navy surgeon when the Fourth Marines left Holcomb barracks on the U.S.S. *President Harrison* from the port of Chinwangtao. Early that morning of December 8 (Peking time), during a scuffle between the eighteen Marines on the docks and several hundred Japanese troops, some of the luggage had been piled up to make barricades, while the rest of it had simply been left on the dock where any looting private soldier could have emptied it. The doctor was eventually interned in Shanghai. But when his bags were returned to him in camp some time afterward, the bones were gone.

to rickshaw home a final time to collect personal effects and two Chinese servants per person, and then put under house arrest at the embassy until the exchange of diplomats could be arranged.

On Tuesday another Japanese officer officially received from Dr. Houghton the keys to the PUMC, which was marked for conversion to a Japanese military hospital. Houghton, Trevor Bowen (the PUMC controller), and Leighton Stuart, president of Yenching University, were hauled away first for questioning to the American Marine barracks in the city and then interned in Houghton's house for the duration of the war.

An order for the confiscation of all radios held by "enemy aliens," was issued, and arm bands (red for Americans and British, green for Dutch, Belgians, and French) were distributed to all but German and Italian Axis allies. In the next few weeks, while the terrified British and Americans kept carefully indoors, Teilhard and Leroy used their Vichy credentials to get back into the lab at Lockhart Hall.

On entering, they found to their dismay that, though most of the equipment was intact, the environmental material had almost totally disappeared. They collected typewriters, cameras, and other equipment which they declared their "personal effects" and hauled them off to the Institute of Geo-Biology. Later some of the missing fossil material reappeared. Much of it they found on sale at the Thieves' Market; the rest was somehow retrieved for them by Chinese friends. Although the collection was never fully reconstructed, they found they had more than enough material to continue with their scientific publications for some time to come.

That bitter spring of 1942, Japanese in the Pacific swept everything before them. By April 1942 Hong Kong, Borneo, Malaya, Java, and finally Bataan had fallen. In the months that followed, despite the muffled blaring of victorious Japanese bands across the courtyard all day long, the Jesuits somehow managed to finish off several scientific monographs, and in Teilhard's case, even to give a lecture on fossil man at the Vatican-protected Fujen University. Teilhard also had the delicate problem of disposing of an invitation from his friend the Vichy ambassador to Japan, Charles Arsène-Henri, to accept the directorship of a Franco-Japanese scientific center in Tokyo, where he was promised he could have all the newest technological instruments he needed for his work. However tempting the offer might have been, it was not worth the price that he would have to pay in the loss of friendship with his British and American colleagues.

The months that followed were drab and claustrophobic, and when the Jesuits' superiors repeatedly put off giving the permission to accept an invitation proffered by Roland de Margerie to come and give a lecture to the Shanghai Alliance Française, Teilhard and Leroy were quietly dismayed.

In France, though, that spring anti-German tension had begun to rise. As early as the previous August a German naval officer was shot down in a Paris subway station. Thereafter, the score of reprisals and counterreprisals between the occupiers and the new handful of Resistance fighters in both the "Free" and captive zones was growing day by day. By the spring of 1942 German pressure forced Pétain's chief of government, Admiral Darlan, to hand his powers over to Pierre Laval, who immediately enacted a series of anti-Semitic and antiforeign restrictions in the south; and later that summer a German gauleiter arrived, empowered to round up 350,000 French workers and deport them to Germany. About the time of the Laval take-over, Robert Murphy, counselor of the U.S. embassy, who had been shuttling back and forth between North Africa and the Métropole, had made contact with the "Group of Five," Resistance leaders who formed the nucleus of the formal Allied-sponsored French underground. By October he had primed them to be ready for an African invasion.

That same autumn Admiral Darlan flew to Algeria. On November 8 Mark Clark led American and British troops in a landing on North Africa; and after a brief, bitter engagement, Darlan, acting as Pétain's representative in Africa, agreed to a cessation of hostilities in Algiers; on November 9 the Allies deposited General Henri Giraud there to rally Frenchmen to their cause. Three days later a furious wave of German troops swept down over the demarcation line in "unoccupied" France and the take-over of Vichy had begun.

Two oceans and a continent away, the French community in Peking was more adrift than ever. If the more politically aware people spoke about the state of things at home, they spoke of it in whispers. Still, as the winter chill came on, a second kind of chill seemed to have dropped over the life of the community.

That November word finally came from Teilhard's Jesuit superiors that he and Leroy would be allowed to go and lecture in Shanghai. On the fifteenth, in a dirty third-class Chinese railroad car in which they were to spend two miserable days and nights, they started south, Teilhard with his eyes closed and his fingers threading the broken rosary he always carried; Leroy eagerly watching the moving landscape just outside.

On the seventeenth, near midnight, they arrived in the frozen half-light of the crowded Shanghai station. There Claude Rivière, a lady broadcaster who had interviewed them in Peking two years earlier, was waiting. After seeing to it that the travelers had a hot supper, she hustled them off to their lodgings in the famous old Jesuit Aurora University in the Zikawei district.

Partly because of their association with the Choukoutien discoveries, partly because of the advance publicity spread by friends who had known them in Peking, the conferences of Teilhard and Leroy had been awaited as two of the principal cultural events of the season. But the wary Aurora Jesuits delayed again. The day after their arrival, Teilhard and Leroy were informed that their talks had been put off some weeks at least.

While Leroy scoured the great library of the university for more material, Teilhard socialized in Shanghai. At the Aurora, he spent time with a bright young economist, Emmanuel de Breuvery, and its rector, Père Germain. He called on the de Margeries and other lay friends in the foreign community. Under the guidance of Mme. Rivière who was still looking for material for her radio program, he went sight-seeing along the Bund, through the International Settlement, and into the Chinese Quarter of Shanghai.

Teilhard and Leroy's visit to the city coincided with a Japanese-sponsored Buddhist convocation aimed at rallying Chinese Buddhists to the support of their "Greater East Asia" program, which included the presence in local temples of two "Living Buddhas," one from Mongolia and one from Tibet, whom Mme. Rivière urged Teilhard to meet. Without much enthusiasm, he agreed. The events of each visit were much the same. After passing courtyards full of mah-jongg players or relatives merrily feasting the memory of departed souls, he and his guide were ushered through shadowy rooms full of terrifying idols and thick with the smell of incense into the chambers where each of the August Presences sat. They exchanged banalities through translators with the Buddhas, received the blessing of each, and then departed.

Both times Teilhard walked into the daylight with the same show of relief. The open pragmatism, the apparent absence of real mystical preoccupation in Chinese religion—Buddhist or Taoist—had always troubled him. In religion-teeming India, where the very sight of the insurmountable misery all around led so many people to give up, the very act of "giving up" had become a genuine "mysticism," with nothingness sought as the ultimate bliss; and though Teilhard could not accept as a legitimate path to ultimate fulfillment the bypassing of the material, he did recognize the impulse as religious. In other oriental countries, such as Burma or Ceylon, where daily existence was not so difficult, men could afford to be "mystical" in a lesser fashion. Teilhard had already met many Burmese and Ceylonese whose kindness and whose radiant inner peace impressed him deeply.

The Chinese, however, he often noted, were too hardy and pragmatic a race to waste much time on the intangible. What most of the Western missionaries and sometimes (Teilhard admitted) he, too, overlooked, was how deep a mark century after century of poverty, hunger, and exploitation—every form of dehumanization possible—had made on a people predisposed, perhaps, by their environment, climate, and history to a more Faustian spirit than their neighbors. The missionaries did not see, as the simplest Chinese peasant did, that while men perhaps could not live by rice alone, they certainly could not live or think or feel without their rice at all. Since most of the people of China in the first half of this century scraped out a short and precarious existence, plagued by misfortune and disease, living by their wits from day to day, disposing of those of their clan who could not pull their own weight and moving on, the primary interest of each individual was his *fan* or bowl of rice, whether he ate it on a curb beside a running gutter or in an exquisite pavilion. "What is the point," the venerable Dr. Ting, long-ago head of the Chinese Geological Survey, had once asked Teilhard, "of tormenting yourself with the insoluable problems of the meaning of life, death, and creation, when these problems are beyond our understanding? . . . True wisdom lies in acting as if such problems did not exist. . . ." And this conversation, unhappily, was the only hint Teilhard ever was to have of the religious possibilities of the Chinese soul.

On December 4 the Aurora Jesuits finally gave Teilhard permission to give his talk.[1] He was to give it at the great hall of the university. But by the time the day arrived, he mounted the podium in some distress. He was painfully aware of what had happened to his listeners. He understood their bewilderment at feeling that they were no longer the proud representatives of that Western incursion into China that had made Shanghai the great port it had been—an unchallenged bastion of the white man's commerce, a legendary city of sin and luxury, the key to the treasures of the East. Gathered before him was a sad grab bag of aliens now drowning in an Eastern sea: a sprinkling of nervous French diplomats and newsmen, some French escapees from Japanized Indochina, and paunchy businessmen with pretty little *snobinettes* in jewels and brilliant dresses. There were also other nationals from the International Concession: Czechs, Poles, and German Jews, who had their own ghettos in Shanghai; and a little group of the blond White Russians, all musty finery and artificial manners, who had been coming south from Manchuria ever since the beginning of the Japanese infiltration there in 1922.

As he began to talk, Teilhard faltered momentarily. "I know too well the trouble and disillusionment that you are feeling now," he said. And insofar as his paleontologist's mind permitted, so he did know. But it was precisely because he could take the long-range view of things—because his stop-action camera mind could go back millions of years, through inundations of seas, violent climactic changes, and all the things that terrified pre-man and man himself—that he felt he had any comfort to offer to his listeners in their time of trial.

Turning to the blackboard behind him, he drew a perpendicular line. It represented, he explained, a rising scale in material mass, going from the infinitely small (molecules which could be broken down into atoms, which could in turn be broken down into their own constituents) to the infinitely large (that apparently endless sea of galaxies which had troubled Pascal long ago). Then, midway across that line, he drew a horizontal one to represent the zone where life arose and evolution's force was concentrated—the level at which things complexified and interiorized. Since solar systems were, geometrically, as simple things as atoms, the real focus of creation, he contended, could be nowhere but at that mid-line where reason lives and human souls exist.

To reinforce his point about the unique quality of human

life, Teilhard posited another hypothesis. At each extremity of the perpendicular line representing rising mass, he explained, all the scientific laws which had operated up to that point, went askew. At the top of the line, which he identified as the "first infinity" (that of immensity), Einsteinian physics took over; time and space curved, and Euclidean geometry became meaningless. At the bottom of the same line, the "second infinity" (that of the infinitesimal), was the world of quantum physics, where subatomic particles moved with apparent unpredictability.

Was it not, then, he asked, entirely probable, that at the extremity of the horizontal line he had drawn (his "third infinity") those stern laws which, up to this time, had governed life, should go awry as well? Was it not entirely expectable that at this point, a creature should appear who possessed real freedom—reason, will, and even so tightly centered a psychological complexity that death itself was powerless to destroy it? Such a being would have inestimable value, since in evolving it, nature arrived at the end of all its blind labor. Man was evolution's great achievement—the one unit in creation whose final satisfaction could be found only in union with the source of evolution itself. Measured against the value and final destiny of such a being, the momentary catastrophes that touched it in its passage toward its end were minor considerations.

Whether because of the content of the speech or the fervor with which Teilhard gave it, his Shanghai conference was a huge success. When the lecture was over, happy and sometimes tearful listeners swarmed toward him. Even the gently cynical de Margerie, who so often wondered at Teilhard's facility for giving highly rational—profound—scientific lectures, then suddenly ending with God, "like a magician pulling a rabbit out of a hat," came up and embraced him.

A few days later Leroy gave his talk at the Alliance on the varieties of life in the deep sea. The eloquence with which he described the strange and monstrous, exquisite and often baffling inventiveness of evolution at this stage of life left most of his listeners about as breathless as Teilhard had done. And as the meeting ended, Leroy himself heard one priest from the Aurora go out grumbling, "Friend of mine he may be, but with one lecture, he has ruined ten years of my teaching!"

The speeches by the Peking Jesuits seriously upset their Shanghai confreres. So vigorously did they deplore Teilhard's extrapolating on evolution "as though it were a proven fact," before "so ill-prepared and heterogeneous an audience," so shocked were they at Leroy's easy acceptance of "transformism," that when, soon afterward, the visitors took the Blue Train back up north, it was with the certainty they would not soon see Shanghai again.

Home in Peking near Christmastime, Teilhard's studied naïveté led him into trouble of another kind. The officers of the Indochina Bank and the French diplomatic staff were giving a luncheon for the upper strata of the colony, but by now the strain among them over France's second fall was distinctly perceptible. As conversation after lunch rambled aimlessly along, Teilhard, who in Mme. Rivière's house had heard and reheard from her Russian secretary the story of the endurance of the Soviets during the year-long siege of Stalingrad, dropped a remark in passing about his admiration for the courage that the Russians showed in fighting for their land.

A Siberian silence descended on the room. Suddenly, over his coffee, Teilhard saw Cosme rise, his face beet-red, gasping "Mon père, I am completely shocked to hear someone of your cloth praising Communists!" Then, he clapped his cup and saucer down and, followed by his devout and gentle wife, stormed out of the room.

Until then Teilhard had not really noticed how strong anti-Allied or anti-Russian feeling was running among his friends. And of all the men he knew, it was Cosme—the man who had given him the roof under which he lived—to whom he was most unwilling to give pain. He had to make things right. After some deliberation, he decided to sit down and write a note explaining that his remark had nothing political about it; it was only a little tribute to human courage. Surely his old friend would understand.

The next morning Cosme hurried to the Institute, note in hand. He threw his arms about Teilhard and made excuses for his display of temperament. It had not really been, he said, Teilhard's observation that had driven him from the room. It was the growing burden of his duties as senior French representative in China during a conflict which became harder for him to understand each day. It was the pressure of keeping silence about the squabbling in Peking between pro- and anti-Vichy Frenchmen, some of whom, like the Jewish Paul Raphael, he considered his closest friends.

As the third slow winter of the European struggle wore into spring, despite the problems created outside Peking by the mysterious Chinese guerrillas from Shensi who continued to harass the Japanese throughout the north, life inside the city was not too difficult for the foreigners. To most of the Europeans, thinking as they did of Chinese resistance only in terms of Chiang's far-off troops in uniform, it was impossible to distinguish Mao's peasant soldiers (who seemed to take small notice of the Westerners) from bandits or simple farmers. Sunday picnics went on as usual.

But the group of picnickers was growing smaller. Paul Raphael died of a heart attack in February 1943. Eleanor Tafel moved away to Shanghai, and Teilhard and Leroy often spent their teatime hour in the Tartar City in the pretty house of a young Belgian writer pen-named Georges Magloire and her baby, Peter, whom Teilhard had just baptized. He knew he was about to lose his American and British friends as well, because after too many of them had escaped into the hills, warnings were posted on the walls of the Quarter demanding that nationals of those countries be ready for deportation to an internment camp at Weishien, south of the city, within weeks.

On the morning of March 12, 1943, Teilhard watched sadly as the British and Americans marched down toward Hata-men Street from the British embassy to the railroad station. They were a brave but melancholy spectacle, six hundred people: priests, nuns, Protestant missionaries, old people, businessmen whose wives had refused to leave them, all straining under their heavy bedrolls and whatever else they could carry, tramping off to the drumbeat of the Salvation Army band.

The Jesuits were desolate at losing so many of their friends en masse. Those who remained now were a politically volatile mix of individuals, many of whom had already taken sides in the war. Teilhard was at great pains to cultivate a most delicate neutrality in order to preserve the affection and trust of both pro- and antifascist friends. He had loved and admired Paul Raphael, who had been violently anti-Vichy; he continued to see even such Germans as Werner Sostman who were so Nazified that they refused to associate with Teilhard's own young German secretary, Claire Herschfeld, because of her Jewish origins. He received inquiring Japanese scientists with faultless politeness, while stubbornly (though secretly) mourning the decline of Western influence in the East. To the despair of certain friends, he always found something kind to say about the most unpleasant people. One day, after someone mentioned a thoroughly despicable local gunrunner, he mumbled something like, "Oh, he has his good points, too." To which Leroy replied exasperated, "I honestly believe that if you met the Devil in the street, you'd think of something nice to say." "Why not?" Teilhard said, shrugging.

That September, when the two Jesuits took a few weeks' vacation to visit with the French community's doctor, an Auvergnat named Bussière, in his tree-planted compound in the mountains, they finally did blunder into politics. Since guerrilla fighting in the countryside around Peking was on the increase, short pitched battles continued to leave casualties. Bussière, a onetime army doctor for whom the sick were only men when they were suffering, never turned any of the wounded from his door. Sometimes the lights burned until dawn in his surgery; and once, after midnight, he even summoned Leroy to the tower, where he held a lamp for him while he probed for a particularly difficult bullet in a Chinese soldier's shoulder. The next day, no one said a word about the incident. It was as though the night had never been.

Unfortunately, before the visit ended, Leroy himself fell victim to a freak accident. One morning while he made his bed, his knee gave out from under him. Bussière treated him as best he could and put him to bed for a week, but the leg did not improve. Baffled, the good doctor finally packed him onto an improvised wooden stretcher carried by two coolies and sent him bumping the fifty miles back to Peking.

At Leroy's sudden return, Père Bornet, the father minister, seemed almost frantic. After Leroy's and Teilhard's spectacular lectures in Shanghai, their superiors had decided that they would be better off in separate houses; and on July 31, while they were still away, Leroy's official order of transfer to Hsien-hsien from Peking had come. But here he was again, immobilized with a useless knee, and all Bornet could do was follow the instructions of a doctor he called in and send his injured charge to the Sisters of Charity in the French hospital next door.

When Teilhard returned from Bussière's, Leroy was still in bed. And there he remained for months, with no sign of improvement. That autumn, when Claude Rivière visited Peking, it fell to Teilhard alone to be her guide. The same thing happened when the elegant Emmanuel de Breuvery came north a few months later. Leroy was still in the hospital and Teilhard became the Shanghai Jesuit's guide all alone.

Immersed as he was in a Japanese world, the average Frenchman in China knew few of the details of the island-hopping American advance in the Pacific which, one year before, had stopped Japanese expansion at the battle of Midway. And that October 1943, it came as a surprise to some Peking French to hear that Chiang Kai-shek refused to recognize Ambassador Cosme's credentials, receiving those of General Petchkov of the Free French Council of Liberation in Algiers.

Fortunately though, getting news from Europe now was somewhat easier. The Allied advance through Sicily and the Italian government's capitulation in September 1943 had immediate repercussions in Peking. Despite their individual protestations of friendliness to Japan, all Italians who were not protected by the Vatican (e.g., papal representatives or employees of the Catholic Fujen University) were branded traitors and shipped off to camps. Two Italian brothers, owners of Peking's largest garage, disappeared one night without a trace. As far as the Europeans could see, the Japanese general staff was acting out of panic now; and every occupying soldier was told to make ten Chinese friends apiece. There was the feel of crisis in the air.

For the French community, at least, darker days were definitely approaching—and more rapidly than anyone expected. In mid-November 1943 Charles Arsène-Henri, Vichy ambassador to Tokyo, died suddenly of a heart attack, and Henri Cosme's days of trial began. With the tide of war in the Pacific turned, and as the Allies struggled painfully but implacably up through Italy, it was plain that the next step in the Allied strategy would have to be an invasion of France. Cosme was the logical man to replace Arsène-Henri in Tokyo and then where would he stand in relation to the new French government?

That winter in Peking was bitterly cold. There was little fuel and even less real food. Near Christmastime "Georges Magloire" went to Teilhard on behalf of the little Sino-French literary society—most of whose members were avoided by the better class ladies of Peking because they were married to or connected with Chinese—and complained, "Oh, we are all so unhappy, mon père! Won't you come and speak to us of happiness?"

On December 28 Teilhard gave his little talk.[2] Happiness, he declared, was always a by-product—a bonus that came only in the pursuit of something else. There was no more point in seeking it for its own sake or in trying to seize and hoard it as a miser when it came than there was in declaring that earthly happiness did not exist and living one's life braced stoically against the worst that could occur. The best way to achieve true joy and peace, he felt, was to remain completely open to the risks of life and to yield with love and gratitude to whatever tasks Providence imposed.

"Everything that happens," he maintained, quoting the pious geologist and philosopher Pierre Termier, "is adorable." And looking at Teilhard's face, serene and beautiful despite the fact that it was the face of an old man who, like his audience, was far from home but who, unlike them, shone with the fervor of a faith in life (a faith which, in all probability, he would never be able to disseminate in his lifetime), his audience could almost believe him.

# CHAPTER
# EIGHTEEN

That winter of 1943 Peking stood isolated in its antique splendor, like a glass paperweight one tips to see the snow fly. Even the appearance of a single American plane over the city the day after Christmas caused little real excitement. Père Leroy, his knee finally successfully operated on by a Chinese surgeon, was discharged from the hospital and came back to the Institute of Geo-Biology, where he helped finish the analysis of the last Neolithic material from Choukoutien. Through the dusty months of spring, he continued with his lab work, while Teilhard worked on his philosophical papers in his study.

Spring flowered into summer. After temporizing for six months over his appointment to replace Arsène-Henri as French ambassador to Tokyo, Cosme bowed to fate and left. At the same time, after delivering a final talk at the Alliance Française, on the agile diplomat Louis de Narbonne,* Roland de Margerie left Shanghai to replace Cosme in Peking, serving (because of his youth) with the title of chargé.

Siesta time on June 7, 1944, was expectably quiet. It was a warm day and a leaden, sticky stillness lay over the Quarter. Leroy, whose luckless year it seemed to be, was once more in the hospital, this time recovering from an attack of appendi-

---

* Comte Louis de Narbonne (1755–1813), French nobleman and minister of war under Louis XVI, émigré to England during the Revolution of 1789, returned to France to serve Napoleon I as ambassador to Russia and Vienna.

citis. In his study at the Institute, Teilhard was finishing a paper he called "An Introduction to the Christian Life."[1]

Just before 1:00 P.M., Claire Herschfeld, his secretary from the days in Lockhart Hall, interrupted him. Breathless and starry-eyed, she rushed in with the announcement that she had just become engaged to marry her biology teacher from Fujen University, Edgar Taschdjian, a widower twice her age with two growing sons. Taschdjian was a Catholic, and Claire wanted to be baptized into his Church; but given her present Episcopalian profession, to say nothing of her Jewish origins, she worried that some problems might arise. Teilhard seemed just a bit surprised. "But you believe that Christ is the Son of God, don't you?" he asked. "And you believe He came into the world to save it? . . . What possible problem could there be?"

As Claire in some relief settled back into the wicker chair, Teilhard went off to the kitchen to prepare a small *goûter* to celebrate the event. He returned downcast. The girl's exhilaration had left her famished, but all he could find to offer her was a hard crust of French bread sitting stiffly on a plate. "It's all we have," he shrugged, proffering the pitiful bite. "Even the mice have left us now."

Undeterred, Claire swallowed the crust, climbed on her bicycle, and pedaled homeward. On the way, she considered how best to acquaint her family with her plans. But she never had the chance. No sooner did her bike scrape the stone of the courtyard where she lived than her father ran out in an almost unrecognizable state of exuberation. Waving the eyeglasses he had broken in his excitement, he was announcing for all the world to hear, "Claire, come in! It's on the radio! . . . Normandy has been invaded!"

And so for the French exiles the turning point of World War II had come. All over the Quarter, radios supposedly surrendered on Pearl Harbor day miraculously reappeared. While the Allies lay pinned down three days on the Normandy beach, those Westerners who were still without sets

pressed the Apostolic Delegate, Bishop Zanin, and the family
of the puppet Chinese governor, Wang Yin-tai, (who were
permitted to keep radios) for any kind of news. For the next
few days, while the inland push began, the atmosphere of
countercharges between Gaullist and Vichy factions in the
city was breathlessly suspended.

While the Japanese kept a pretense of normalcy, most foreigners tried to do the same. Mme. de Margerie and her children arrived by train from Shanghai on July 1 and went to the
resort of Peitaiho for a few weeks. On her return to Peking,
she began holding her own small Sunday outings in the city
for Teilhard and others. Because of increasing guerrilla activity, the picnics were held less often in the Western Hills and
more frequently on the great marble boat that the empress
dowager had constructed in the Summer Palace gardens.

Back in Europe things were moving now at breakneck
speed. While the Allies fought the Germans furiously up the
boot of Italy, old Marshal Pétain was carted off from France
by the Germans to Sigmaringen Castle in the Black Forest.
Pierre Laval was captured by the Americans.

On August 25, when General de Gaulle led the Free
French and the Americans down the Champs Élysées in Paris,
the citizens went mad with joy. In Peking, where the celebration was necessarily subdued, feeling ran as deep. Lunching
that noon at Mme. Raphael's, Teilhard and Leroy were startled to hear an agnostic friend André d'Hormon, announce
that when he heard the news he fell on his knees and
repeated the Our Father for the first time since he was a
child.

That evening, under the expressionless gaze of Japanese
guards, the Jesuits joined fifty or so casually dressed, shirt-
sleeved Frenchmen at their embassy to drink the last of the
champagne in its cellars. Wherever Frenchmen met that
night, there was an emotional exchange. The next morning,
according to Mme. Raphael, she found a black North African

colonial at the corner of the Rue Labrousse, weeping openly with joy.

After that night, life in Peking was never quite the same. Up to then, though Vichyites and anti-Vichyites had clung together for mutual protection against the Japanese, they had bickered endlessly. But now uniforms changed overnight, and the community was suddenly politically unanimous.

The patchy French Far Eastern empire (Laos, Cambodia, Vietnam, Pondicherry on the Indian subcontinent, as well as the "leased" Chinese territory of Kwangchowan, and the concessions in the Chinese cities) came suddenly unglued. Since, whatever their new profession of allegiance, its diplomats all had their posts assigned or at least confirmed by Vichy (the only Metropolitan government that existed in 1940), their new positions were ambiguous, to say the least.

Unlike France's African empire, where a "government" opposed to Vichy had existed since 1942, most of the French in the Far East had never really formally changed their allegiance. In October 1944, when Admiral Decoux, the French supreme commander in the East, returned to Hanoi from vacation, he found to his amazement the two French generals Mordant and Aymé, who had been appointed "Chief of Resistance" and "General Delegate of the Committee for the Liberation of Indochina" by the Free French Council in Algiers, sitting at his desk.

Decoux wired General de Gaulle for new instructions. Three weeks passed without a word. Finally he received an icy telegram, reminding him that, whatever he had been doing, the new French government had been at war with Japan since 1941. Still, the new government had responsibility for protecting its Far Eastern colonies. Therefore, the cable continued, Decoux was formally instructed to stay on as the nominal chief French representative in the East and to keep up a façade of friendship with the Japanese, while the real Resistance to Japan was run by Paris appointees.[2]

M. de Margerie, as well, was under orders to behave correctly to the occupiers. But more and more often embarrassed silences fell over the ring of Baccarat crystal and Sèvres china at the embassy luncheons. Encounters with the Japanese grew more irregular. But, no matter whether or not the unwelcome luncheon guests had come, every afternoon, as soon as the meal was over, Jenny de Margerie hurried to telephone selected friends such as Teilhard and ask them to her upstairs sitting room, where she dispensed the latest bits of diplomatic gossip like delicate tea cakes.

That autumn there was really something to report. The war in Europe had just come to climax. While the Allies, airdropping Resistance fighters into Auvergne, dashed through Normandy toward the Rhine, and while General de Lattre de Tassigny (with Teilhard's nephew Olivier serving as interpreter from the time the general reached Lake Constance) fought his way northward from Provence, the Allies now paid bitterly for every inch of ground they gained. At Christmas, bad weather and the fact that they had outraced their supplies caused the Allies fighting in the north to halt. The English still had not secured the northern ports. And near Bastogne in the Ardennes, the gallant U.S. 101st Airborne was cut off in a blinding, suffocating snowstorm until a salient of General Patton's Third Army from the south rescued them.

By the end of February the Americans had taken back the Philippines. Sure that an invasion of Indochina would come next, Japan, on March 9, 1945, invoked the Mutual Defense Pact signed with Vichy France, in 1941, which specified that in the event of an Allied invasion the Japanese should have free entry into the peninsula, and began flooding Indochina with their troops. That night, while fighting flared in the streets of Saigon and Hanoi, the Japanese occupied French Government House and made temporary prisoners of Decoux and his aides.

With that, a rumor flew through Peking that, like the Italians, the entire French community was about to be deported to a camp. Some people even started packing bags. Since the

Japanese had already taken over the embassy's enlisted men's barracks, Leroy and Teilhard were seriously worried that their barracks would go next. Ever since the reduction of field work that resulted from the Japanese expansion, they had known that there was little to justify the existence of their Institute. Still, it was a place for Teilhard to keep working on his papers and for Leroy (who had advanced from working with earthworms to studying chickens) to continue with his experiments in endocrinology. The lab work was a process fraught with difficulty, mostly due to the specimens' propensity for awakening too rapidly from anesthesia and flying wildly out the windows to the nearby Japanese parade grounds. This meant Leroy had to go time and time again to Japanese headquarters to fill out reams of papers (including maps of the chickens' probable "escape route") in order to retrieve them.

In April 1945, while the English and Americans were making their last thrust to the Elbe, the Russians roared in from the east. At Rheims on May 7 the Germans signed the instruments of unconditional surrender. Two days later, in the presence of General de Lattre de Tassigny and Air Marshal Sir Arthur Tedder, Marshal Zhukov and members of the German general staff ratified the document in Berlin.

Meanwhile, in the Pacific, sick and desperate Japanese soldiers continued fighting, or turned to suicide. The soldiers in Peking took on a hangdog, ragamuffin look: their uniforms showed patches; their boots were shabby and broken; they took to making their patrols at night now to avoid appraising eyes. The "best" Japanese civilians, on the other hand, showed even more abrasive manners, and snatched up the few vegetables still in the markets from under the noses of the other foreigners.

There was considerable speculation as to how long the strange state of affairs could last. The Jesuits' worry over their possible eviction ended when the Japanese announced they needed no more space and made Leroy paper over the windows facing the parade grounds. But all that spring and sum-

mer life in the world outside the Institute seemed as unreal as
the shadows on the paper walls.

Then in August 1945 the unbelievable occurred. For
months—even before the German surrender—Teilhard's
friends had been gossiping about new Allied and Axis "secret
weapons": flying missiles, bombs of enormous power, germ
warfare, and other monstrous fantasies of death. On August
6, when Leroy, returning from a luncheon at the Indochina
Bank, stopped at the corner of Hata-men Street, the French
attaché Guy Dorget flashed past him in a rickshaw. "Go
home and turn on your radio, Pierre," he cried. "They've
dropped it!" But dropped what? . . . It was nine in the evening before Leroy and Teilhard heard a crisp British account
of the explosion of the atom bomb in Hiroshima. But without pictures or adequate press coverage, they could have no
idea of the terrible storm of fire and death that had wiped out
the city.

The first real aftershock came in the muted murmur of the
Japanese official who accompanied Rhineholt Höppeli (acting as Swiss consul) to visit Dr. Houghton and to tell the five-
year prisoner politely that he was free. On August 14, Japan
officially surrendered. The next day Allied planes appeared
over Peking dropping leaflets and food packages and para-
chuting down Red Cross teams. It was perhaps not until they
saw that gentle summer storm of paper and food packages,
then felt the warmth of handshakes from Red Cross people,
that the exiles began to feel part of the living world again.

The night after the surrender, however, they crouched
down in their houses listening in horrified silence to the
sounds of slaughter and pillage that came from the Japanese
sections of the city as the long-humiliated Chinese citizenry
threw themselves upon their former masters. From dusk to
dawn, crowds smashed and looted the big, new Japanese department store and broke into private houses, leaving the
glacis in the morning strewn with bloodstained kimonos. The
Japanese military retained a defense perimeter around their

installations. They could not fight, and, according to Mac-Arthur's General Order No. 1, they could not surrender either to Chinese irregulars or to the Communists who surrounded the city to the south and west, but must wait until a Chiang Kai-shek representative could be airlifted from the south.

On September 9, 1945, a Nationalist general named Li was brought up from Chungking for the surrender ceremony, and tension eased a little. In Indochina, however, things were getting out of hand. The wispy-bearded Ho Chi Minh had moved to fill the power vacuum left by the defeated Japanese and declared himself president of Free Vietnam. De Gaulle sent the Carmelite warrior-priest Georges Thierry d'Argenlieu to try to restore French sovereignty.

Toward September's end, just as French paratroopers were beginning to drop back into Vietnam, Teilhard returned from a vacation he, Leroy, and a French businessman had taken to the temple country of the Western Hills, carrying (at de Margerie's suggestion) a copy of Tolstoy's *War and Peace*. A few days later, when a junketing American Marine colonel† out of Guam landed a C-47 at one of Peking's airstrips, a Red Cross worker offered him a Chinese guide for a short trip around the city in exchange for taking some "important" passengers with him when he left.

While the colonel went off sightseeing, the Red Cross man rushed from embassy to embassy collecting passengers. He stopped at the Institute of Geo-Biology to ask Teilhard and Leroy if they wanted to leave that afternoon—even with the restrictions on heavy baggage. Both men were content to wait. Teilhard still did not have his religious superiors' permission to come home, nor even a reply to the letter he had written to d'Ouince in August asking that a place be held for him at *Études*. In any case, the Americans, led by his old friend the prewar military attaché from the U.S. embassy, William Arthur Worton (now a brigadier general), had been in Tien-

† Now Major General Carl S. Day, USMC (Ret.).

tsin with a small party since September 19. It was only a question of time before they came to Peking.

What Teilhard did not know was that General Worton was then having troubles of his own. On the thirtieth of the month, the First Marine Division had landed at Taku Bar to be met by sampans full of smiling Chinese scullers. Though they were cheered by peasants all the way up the Hai River to their old barracks in Tientsin, the temperature of welcome dropped abruptly the next day. The increasing American airlift of Nationalist troops from the south to territories where the Red guerrillas had fought alone so long was too much for the patience of Yenan. Sporadic fire fights began to break out between American troops and the peasant soldiers of Mao Tse-tung. A few days after the division's landing, Chou En-lai himself issued a formal warning to the Americans to stay out of Peking.

Nevertheless on October 5, after trudging westward eighty miles through roads so blocked that it took the corps of engineers, working under rifle, tank, and air cover, a day to clear, the first American contingents entered the ancient capital.[3]

Returning from a visit to the de Margeries, Mme. Raphael was suddenly surprised to hear a far-off, grumbling sound like an approaching thunderstorm. Then the ugly green metal amphibious trucks bearing two thousand fresh-faced Marines, waving gaily to anyone who would wave back, appeared at the end of the Rue Labrousse. Almost in disbelief, she stood and watched a moment as the trucks stopped to collect prisoners and papers at the Japanese and German embassies, then moved away, down the street, with a broom acquired from the Germans sticking upright from the collection like a trophy.

While Mao's troops waited patiently outside Peking, the Kuomintang and the Americans staged an elaborate victory parade, and a carnival of delirious rejoicing in the Foreign Quarter began. The internees came back from Weishien; the Marines, who at once set up headquarters in the German embassy, shared their whiskey and K rations with the Legation people and were amazed to find their powdered eggs, their Spam, their cheese and chocolate susceptible of miraculous transformations at the hands of able Chinese cooks; the Russian chargé distributed Crimean oranges flown in from Manchuria; and everywhere, in embassies and private houses, journalists showed the exiles newsreels of battles, some of which they had not even heard about. In October, emerging from his annual retreat, Teilhard wrote to his brother Joseph, "Our French embassy, which has the great good fortune to have Monsieur de Margerie in charge, has become a brilliant social center once again. . . ." And in the giddy joy, the easy camaraderie, in the mélange of races and nationalities around him (even though he knew it was considerably helped along by alcohol), Teilhard also thought he caught a glimpse of "those mysterious and profound affinities among all men, which are still manifest furtively and at intervals, but which must surely be among the strongest energies of the earth."

"The Peking club came back to us at last!" one Westerner remembers. And for the moment, to the victorious foreigners it seemed that everything "came back." But that was all illusion. China in 1945 could no more return to its old way of living in patient poverty and ignorance or under foreign tutelage than it could turn back the clock.

This was the fact that Chiang Kai-shek, with his "Westernized" warlord mentality, had never understood. But the wily Mao Tse-tung had known it all along. Since 1920, with his own adaptation of "Marxism" to a rural rather than industrial society, he had worked to give the land back to the tiller that he might be a man again.

At his "Anti-Japanese University" in the village huts of Suiteh, Mao taught his once-illiterate soldiers to read the simplistic manuals of faith he wrote, and to fight the guerrilla way—striking where the enemy was weakest, and retreating when they saw that he was strong. He entertained and educated his followers with propaganda "guerrilla" theater which further explained their struggle for self-betterment to them, and formed in them a new idea of "community" with a list of "crimes" and "duties" relating to it.

By 1945 Mao commanded a force of 910,000 regular troops and two million militia and laid claim to a territory of almost 400,000 square miles; and the Americans (who from the beginning, because they supplied Chiang against the Japanese, inadvertently became more and more involved with him) found themselves acting as referees between the Kuomintang and the once "simple, pliant" Communists.‡

By the fall of 1945 Major General Patrick Hurley, the war-whooping Oklahoman who had gone to China as President Roosevelt's special envoy, threw up his hands over the complexities of the quarrel between the Kuomintang and the Communists and went home. Roosevelt's successor, President Harry Truman, immediately asked George C. Marshall to work out some kind of agreement. In December 1945 Marshall managed to effect a cease-fire at a conference in Chungking.

Among the Western Pekingese, still stranded in that island of irreal gaiety, uneasiness grew rapidly. Since the only escape route was by air, and that route was much occupied by political and military traffic, civilian transportation on American planes was at a premium. While waiting for permission from their religious superiors to leave China, Teilhard and Leroy worked at transferring some material from the Geo-Biology Institute to the reconstituted Geological Survey. More and more often now, Teilhard's essays took for their theme evolution *after* the appearance of man and the new physical, economic, and social interdependence of humanity that the

‡ The American "Dixie" mission (the group of foreign service and military men sent by the U.S. government to make an independent judgment on the "rebel" Red Chinese, and to find out whether, as the old song says, it was "true what they say about Dixie") arrived in Mao's capital of Yenan, to be much impressed by the contrast between the apparent simplicity, disinterest, discipline, and courage of the Communists and the bumptious, restrictive, self-interested movement led by Chiang Kai-shek.

conflict had effected. Communications and up-to-date transport now extended to such out-of-the-way places as the islands of Polynesia, and suddenly, men had the ability to extend their "psychic" influence, at least electronically, to almost any place on earth.[4]

At Christmastime, Teilhard's official permission to return to Paris came. Since Père d'Ouince had already offered him his old place at *Études,* and since Teilhard's passport had long ago been cleared with the new French government, he was anxious to get home as soon as possible. The manic entertainments of the Legation Quarter had by now begun to pall on him. Though Leroy, who intended to return to China, was satisfied to fly quickly home without luggage on a British plane in late March, Teilhard decided for a longer route. He asked General Worton to get him air transport to Shanghai, where, with luck, he might be able to find a ship to take him and all his baggage home. To Mrs. Swan, who shot him a delighted cable the moment the war was over, he wrote he felt that he had "been living in a twilight or a fishbowl" . . . and was eager to get out. And despite the difficulties, he wrote that he was hoping to get some kind of air transport to a seaport where he could take a ship home via America. Seeing her again, he said, would be a "real breath of life" to him, and strengthen him for the work ahead of him in France. "Don't think, though," he wrote her in another letter, "that I regret having spent these last months in Peking at the flash point of the battle between Communism and the democracies. I've learned a lot. . . . But now I must go home and speak, and you must give me the heart for it."

Teilhard probably never wrote a truer sentence in his life than he did when he said he was fortunate to be in Peking at that moment. And perhaps never in his life did he make so little use of his good fortune. In the communes all around the city there was taking place, under almost laboratory conditions, a measurable evolution to near twentieth-century humanity, of a human mass most of whose individuals had been living at an almost animal level, that was a concrete proof of his own theory of social evolution. Once their mininal physical needs had been filled, the Communist Chinese seemed to be transforming themselves almost instantaneously into individuals with united and outward-directed goals, thus illustrating something very like Professor Édouard Le Roy's theory of "conspiracy." Though the emerging Chinese civilization was still being paid for in blood and terror, and though it as yet had an extremely limited intellectual and spiritual content, it represented for most of its participants a human advance on an enormous scale.

Teilhard, however, was so absorbed by his own homesickness and so convinced that it was "really in the West that the axis of social evolution lay" that he never took the time to look into it. By mid-March 1946 worry about how to get out of Peking was spreading like a panic in the foreign population. By then, though, General Worton had completed arrangements for Teilhard's air passage to Shanghai as well as for his neighbor, Mme. Raphael. From Shanghai, Worton proposed to book them both on ships bound for America. On the snowy morning of March 17, Leroy and Mme. Raphael accompanied Teilhard to the airstrip in one of Worton's cars and watched his plane, its wings heavy with ice, take off into a leaden sky. At Tsingtao through sheer luck he found his mail waiting for him; then he immediately changed planes for Shanghai.

So deliriously happy was he at the thought of getting home that he scarcely noticed how changed the city was from when he and Leroy had last visited there in 1942. Shanghai was gray, cold, and humid—a jerry-built camp where refugees speaking almost every tongue imaginable fought one another for space on outgoing ships. The harbor, from which Japanese civilian and military personnel were also being shunted home, was crowded. And the Americans were supplying the supposedly impoverished Nationalists with 100,000 tons of American coal a month, just to keep the city's factories and public utilities functioning.

On his arrival, Teilhard went directly to St. Joseph's

Church on Rue Montauban, where Père Germain was living. A few days earlier a friend of Worton's had left most of his baggage there, along with the great part of his papers and other memorabilia. He really planned to wait for Mme. Raphael. But when, soon after he arrived, a British ship, the *Strathmore*, bound for England, swung into the harbor, he rushed to the ship's agent and signed on.

Though he regretted not being able to go home through America, or even spend a few days in Shanghai with his neighbor from Peking, the thought of being able to leave at once made these seem a small price to pay. Of course the ship he signed on promised none of the comforts he was used to when he traveled. Food, though plentiful, would be hopelessly plain; hammocks strung back-to-back below decks to accommodate the crowd would replace cabins; traveling with a boatload of gregarious expatriates would leave him little time to write or think. But all that he could think of was that, after six years of waiting, he could be home in six weeks' time.

When the *Strathmore* moved out of the harbor on the evening of March 27, Teilhard stood among the Europeans at the rail and took a last look at China—the exile he had tried so hard to escape from, the refuge he could always count on to receive him if he needed one. The thought that he might one day need another refuge never crossed his mind.

As the skyscrapers of the Shanghai Bund receded black and window-lighted against a sky now blazing red, it may be doubted that any of the other passengers wondered about seeing Shanghai again either. Most were occupied with thoughts of home, of long-lost friends and relatives, of peaceful countrysides and English gardens. Among the anxious passengers departing China, there was not much nostalgia or even much interest about the land they left behind.

Still, beyond the odd façade, fading into mist like the backless flat of a Hollywood set, Napoleon's "sleeping giant" had begun stirring—and one way or another, once that giant was awake, his movements would touch them all before they died.

# IV

# JUDGMENT

# CHAPTER
# NINETEEN

On May 3, 1946, the boat train brought Teilhard into the Gare St.-Lazare on the last lap of his trip to France. Almost dizzy with delight at being home, he hailed a porter to carry what little baggage he had not sent to be stored at the Rue de Châteaudun, then walked outside to find a taxi for *Études*.

He was sixty-five now, thin and old; his hair was almost completely white. But as he rolled the taxi window down to admit the sights and sounds of the mechanized West, he felt like Lazarus revived. The sight of so many querulous Parisians queued up outside stores with ration cards was distressing; but the pungent scent from an *épicerie* or the soft, sweet smell of a pastry shop brought back memories of brighter, better days. The cab headed toward the Concorde, crossed the Seine, then followed the Rue de Babylone into the narrow streets full of whitewashed religious houses, hospitals, and rest homes behind the Rue du Bac. Finally, just before noon, it stopped at *Études*.

Teilhard pushed the buzzer at the dark wooden door. Within moments, smiling little Brother Cochet opened his arms to him. Since Teilhard had not been certain of the time of his arrival, he had sent no message to expect him. But the news of his return spread quickly through the house. D'Ouince rushed to embrace him; Fessard clapped him on the back; Huby and du Passage appeared, quite out of breath.

Unlike the Jesuits of the larger and more politically divided

house on the Rue de Grenelle,* the Jesuits of *Études* had
been drawn closer together by the war. It left them with a
new sense of purpose and mutual solidarity. It tightened the
bond between them and their brothers at Fourvière in the intellectual warrior city of Lyon, chief, under the leadership of
its cardinal Pierre-Marie Gerlier, of the cities of the French
Christian Resistance. Gaston Fessard, for example, (the "Silver Fox" to his admirers), passed much of the war helping
Jews to escape across the Pyrenees; and in 1941, on the eve of
his transfer from *Études* to Lyon, the young Yves de Mon-
cheuil was shot by the Nazis while attending some wounded
*maquisards* in a cave near Grenoble.

While the magazine *Études* had taken a public stand
against the German politics of blood and race even before the
war began, Fourvière in 1941 could boast of writings published in Switzerland against Nazi racism and irreligion by
Père de Lubac. As Nazi anti-Jewish persecution in the Vichy
Zone grew more cruel, Gerlier appointed the Fourvière theology professor Pierre Chaillet director of Les Amitiés
Chrétiennes, a group of Christian families pledged to shelter
refugees. At the same time, with the assistance of Fessard, de
Lubac, Pierre Ganne, and Victor Fontoynont, Chaillet published the fiery anti-Nazi pamphlet *Témoinage Chrétien,*
whose first issue, "France: Prends Garde de Perdre Ton
Âme," was written entirely by Fessard.†

Rather than submit their prestigious magazine to Nazi censorship, the Jesuits of *Études* early in the Occupation
suppressed it in favor of a less incendiary paper called *Con-
struire*. In their work for the Resistance, many of them paid
dearly. D'Ouince, for example, who spent a year as a prisoner

---

* Grenelle, too, had its share of heroes. Most prominent among them were
Michel Riquet, Aloysius-Gonzague Pierre, and Jacques Sommet, all of whom
were eventually deported by the Germans to Dachau.
† The first four issues of *Témoinage Chrétien* were entirely the work of the
Jesuits; the next ten, which were distributed alternately with *Combat* by the
Dominican-trained Young Christian Workers, were condemnations of various
aspects of Nazism by representatives of other Catholic and Protestant groups.

of war in Germany (and who, after returning to Paris, had the distinction of being the priest who obtained from Cardinal Suhard of Paris permission for all Resistance chaplains to adminster the Last Sacraments at any appropriate moment to their companions because they were always to be considered *in articulo mortis*), later spent two more weeks under Gestapo interrogation at a deportation camp outside the city, after having decoyed German agents who had come to the house looking for Fessard.

In those first years after the liberation, the Jesuits of *Études* and those of Fourvière shared with the Dominicans of the priory of Le Saulchoir as well as with other liberal Catholics a prophetic sense of new beginnings. For Teilhard, who had spent the war shut up inside the little Vichy colony in Peking, there was considerable catching up to do.

Through ecclesiastical channels kept open in China, he already knew that the French Church was in ferment. It was re-examining its social ethic, its philosophy, its art, its ceremonies, its biblical criticism, its very definition of the Christian life. Priests and faithful who had gone through a harrowing period where they found themselves deprived of their libraries, seminaries, cathedrals, and other old familiar comforts had realized with sharp intensity (as the Dominican Yves Congar has said) that their true and only "liberation" was their faith.‡

In 1943 a statistical study of religious observance in France compiled by the Abbés Godin and Daniel, proving that in many sectors of the nation 84 per cent of the people were "paganized,"[1] had caused considerable shock. It corroborated

‡ "Anyone who did not live through the years 1946–47 in French Catholicism has missed one of the most beautiful moments in the life of the Church. Throughout that slow awakening from misery, everyone sought in the grand freedom of faithfulness as strong as life to re-enter evangelically that secular sphere with which he had just been involved as few had been involved for centuries. That the future of the Church is bound to the future of the world is a thing that we have since rediscovered. But at this time it was a truth brought home to us by experience itself." Yves Congar, O.P., "The Need for Patience," *Continuum*, Vol. II, No. 4, (Winter 1965).

the intuitions of Cardinal Suhard, who in 1941 had already set up an organization of extraparochial priests which he called the Mission de France, dedicated to preaching the gospel, making the liturgy more relevant to the common people, and reintegrating religious practice into family life in the more abandoned regions of the nation. When religious and priests (the Jesuit Henri Perrin among them) who had accompanied the forced workers to labor camps in Germany returned home at the war's end, they confirmed out of their personal experience the fact that most of the French lower class was completely alienated from the Church. As a result of their testimony, Cardinal Suhard established a second experimental group of missionary priests, dedicated to sharing the lot of laborers of the industrial suburb of Aubervilliers and Montreuil, which he called Mission de Paris.

Though obedience has traditionally been called the "genius of Catholicism," in those first years after the liberation, French Catholics were re-examining the attitudes of their ecclesiastical directors as closely as they were examining their own. While a mere handful of churchmen, such as Archbishop Saliège and Msgr. Bruno de Solages of Toulouse and Cardinal Gerlier of Lyon, as well as (more ambiguously and under more difficult circumstances) Cardinal Suhard of Paris, had, with varying degrees of vigor, resisted Nazi paganism, most of their brothers in the episcopate had not; and after the liberation of France, General de Gaulle's government vainly petitioned the pope for the removal of the collaborator bishops. But from about 1943 the dedicated Chrisian Frenchman had often found the only way he could live his faith was by acting in direct disobedience to the instructions of his bishop. Now, with the war over, this atmosphere of reappraisal permeated everything; and for a moment, more enthusiastic souls really believed they were about to see "the old husks crumble into dust."[2]

Luncheon conversation on the afternoon of Teilhard's return to Paris was a Babel of unfinished sentences. When it was over, d'Ouince and Jouve led him to his quarters, a large room on the fourth floor overlooking the courtyard, with a desk, a chair, a day bed, bookcases, and filing cabinets for his papers. There they sat awhile and talked to him of acquaintances or relatives about whom he was concerned. They talked about his protégé Maurice Trassaert, who had broken off his wartime marriage and tried to return to the Jesuits, only to disappear again, after an insensitive superior sent him off to do penance at the Trappists. They regretted with Teilhard the death of his beloved brother Gabriel in 1941 and of Marcellin Boule in 1942. They chatted about the return to Paris from Morocco of Max de Begouën and his ailing wife, who, because of the housing shortage, were now sharing the apartment of Teilhard's cousins Marguerite and Alice Teillard-Chambon. They told him about the Abbé Breuil, who had been working in South Africa since 1942, when he had been helped out of the country by Marshal Smuts; and about poor old Licent, who, since his return from his outraged trip to Rome in 1938, where he had gone to argue back his place in Tientsin, had been assigned to Paris and who was then living in a little apartment across from the Jardin des Plantes, studying insects.

D'Ouince was eager to discuss his own new projects with Teilhard. At the very least, he wanted to talk about the dialogue that he, like the Dominicans on the nearby Boulevard de La Tour-Maubourg, was supporting between believers and nonbelievers who had fought together in the Resistance. But the traveler was obviously so worn out, he decided to cut the visit short. That night, as d'Ouince left Teilhard in his room, the picture he took with him was of the old man standing in an attitude of exaltation staring from the window at the violet Parisian sky, like an old soldier who had been hoping hopelessly for one last taste of battle before he died, and who —almost miraculously—was granted it.

That first night home Teilhard slept easily. The next day he awoke to find, to his surprise, that during his absence, he

had become something of a celebrity. All through the intellectual famine of the Occupation, he discovered, mimeographed copies of his essays had been passed from hand to
hand, and an audience had grown which, that first day, almost overwhelmed him with visits and phone calls. In a letter
to Mrs. de Terra written during those early weeks, he complained there did not seem to be enough hours in a day to do
all he wanted to. "Sometimes," he told her in a rather inexact
simile, "I wish that, like the Buddha, I had ten pairs of hands
and ten heads—or only a good and efficient secretary."

As a matter of fact, he already had a secretary—a devoted
and utterly indefatigable one. In 1938 Jeanne Mortier, a pious
gentlewoman with a perpetual oriental smile and a pork-pie
hat, whose small but independent means enabled her to live
as a pensioner at a convent on the Rue de l'Abbé Grégoire
and spend her time working for various religious organizations, had read the *Milieu Divin*. So impressed was she by
that single essay that from the time she finished reading it,
she had tried, unsuccessfully at first, to track the author
down. One day, providentially, she received an invitation to
one of Teilhard's scientific lectures, and at the end of it went
up to him and offered to do anything she could to help his
work. "Come to *Études* tomorrow," he had said, "and we will
talk about it."

From that time on, Mlle. Mortier had become a very
"demon or angel," Teilhard said, of activity on his behalf,
gathering his old essays together, keeping whatever papers he
was able to smuggle back from China, making sometimes
three hundred copies of the essays he wished distributed to
various "discreet admirers."

The afternoon after his return to Paris, she came to see him
in the old parlor of *Études* fronting on the leafy garden courtyard. She had expected to see an old man, worn and drawn
after seven years of exile. But to her surprise, she later said,
the joy in Teilhard's face seemed to erase any pain lines that
the war had left. He was gay, excited, full of hope for the fu-

ture, and thoroughly convinced that the time for his philosophy to be accepted had come at last.

Two days after Teilhard's return, Pierre Leroy, too, came back from China. Though he had left Peking by plane in March 1946 with very little luggage and the intention of going back to China, a series of unforeseeable small disasters in both Calcutta and Cairo, where the plane stopped to pick up refugees, had delayed his return long beyond the time he expected. He and Teilhard spent the next afternoon together, first picking up the luggage the older priest had left in storage, then lunching with Leroy's sister-in-law in Paris. At that moment Leroy's future was uncertain. His application to return to China was refused, and his superior suggested he accept instead a post in Paris teaching Latin. It was only two months later that, with the help of d'Ouince, he was re-established in a more appropriate situation, teaching biology at a boys' school in Versailles, and spending his free time in Auteuil, doing endocrinological experiments at a laboratory attached to the Collège de France.

Never in his life had Teilhard been so busy or so sought after. He did his best to keep up his contacts with relatives and old friends, but requests for lectures and for private counseling continued to pile up. Besides Parisian students, societies of young Catholic intellectuals as far away as Switzerland and Italy now solicited his presence. ("If you want to fill an auditorium," a student chaplain told d'Ouince around that time, "all you have to do is advertise that you have Teilhard or Jean-Paul Sartre.") One thing he made a point of doing was reopening his contacts overseas as soon as possible. Within days of his arrival, besides Mrs. de Terra, he had written to Franz Weidenreich, Hallam Movius of Harvard, and even Lucile Swan, the thought of whose disappointment at his changing his mind about returning home via America, still plagued him. Lucile answered his letter by return mail, sending him her picture, which (he wrote in reply) he kissed joyfully on sight. His apparent "neglect" of her, after all she had done for him in China, he explained by telling her, "I am burning the coal I accumulated in Peking. . . ." But it was cold comfort three thousand miles away.

As the spring faded, Teilhard kept up the same feverish pitch of activity. His China-written essay "Vie et les Planètes" was published in *Études* in May in a slightly truncated version; another China-written essay was scheduled for publication in September.[3] At a gathering of intellectuals in the apartment of the then-political former Resistance hero of Grenoble, the Abbé Pierre,* he held a long dialogue with the bearded, pessimist philosopher Nicholas Berdyaev. Later, he talked to a group of young priests about a new mystique based on a "love of evolution." On June 26 he debated the Dominican scientist Dominique Dubarle and the philosopher Emmanuel Mounier, for whose magazine, *Esprit*, he agreed to write a short essay exposing again the illogic of the still-standing antagonism between science and religion.[4]

Mademoiselle Mortier's observation that she "had never seen Teilhard happier than in those first few months at home" is a tribute to his long-cultivated ability to disguise his feelings whenever he could. It is true that, for the first few months, he was so loaded down with work he had simply yielded himself up to the joy of his welcome without questioning his future. He even wrote excitedly to Père de Lubac that because of all that was going on in postwar French theology, he wondered whether this re-Christianized France might not—two thousand years after the first Epiphany in Bethlehem—be "the cradle where Christ might be pleased to be reborn again . . . this time universally."

But from the time of his first visit to Lyon on his return in July, Teilhard had known all was not well. It was then that it

---

* In 1954, abandoning politics, the Abbé Pierre was to create the Communauté d'Emmaüs for the ragpickers of Paris, and when a woman with an eviction notice in her hand was found frozen to death on the Boulevard de Sébastopol, his radio speech on the subject caused an outpouring of jewels and money for his Communauté which is still remembered as the "insurrection of kindness."

was confirmed that the manuscript of *The Phenomenon*
which he had sent to Rome from China had been summarily
rejected. All the wartime regents who had ruled the Society
since the death of Ledochowski in 1942—from the Italian Assistant Alexius Magni to Teilhard's old adversary Norbert de
Boynes—had apparently concurred in the decision. Still, no
matter what might happen to him personally, he desperately
wanted, at least, to leave behind him the theological statement of *The Phenomenon* for the guidance of future thinkers.
He therefore saw but one way he might save his book: redo the
text completely, and rephrase it all, in a less "offensive" way.
To do this, he knew he needed the guidance of the surest and
most accomplished sympathetic theologians he could find.
Early in the summer, therefore, he wrote to Bruno de Solages
in Toulouse, and to the now highly influential de Lubac, asking them to help with the revision. They agreed. But since all
three were extremely busy at the time, a date for a discussion
at Toulouse was put off until the following January.

D'Ouince saw to it that three clean copies of *The Phenomenon* and its Roman criticisms were made. At summer's end,
Teilhard sent one to de Solages and personally deposited another with de Lubac at a meeting at the hilltop pilgrimage
place of Dôle near Lyon. Then he stopped at Auvergne,
where he stayed with his brother Joseph at his château, Les
Moulins, near Clermont, to bless the marriage of Manette,
the daughter of his brother Gabriel, to the young Gonzague
de Lavergnie of Lyon.

In September 1946 the first general election of a superior of
the Jesuits since Ledochowski's death was held in Rome. On
its outcome, Teilhard knew, his own future and the future of
his proposed revision of *The Phenomenon* depended. "*Everything*," he wrote Mrs. Swan in ill-concealed anxiety, "hangs
on the kind of general we get." But when he returned to Paris
in the autumn, he was greeted with the news that Jean-
Baptiste Janssens, a Belgian, a conservative, and a specialist in
canon law, was the new head of the Order. Though Janssens

had a reputation for kindness and was as pastoral as Ledochowski had been political, it was only by concentrating on the new general's humane qualities that Teilhard—grasping at straws—could still hope to gain the day.

In Rome that year, except for a sharpened paranoia about Communism, life went on as though the war had never happened. For six years the pope had floated "lonely as a cloud" above a holocaust. In his Christmas messages, with impeccable impartiality, he had deplored the atrocities he said both sides were committing and bemoaned the pain they caused his "paternal heart." He complained far less about the excesses of Nazism than about the threat of atheistic Communism. While many of his confederates had wined and dined luxuriously with their German visitors, his "diplomacy" of silence in the face of such outrages to humanity as the Nazi brutalization of Catholic Poland, the systematic extermination of Jews in the death camps, and the forced Catholic baptisms in Croatia prepared the way for the eventual loss to Communism of almost half of Catholic Europe. However, like the Bourbons of France, the pope and his advisers did not learn from their mistakes. They were just as tenacious in their resistance to change as their predecessors had been when the young Teilhard first complained about that very thing twenty-five years earlier.

Of all the Vatican power brokers of the bad last days of Benedict XV, only Nicola Canali—now backstage watchdog of orthodoxy in the Holy Office, Cardinal of the Propaganda, in his slapdash way manager of Vatican finances, and so powerful a man in Rome that the SCV of plates from the Vatican Bureau of Automotive Traffic was said to mean "Si Canali Vuole," along with other less printable Italianism—survived. But men brought up in the tradition and under the patronage of Merry del Val and De Lai continued in their stead. Between them, Pius XII's close friend Cardinal Adeodato Piazza and the exquisite little Cardinal Giuseppe Pizzardo alone wielded enormous power on the congregations of

Religious, the Propaganda, the Vatican foreign service, and the Holy Office. The caustic Francesco Marchetti-Selvaggiani, who served prominently in the Holy Office, as well as Vicar of Rome, was a member of the Congregation for Seminaries and University Studies, the Concilium (a kind of ministry of internal affairs in the Church), and the Commission of Canon Law; Ernesto Ruffini, the prelate of primitive Sicily, also sat on the congregations of Seminaries and the Sacraments; the aged Domenico Jorio, prefect of the Congregation of the Sacraments, also had a place on the Propaganda, Seminaries, and the Concilium; and the half-blind Alfredo Ottaviani, while he gentled the poor children of his city's orphanages as a private priest, in his capacity of Holy Office *Assessore* defended the "orthodoxy" of the rest of the Catholic world with the autocracy of a Victorian father.

Just about the time Teilhard returned to Paris, and to the news of the election, a sudden storm had drifted up from Rome. The July–December issue of the influential theological review *Angelicum* had featured an article by the apparently indestructible Réginald Garrigou-Lagrange (who, as early as 1941, from the Vichy Zone had violently condemned the "modernism" of the Dominican house of Le Saulchoir and sent a message there with an order for the deposition of its rector, the great Marie-Dominique Chenu) which launched a frontal attack on all the "new theology" in France, and this time, on its Jesuit teachers. Though in this decade after Vatican II, Garrigou's charges sound like anathemas out of the Middle Ages, in 1946 they could draw blood. De Lubac was rebuked for taking a stand on something so apparently academic as whether the "fall of the angels" was "natural" or "supernatural" to them. Henri Bouillard, his colleague in theology at Fourvière, was criticized for his inquiry as to whether one must consider Divine Grace in the Aristotelian sense of a new "form" added to human nature; Fessard was soundly rapped on the knuckles for daring to speak of Thomistic thinking as "blessed drowsiness that canonized and (in the words of the poet Péguy) 'interred' real religious thinking." The article left Teilhard and his philosophic work in the most dangerous position of all. When the mighty Garrigou got around to his ideas, he tossed them aside as "the wildest dreaming and fantasy." For a moment, it seemed the prophet of the *Angelicum* was asking his readers whether or not all postwar religious thought in France might not be basest heresy.

Teilhard again began to look about him for a refuge. His one security had always lain in knowing that he had a scientific job to go to in the field. But now, with China torn apart by civil war, that hope was gone. He therefore fixed his eye upon a new frontier in the search for early man.

The place he chose was Africa. Digging there had begun in 1924 almost unnoticed by most of the scientific world, when an anatomy professor named Raymond Dart had catalogued the face bones of an astonishingly manlike little creature dug out of a limestone quarry at Taungs, South Africa, with a muzzle and tooth formation definitely smaller than that of any existing African ape. Although the music halls of the world at first had rung with jokes about "Dart's Baby," within weeks of the announcement of its discovery, a Scottish physician named Robert Broom arrived at Johannesburg to help with the research. Then in 1936 at Sterkfontein, about thirty miles away, Broom found a well-preserved braincase of an adult of the same species. In 1934 at Kromdraai he had identified the lower jaw of a near-man of an even more advanced and younger species but with a flatter, longer skull. Since these specimens, which seemed to lie at the evolutionary fork from which both man and ape had issued, were lower on the evolutionary scale than any other "fossil man" and since they did not conform to any previously known line of human antecedents, their discoverers had called them "Australopithecus" (southern pre-man).

For some months Teilhard had hoped that if Rome should exile him again, he, George Barbour, Helmut de Terra, and

Alberto Blanc might form a scientific team to join the new researchers on African terrain. That summer he had, in fact, already written to Franz Weidenreich at the American Museum of Natural History, indicating his anxiety, and at Weidenreich's request the Viking Fund, a New York City–based institute for anthropological research, awarded him $2,500—only enough for him to go alone.

For the moment, all he could do was keep a weather eye out, and go on lecturing. In early October he spoke to the students at the École Normale Technique, and late in the month, to a Catholic workingmen's group. In December, beneath the imperturbable smile of the Golden Buddha under the cupola of the orientalist Musée Guimet, he read the paper "Ecumenicism"[5] to the Union des Croyants, a group of intellectuals of various religious persuasions which numbered among its members Georges Salles of the Louvre, René Grousset, curator of the Musée Guimet, the Islamic scholar Louis Massignon, the Comtesse Béatrice d'Hauteville (daughter of one of France's oldest Protestant families), and the tiny, Chinese-looking orientalist Solange Lemaître. At about this time he also wrote a paper on the importance of education as a "biological impetus in human history,"[6] sent a second paper (since he dared not appear in person) to be read to a congress at the Instituto di Studi Filosofici in Rome, and completed an argument for the process by which matter gradually "spiritualized" itself in evolution.[7] Then, at the year's end, hoping he could sound "scientific" enough to be printed by the *Revue des Questions Scientifiques* in Louvain, he finished another essay, updating his noosphere theory.[8]

The eyes of all the academic world of Paris seemed fastened on Teilhard that year. He had the satisfaction of being asked to stand as candidate for the prehistory chair at the Collège de France then held by the Abbé Breuil, who had reached the retirement age of seventy, and every day, at social gatherings, he wrote, he met "new and curious people . . .

who had set their minds to bringing about a new world, a new
economy, even a new morality." Among them were Marshal
Smuts, who was passing through Paris, and the eccentric
Julian Huxley, director of the newly begun UNESCO, which
was still operating in temporary offices in the old Hôtel Majestic. In memory of their first meeting, Teilhard sent Huxley
a copy of his "Planetization" essay. The Englishman seemed
pleased.

As the date set for the critical meeting with Bruno de
Solages and Père de Lubac at Toulouse to correct *The Phenomenon* drew near, Teilhard's dread of one more failure
grew unbearable. Though he continued to maintain his winning public face, old friends like Leroy, d'Ouince, Jouve,
Huby, Lecler, and du Passage (who had the rooms at *Études*
beneath him) could see the pain behind it. His always broken
worry-bead rosary was constantly in evidence, and the dark
floor boards of his room squeaked so much late in the night
that du Passage made him a gift of a pair of carpet slippers.

On January 5, 1947, Teilhard set out to meet his fate. The
discussion was scheduled to be held at the château belonging
to the Msgr. de Solages's cousin in the countryside outside
Toulouse. Teilhard's arrival at the rector's apartment of the
Institut Catholique in the old part of the city was almost simultaneous with that of Père de Lubac, who came down
from Lyon for a few days.

After exchanging a minimum of pleasantries, the three
drove out in the monseigneur's car past the ancient pink-brick
Catharist city of Albi toward the village of Carmaux. Though
the Solages château had been burnt down a century earlier
and was replaced by a series of comfortable little *haut bourgeois* houses, the elegantly terraced park remained. After
lunch with the family, the monseigneur and the Jesuits spread
their papers on the dining table. From then on, they concentrated solely on the book, stopping from time to time to
warm their hands before the gas heater in one of the fire-
places or to walk along the gravel terrace near the house in

the cold and brilliant winter light. Though the meeting lasted
two full days, to Teilhard, who had to defend almost every
proposition he had written, the time seemed endless. When
all was said and done, his friend de Solages suggested 50
major revisions; de Lubac, 240. Though in the hierarchy of
the Church the rector of the institute outranked the Fourvière professor, Teilhard knew that de Lubac better understood the mind of the Society. The three men left Carmaux
together on the seventh, de Solages riding beside the Jesuits
down to the old Toulousian station facing the Canal du Midi
with its curious hand-worked locks. From there du Lubac
went to Lyon, and Teilhard straight back to Paris.

Even though his companions had tried to draw him into
conversation in the wait before his train arrived, Teilhard was
silent and distracted. No matter what anyone said, he knew
that he was traveling to Paris in defeat. Clutching the manila
envelope that held his manuscript, and staring blindly from
the window of the northbound train, he felt a little desperate
again. The weather was severe that year, and the fields he
passed were frozen hard as rock. Everywhere about him the
landscape was the same. Rivers were afloat with ice, and snow
was deep on both sides of the train. It was as though a shroud
had dropped around him. Everything that could be seen was
colorless—cold and white as the end of the world.

# CHAPTER
# TWENTY

The relief in the air that marked the end of 1946 was almost tangible. Goods and services were still in short supply; the black market flourished; and legitimate prices spiraled out of sight. The previous January de Gaulle had left the government; the Catholic MRP party continued to be wracked by internecine strife; and in the Assembly the power of the Communist party increased each day. In July, just before the delegates from the victor nations of World War II met in Luxembourg Palace to iron out treaties with the German satellites, the United States tested its A-bomb on Bikini Atoll. And even though the peace talks were conducted in the afterglow of that terrifying blast, the onetime Allies argued long and hopelessly. In October, when the conference ended, when the flags were drawn, the gilt chairs returned to the cellar, and the reams of unused paper carted off by army lorries, one fact emerged with absolute clarity. Despite the new and terrifying weapons at man's disposal, the world was now definitely split into two antagonistic camps.

Teilhard refused to be discouraged. Unlike most people, he had faith in the power of reason to understand the new weapons more as a deterrent than a spur to war. In "Faith in Peace," an essay published in Pierre Chaillet's new review *Les Cahiers du Monde Nouveau*, he argued the point at length. Once human consciousness appeared, he held, there was no longer any biological necessity for animal species to keep on replacing one another in evolution's rush to self-awareness. The murderous instincts of the cave could not, of course, be expected to have vanished overnight. But now that man had at his fingertips the power to destroy himself as well as the very planet that he stood on, it was plain he had reached the point where he must weigh the advantages of using force against the disadvantages.[1]

Early that year Rhoda de Terra, divorced from her husband since before the war, arrived in Paris, searching, she said, for atmosphere for a book. Though in letter after letter from America Mrs. Swan fretted that Rhoda might become "too possessive" of Teilhard during her stay in Paris, the Jesuit reassured her he was much too busy to be able to devote his time to any single visitor. He was, he insisted, finally moving in an intellectual atmosphere where his "message" had a chance of spreading, and he was not about to lose the opportunity. He continued writing at a furious pace, finishing early in the year a new essay comparing twentieth-century man's leap toward unity through the spread of technology to the advance early man made when he discovered hand tools.[2] He was extremely active in the Christian intellectual community. With Père Leroy and another Jesuit scientist, Pierre de Saint-Seine, he attended the regular conferences given by the geophysicist-priest Pierre Lejay in his apartment on the Rue de Sèvres. Teilhard gave a series of scientific lectures at the Sorbonne and innumerable private philosophical talks. At least once a month, too, he talked to groups gathered at Père Dubarle's, rejoicing that, after all his years of intellectual isolation, he at last had an opportunity to hone his thought against that of his peers.

To some of his adversaries, Teilhard's optimistic viewpoint seemed more than a little naïve. Once in a debate with Gabriel Marcel on the subject of "Science and Rationality," he shocked his opponent by refusing to permit even the appalling evidence of the experiments of the doctors of Dachau to modify his faith in the inevitability of human progress.

"Man," he asserted, "to become fully man, must have tried everything. . . ." Of course, he added as a corollary, since the human species was still so young and still prone to fall back into the dark from which it came, the persistence of such evil was to be expected. But since, unlike the lower animals, man no longer acted purely out of instinct, he would presumably abandon every new experiment the moment he saw it did not lead him to greater personalization. . . . "Prometheus!" Marcel had cried, articulating the astonishment of most of the audience. "No," Teilhard replied; "only man as God has made him."

Through February the Jesuit continued scientific lectures at the Sorbonne and philosophical ones at the Musée Guimet.[3] By now he was a more or less unofficial member of Julian Huxley's "think tank," for which he wrote about human rights.[4] He also made time to work on a revision of *The Phenomenon*, following the suggestions given him by Père de Lubac and Msgr. de Solages. In March of 1947, still with an uneasy mind, he repacked the manuscript and sent it back to Rome.

Though he continued to protest a patient disinvolvement about the future of his book—even with the changes—he never ceased to worry about it. As the time wore on, he began to look more urgently about him for field work that would take him out of France.

In April an international conference of paleontologists and philosophers on "Paleontology and Transformism," was held in Paris under the auspices of the Rockefeller Foundation and the French National Center for Scientific Research. About that time, Teilhard petitioned the Rockefeller Foundation to back his trip to Africa with Helmut de Terra and Alberto Blanc. If he despaired when his petition was refused, it was only momentarily. A letter from his Burma field companion, Professor Hallam Movius of Harvard, told him that another mutual friend, Professor Charles Camp of Berkeley, was going in July. Teilhard, who still had the $2,500 that the Viking Fund had voted him the year before, wrote Camp at once, asking to accompany him.

When Camp agreed, Teilhard grew dizzy with relief. His mood remained unchanged all spring, even when *Études* was called on to entertain an ominous visitor from Rome. There had been, of course, no objection on the part of his superiors to the idea of Teilhard's trekking off to Africa. But the generalate had decided to update the dossier it was keeping on him in its archives just the same. The visitor they sent was a gentle Belgian priest with the pained look of a soldier who has been issued shoes too tight but is too loyal to complain, and he was quite open about the purpose of his visit. He had lived most of his religious life in the Eternal City and remembered Ledochowski with affection. The very energy he felt in the house on the Rue Monsieur—its overload of work, all the rushing to and fro about the building—distressed him, and he showed it. Knowing too well now how little Roman thinking had evolved since the war, d'Ouince took umbrage at the very sight of him. He also begged Teilhard, no matter how truly ingenuous the visitor might be, to be careful *just this once* of what he said.

But that had never been Teilhard's way with interrogators, and the advice hardly sat well with his mood. Whether because he was still so driven by his vision that he felt he had to talk to anyone who would listen, or whether because, sensing the genuine goodness of the Belgian, he could not but believe he could make him see the light, Teilhard did just the opposite of what d'Ouince suggested. He took the stunned young priest in hand, brought him to his room, and bombarded him with theories. He even dragged out new unpublished papers to substantiate his points.

When d'Ouince heard what had been going on that morning, he was horrified. At the noon meal, he tried to reassure his caller with his more sophisticated pious charm. "Now you know," he said, "that I and my friends are just as interested in the truth as you and your friends are." Too open, worried, and at that point too worn out for repartee, the Belgian shook his head. "I only wish," he said, "I could believe that."

May of 1947 was probably Teilhard's busiest month since his return from China. He debated the Sorbonne professor Louis Lavelle on Idealism, and later Jean Hippolyte, the disciple of Heidegger. In making his adieux for the African trip, he called on as many friends as possible. Considering the pressures on him at the time, his cheerfulness and thoughtfulness were remarkable. Whenever, at his entrance into Solange Lemaître's apartment, her cat deserted René Grousset's lap for his, he would explain that the little beast preferred him "because I wear a robe." One night, when Juliette, her cook, having done her utmost to prepare a succulent omelette for a small group of Mme. Lemaître's friends, tripped in the doorway and spattered it across the floor, Teilhard bounded to her side and, once he had reassured himself that she was unhurt, looked up in mock confusion, inquiring, "Which do I pick up first, Juliette or the omelette?" When he visited Mme. Lemaître again in mid-May, he talked of the forthcoming feast of the Ascension, a feast he said he always loved, when Christians celebrated Christ's return to his Father bearing the rest of humanity with Him in His arms. It was the great feast of hope, he said. But if anything, Teilhard was much too full of hope that month. He was visibly overexcited, tired from rushing about getting visas, vaccination, and shots and making other arrangements. Until that time it had been his habit to walk in the ambulatory of the courtyard of *Études* after lunch to chat with the caustic, witty Raymond Jouve. But in those weeks he was so busy he was rarely in the house.

On the evening of May 31 Teilhard returned home late and weary. He had a touch of indigestion and avoided conversation. He announced he was going to finish his breviary and examination of conscience in his room. But when he climbed the wooden staircase he had climbed a thousand times before, he wondered that it seemed so endless. He was so tired he was almost numb.

After hurrying through his prayers, he tumbled into bed. The night was balmy, and sleep came quickly to him, strangely sweet and very deep. The scent of greenery from the courtyard hung heavy in the room. It is in such a sleep that old adventurers dream of gardens in Kashmir, white mountains in Tibet, and night calls in the jungle dark. . . .

Suddenly, though, just as dawn lightened the room, Teilhard found himself awake—more so, perhaps, than ever in his life. He was terrified, lying sideways on his cot, as though he had been wrestling with his bedclothes. His heart was squeezing with a pain which corseted his chest and moved along his left arm. There seemed no air around him. At first, he tried to lift himself. It was no use. He sank back into a kind of sleep again, struggling like a drowning man. An hour or so later he reawoke. He struggled to his feet and stumbled to his phone.

It was there by the desk, that Père Fessard, who acted as a paramedic to the house, found him, moments later, pale as the shirt he was trying to put on, staring like an upright corpse. At a little after 7:00 A.M. Fessard had just finished his Mass and was returning to his room when he was accosted by a breathless Brother Cochet, who had just received Teilhard's phone call at the porter's box. "You'd better hurry upstairs and look at Père Teilhard," the brother said. "He may be very ill." Fessard dropped the papers he had just begun to gather and hurried to the floor above. One glance at Teilhard, and he pressed him down into an armchair. Then he phoned an eminent cardiologist and old Resistance companion, Étienne de Vericourt, and urged him to come by at once.

On his arrival, the doctor ordered Teilhard to lie in bed and not to budge. He called the brothers at the little hospital of St. Jean de Dieu on the Rue Oudinot at the foot of the street, who sent two stretcher-bearers for him. With Fessard at their side, they carried the litter the half-block to the hospital. Fessard stayed a moment, then hurried back to talk to Père d'Ouince.

On the way up the street he passed Père Jouve, his ruddy

face more flushed than usual, heading for the hospital. Jouve
stayed a long time in the corridor waiting for news, then
talked to the doctors. The attack had been a massive myocar-
dial infarction, the consequences of which were difficult to
assess immediately. When Teilhard's infirmarian first saw
him, he found his patient fully conscious, silently absorbed in
his thoughts.

Alone in the ice-white clinic cubicle, Teilhard had much to
think about. No matter how long his recovery might take,
there was now no question of his being able to make his trip
to Africa. And with the trouble heading his way out of Rome
and no escape to field work possible, what was left for him to
do?

The next day, when his fever had subsided, d'Ouince and
Jouve came by to visit. D'Ouince asked just two questions.
"Are you in pain?" "No," came the crisp retort. "Are you
happy?" "No."

On the third day, in the middle of an avalanche of flowers
("In fifteen years of work at Oudinot," says Brother Déodat,
who cared for him, "I never saw a sick man receive so
many. . . . They were everywhere—in the chapel, on the
other floors"), Leroy, who had been stopping in each day to
check on Teilhard's progress, was allowed into his room. He
came with their China friend Françoise Raphael. Both the
visitors were pained at how white the patient looked against
the headboard of his hospital bed. Plucking agitatedly at the
plumb of his bell pull, he still spoke very little and, for the
first time since they had known him, showed little interest in
their gossip. He simply grasped each of them by the hand,
looked at them deeply, and then whispered, "Don't work too
hard! . . . One mustn't work too hard!"

On doctor's orders, Teilhard stayed in bed a month. But
even in these circumstances, it was difficult to keep him from
writing. A few days after his attack, he wrote to Mrs. Swan,
who was traveling in Switzerland, to assure her of his safety
and to beg her not to rush to France just then. ("I have too

many skirts around me now," he complained to Leroy.) To the faithful Mlle. Mortier, who had waited patiently in the corridor with his cousin Marguerite, he sent a note asking her to explain to the newly converted Mme. Goldschmidt-Rothschild why he could not attend her baptism that week.

By the time he got around to writing the Abbé Breuil again, the Berkeley expedition was in Africa. From the cool of the pretty little hospital garden where he spent some hours every afternoon, he wrote the prehistorian (one of the few people who could really understand) a detailed letter, articulating his distress. "It takes all of my philosophy and faith," he concluded, "to make constructive use of this heartbreaking event."

In mid-July, still brooding over his missed opportunity, Teilhard was sent to the Blue Nuns' clinic, a rambling bourgeois house near the forest of St.-Germain-en-Laye. Behind the clinic was the breathtaking loveliness of the woods, and before him, the suburban quiet of the town. Teilhard had tablet, pen, new books, and a carefully supervised procession of visitors. He rested there six months while he recuperated, with no stairs to climb, no cigarettes, twelve hours' sleep a night, and doting nuns who tried unsuccessfully to fatten him.

Like any man who has brushed so close to death, Teilhard found that he had subtly changed within. Despite his disappointment about Africa, he was surprised to find in himself an occasional euphoria over the freshness and beauty of life, accompanied by a strange detachment from the worries which had so recently oppressed him. It even seemed to him that since he was definitely "out of the scientific circuit," he might find a new vocation. For decades now, while studying man's past in his function of paleontologist, he had felt himself drawn more and more strongly toward trying to understand man's future. Ever since he returned from China, it had been the main thing on his mind. If he could no longer dig in the field, he wrote a friend, he still could speculate—at least on the purely scientific level—about modern man and social

biology. In point of fact, freedom from obligation to the
world of fossils might well be the true "meaning" of the or-
deal he had just been through.

But scarcely one week after he arrived at St.-Germain he received another blow. News came that his nephew Olivier,
then only twenty-five years old, the only son of his last
remaining brother, Joseph, had drowned when he was caught
in the weeds growing in a pool near Les Moulins where he
was swimming. Olivier had been to Joseph as Albéric had
been to Teilhard's father. In him rested his pride and hope. It
had been Olivier whom that grand gentleman, who now had
only a daughter left to him, had counted on to carry on his
name.

Some days after the accident, Joseph came up to visit his
brother. His reaction to the loss struck the convalescent with
a kind of awe. His patience when he talked about his son was
deeply moving. And Teilhard, in his strangely half-euphoric,
half-depressed condition, could not help wondering at the
ways of a Providence that took the life of a promising young
man (one whom he himself had loved) and spared him, a
sixty-six-year-old with no apparent future.

Joseph might have wondered too. But he did not. More
than an aristocrat, he was a man of faith; and he bowed his
head to the will of God without a word. "You see," Teilhard
wrote to a friend after the encounter, "how much it helps to
have something to believe in? Without it, why should anyone
go on?"

In those days the Jesuits of Paris, Mme. Raphael, who had
just taken a post with a United Nations welfare agency, and
Georges Le Fèvre (his old comrade of the Citroën expedition,
who lived in St.-Germain) came to sit with him in the garden
of the clinic. In August Mme. Dorget and some friends even
took him on short drives around the countryside. By the end
of August Teilhard was well enough to travel short distances,
and Père d'Ouince decided he could safely kidnap him briefly
to attend a Jesuit convention to be held at a boys' school near

Versailles late that month and give a paper. Early in the morning of that day, a car was sent to fetch him.

Out at Versailles, Teilhard lunched with his provincial, with de Lubac, and the visiting John Courtney Murray. That afternoon, sitting on a stiff little chair in the grande salle of the central building of the school and staring absently at the still-empty students' riding ring under the turning leaves, he listened while d'Ouince read his paper "The Religious Value of Research."[5]

The essay discussed the "rebound of evolution" on itself that Teilhard believed was presently in progress in the world, since man in his manipulation of biology and physics (and certainly since the smashing of the atom) had finally laid hands upon the springs of his own being and was moving them to his design. The strongest force then whipping mankind, he contended, was a sense of future. But, sadly, his own religious Order, instead of moving with the drive, was resisting it and, in the process, reversing the original Ignatian ideal of relating everything to the Divine.

The paper did more than cast a new light on old ways of thinking in the Society. Fundamentally, it was a criticism of the whole Jesuit seminary system, whose scholarship had been born in the Renaissance and had not changed its perspective since then. Though that training had been effective in its time, the times had changed. In the twentieth century, instead of sending their sons off to work in the outlands of research where the real curiosity of humanity was engaged, Jesuit seminaries, Teilhard held, still taught men to broaden their humanity through literature and mathematics. And how many generous young novices, he asked, who came to the Society, zealous to be thrown into the thick of human combat, were sent back to the world cooled into quiet classics masters?

In general, the French representatives at the conference were delighted with the paper. But four important Roman theologians who were present that day found the paper shocking. Discussions at the meeting, they were aware, were meant to be self-critical, but not to this degree! Even worse, it seemed to them incredible that they were forced to sit quietly in the company of other priests, listening to a lecture from one whose vocabularly seemed to give the same weight to words (or neologisms) like "super-Christianity," "ultra-humanity," "rebound of consciousness" as to the words "incarnation" and "redemption."

After the session, quite unconscious of the stir he had created, Teilhard was hurried back to St.-Germain. Visitors continued coming: the young Canadian painter and wife of a French diplomat Simone Beaulieu; Ida Treat, the American journalist and friend of many years whom he first met when both of them were going to Boule's lectures; his Jesuit friends; and of course Mrs. de Terra. Besides carrying on a correspondence with Emmanuel Mounier about a conference of Catholic intellectuals to be held that fall, Teilhard read the concentration-camp essays of Michel Riquet, a Jesuit who had spent the end of the war interned at Dachau and was preparing to give the next year's Lenten sermons at Notre Dame. A Benedictine of Beuron, on his way to found a monastery in Chile, visited him. In what time he had alone, Teilhard wrote an essay on "The Rebound of Consciousness"[6] to clarify any confusion his use of the term might have caused at Versailles.

But, quite unknown to him, two days before that Versailles congress the autocratic ax had fallen once again. As if to prove how contrarily slow is the pace of Roman thinking, a letter from Janssens concerning the then year-old article by Garrigou-Lagrange in *Angelicum* finally reached him through his provincial in Lyon.

Even though an answer to Garrigou in defense of Teilhard had been written by Msgr. de Solages for the April 1947 issue of the *Bulletin de Littérature Ecclésiastique*, it had made little stir below the Alps. All year long, the sleek black Cadillacs that carried the consultors of the Holy Office from their various convents to biweekly theological discussions at the Holy Office continued to move steadily through the narrow streets. The "new theology" in France was now under still more serious scrutiny. By summer the discussions by the consultors (in which the voice of Garrigou was still the loudest) had turned to action. Prodded by a serious letter from Marchetti-Selvaggiani, a chastened Father Janssens on August 22, 1947, again sent Teilhard strict instructions, under no circumstances to speak or write on anything but scientific subjects. This time the tone of the injunction was as stiff as any he had received from Ledochowski.

"Well, *someone* had to take the blame for everything," Teilhard commented sadly to a friend. He was the most visible offender, and therefore the natural target. On September 22 he wrote his general, reassuring him of his fidelity. Most of the criticism in his letter, he recalled, referred to papers he had written before 1939, and "since then, with the advice of authorized theologians who are familiar with my work, I believe I have made great progress toward explaining clearly a point of view, which—given my experience among the 'gentiles'—seems ready now to have a chance of serving God. . . . Don't you think," he finished rather plaintively, "it well could be unfortunate if a fruit which may be on the point of ripening were to be tossed aside without examination?"

Teilhard returned to *Études* in October, earlier than expected. He worked quietly (and rather quixotically, it seems) on another essay requested by de Solages. In it, he suggested once again that the old problem of "original sin," which was still disturbing Roman thinkers, would simply dissolve if they would only stop considering the fall of man as a *serial* event in human history.[7] In his next paper, "Turmoil or Genesis?"[8] he suggested that—despite the existence of free will—once the floodgates of reflective thought were opened, a new evolutionary drive had taken over, pushing the individual thinking units ever closer together despite their resistance. If "man to become truly man" had first of all to become "legion," then, a superior humanity could only be achieved as a result of the close unity (and the interchange of information, need, purpose, and love) of all its members.

At the time the restless Mrs. de Terra popped up again in Paris that November, Teilhard was being very chary about making philosophical statements in public. He kept his essays locked in his desk, and eased himself back into his old regime of talk and tea in the great salons of Paris.

# CHAPTER
# TWENTY-ONE

Despite the beginning of the influx of U.S. aid to Western Europe which had been announced by Secretary of State George C. Marshall in June 1947, economic recovery in France was slow, particularly as it affected the working class. Among the poor and dispossessed, Marxism still flourished. In late 1947 a wave of strikes—the first in which Suhard's beloved worker-priests participated as a group—broke out, and employers, who up to then had regarded the priests as a probable "good influence" among the working class, began to question their usefulness. At the celebration of the fiftieth anniversary of his ordination, Cardinal Suhard rededicated himself to the task of saving the lost souls of his diocese, and expressed his pain over his helplessness to break the barrier that stood between the blooming boulevards of Paris and the wretched flatlands of the factory suburbs.

Early in 1948 Teilhard produced "Trois Choses Que Je Vois,"[1] in which, after pointing out the coincidence between Saint John's conception of the Second Coming and his own idea of the maturation of the human stock, he once again suggested that the adoption of a truly *human* faith, one that combined the "rational force of Marxism" with the "human warmth of Christianity" was the only antidote to the economic and social problems of the postwar world.

As new lines of contention began to be drawn up in France, old ones disappeared. Wounds left by the factionalism of the war slowly healed; and Teilhard's China friends began resurfacing. After a series of shattering interrogations at a Paris commissariat, French Tokyo ambassador Henri Cosme retired to his old château of Foucaucourt, at last to cultivate the garden Vichy had denied him in Peking. The former Peking chargé Roland de Margerie, who had come home quietly in 1946 on a U.S. warship and retired to the library of his old apartment overlooking a garden courtyard on the Rue St.-Guillaume to read and write, began accepting invitations. Claude Rivière, the sympathetic lady broadcaster who had been Teilhard's unofficial Shanghai guide during 1942 and was also repatriated by warship in midsummer 1947, found him again that autumn and promptly arranged to have him and Père Leroy invited to a dinner party with her at the house of the sculptor Delemarre.

Like Françoise Raphael before her, Mme. Rivière was shocked by the gracelessness of postwar Paris. The boorishness of its new breed of bourgeoisie who fought like wildcats for their share of the few comforts just beginning to be available contrasted painfully with her memories of the city she remembered twenty-five years earlier. In January 1948, carrying a letter from Teilhard to Auguste Valensin, who, since his shift to Nice in 1935, had become one of the ornaments of its Centre Universitaire Méditerranéen, she left to settle in the south.

Teilhard had just come back to Paris from the snowy mountains of Auvergne, where he had gone to the château of Les Moulins to attend the betrothal ceremony of his brother Joseph's daughter Françoise to a young French businessman. Though the death of Olivier the previous summer still left shadows in the old château, the happiness of the engaged couple sent him back to Paris more convinced than ever that "sorrow and sadness are not the same thing."

And there were other things to lift his spirits. Three months earlier Paul Fejos, director of the New York–based Viking Fund, whose interest continued to be piqued by Franz

Weidenreich's stories about the strange priest with the daring lyrical philosophy who had shared his China years, suggested that Teilhard use the money the Fund voted him for Africa in 1946 to visit in America. Before January 1948 was out, Teilhard wrote Fejos that he had arranged passport and visa and would be ready to come by early March.

But first he paid a social call on his World War I friend the old geologist Emmanuel de Margerie. Scarcely was he settled in the drawing room when de Margerie's nephew Roland sailed in, ebullient as ever, full of news about a bungled burglary at the d'Ormesson château. Everything, he said, had ended happily because the robbers in removing "Tante Yo-Yo's"* famous string of Japanese pearls from the bedroom vault, had tripped on them and awakened the house. To Teilhard's delight, a few days after his encounter with Roland de Margerie he ran into his lively wife as well, quite accidentally, at an exhibition of the art of *femmes peintres* where the Duchesse Edmée de la Rochefoucauld was showing a portrait she had done of him years earlier.

That winter, while Teilhard held court in the salons of the *grand monde* of Paris, he also suffered silently through several dinners in the company of an Indian mystic, the Swami Siddirswaranda, who at that time was lecturing to packed houses at the Sorbonne. As a scholastic, Teilhard himself had come too close to raw pantheism not to know how seductive it could be, particularly to the young and influenceable. It had taken him a lifetime of experience to reassure himself that the only way to reach the absolute was through the conquest rather than the suppression of the tangible. Though always impeccably polite to the Hindu when they met in public, in letters to his friends he called his message "nebulous" and "dehumanizing." There could be no real love of neighbor without individuation—a thing impossible in the pantheist perspective. Under the economic and technical pressures that were growing on the planet, he protested, even India, resist it

* Yolande Arsène-Henri, née d'Ormesson.

though she might, would eventually be forced to recognize that without the "vital upthrust" of the physical it was impossible to reach pure spirit.

In late February Teilhard sailed for New York. When he arrived, he was dismayed to find both Mrs. de Terra and Mrs. Swan (ostentatiously ignoring one another) waiting for him on the dock. Unlike her younger competitor for his attention, Lucile had not seen Teilhard since China, and in New York she was determined to make up as much time as possible. Thus began an embarrassing tug of war that lasted through the visit. Somehow, however—even during his first few days in America—he managed to escape his social obligations long enough to drop into the American Museum of Natural History to visit Weidenreich, the wry, white-bearded geologist George Simpson, and the courtly Harry Shapiro and to examine the vertebrate collection of the museum's backstage workrooms.

While he was in New York, Teilhard stayed with the Jesuits at the residence of the staff of *America* magazine. Unfortunately, except for moments with the sophisticated John LaFarge, whose pioneer work for black civil rights left him little time to spend with the visitor, and Robert Graham, with whom he maintained a tenuous friendship, he was painfully ill-at-ease among his brothers. As he wrote to Leroy, his reception at America House was "cordial and hearty, as is the custom here. . . ." But he confessed, try as he might, he could not manage to "feel spiritually comfortable" in that setting.

The discomfort he experienced was mutual. The "Villanova incident" of 1935 was not forgotten, and at that time the outlook of the American Jesuits was far too narrow for them to be able to accept him for the man he was. Like most Irish-American priests at that time, they had a deep and solid Jansenistic streak. Close-minded, almost monkish in their rigidity, they found Teilhard's easy freedom of movement, his curious contacts, his odd-hour appointments, his evenhanded openness with men and women, his retinue of lady admirers, even his worldly European manners quite bewildering. All through the visit Teilhard remained an alien presence among his brothers, troubling their days with thoughts or memories they had long suppressed. At his entrance into a room, sudden silences would fall. The flash of his passing in a hall, caught in the corner of an eye, could send a conversation into aimless drifting.

In his first real close experience of her, Teilhard was distressed to discover how rigid, unimaginative, and sectarian was the American Catholic Church. It seemed to him unashamedly bending its energies toward "hiding the world rather than revealing it." Further, the cultural climate of the United States—that New World which had elicited his lyrical paper "The Spirit of the Earth" when he passed blithely (and a bit blindly) through it in 1931—seemed to have changed completely. So paralyzed was it by the anticommunist hysteria precipitated by Stalinist imperialism, so sleepily self-satisfied with its plenty, and so unconscious of the responsibility that its immense technical power placed on it to help bring about a fuller life for all the world that Teilhard found himself dreaming (as he wrote in a letter to a friend) that "a good dip into Marxism might start things moving again."

On March 2 he paid his visit to the Viking Fund and met its director, Paul Fejos. Like Teilhard, Fejos was a figure somewhat larger than life. A fifty-one-year-old Hungarian with bright blue eyes, a pixyish grin, and eloquent, expressive hands, Fejos already had behind him a career which bettered even Teilhard's own life for extravagance. A medical doctor by training, and also something of a cinematic genius, in the late 1920s he had walked out on one of Universal Pictures' "super-jewels" to make his own kind of film in Europe. Once there, quite accidentally, he fell into doing ethnographical films, and in the course of one such venture near Singapore he met Axel Wenner-Gren (then touring the world on his yacht). When Wenner-Gren subsequently decided to found an anthropological institute called the Viking Fund in 1941, he named his friend its first director.

A product, as Teilhard was, of the European landed gentry, Fejos had an imperial manner and the ferocious temper of a man who expects to be obeyed. He spoke with a delicious "Mittel European" accent that he never tried to lose. Like Teilhard, he believed in the necessity of gathering all the sciences into a single "science of man," and mourned the inability of representatives of one discipline of human investigation to communicate with another. "For effry anzer," he used to say in what he called his "baseball English," "dere's a qvestion. . . . And to effry qvestion, dere's an anzer. Unhappily, de men who know de anzers do not even know dat de odder men exist."

From their first encounter, Fejos and Teilhard got on famously, and the date for Teilhard's lecture at a Friday supper meeting of the East Coast anthropologists was set for April 11.

When that night came, Teilhard gave his talk in the front upstairs library of the Foundation, on "The Trend and Significance of Human Evolution." Before the mixed bag of humanists, archaeologists, and anthropologists he repeated his theory that, since the union of all men increased the psychic awareness of each man somewhat to the "mathematical power" of the number of men involved, the economic and psychic pressures then forcing humanity more closely together on the unexpandable surface of the planet were actually individualizing rather than depersonalizing each human unit.

When he finished, he was happily surprised at how "passionately and easily" he had been able to express himself in English. Still, it troubled him to find that even in that thoroughly secular intellectual atmosphere where he spoke, there was a fissure (seemingly peculiar to America) between humanistic and scientific approaches to the study of man. The division seemed to him that night perhaps as deep as the one which he had, to his misfortune, discovered long ago between science and religion.

In the days that followed, Teilhard stopped frequently at the Foundation to see Fejos, who, he found, had also recognized the problem years before. It was, the Hungarian said, because such a gulf existed that the Viking Fund had been created in the first place. "Our primary interest," he told Teilhard, "is communication."

Fascinated and entertained though he was by his continued talks with Fejos, not long after he had given his Foundation talk Teilhard began to realize that there was nothing else to hold him in America. For a few weeks he continued rather aimlessly stopping at the Museum of Natural History to chat, meeting privately with a few young avant-garde American priests, and looking up American friends out of the past as far away as Washington.

He was, however, still sufficiently intimidated by the lack of understanding between him and his American brothers that he remarked—after giving a very careful talk before a group of scholastics in Fordham's Spellman Hall—"I hope I said nothing to trouble anybody!" He sat to have his portrait done by the sculptress Malvina Hoffman in her studio on East Thirty-fifth Street, but proved so stiff and sad a model that four months later, when the bust crashed onto the Cherbourg dock in France, where it had been sent for casting, Miss Hoffman was relieved to have the chance to try again.

Slowly and surely he was sinking once again into one of his terrible depressions. Even the arrival of the sympathetic Raymond Jouve, who came to the United States that spring to write some articles for *America* magazine and brought with him a copy of Valensin's latest book,[2] did not do much to change his feeling that he was living in a limbo. By now, his discomfort had become apparent even to his friends. Some of them tried to help. Fejos, for example, arranged to have Teilhard invited back to the States the following year to give a series of lectures at Columbia University—a project which would make a lengthy visit more worthwhile. And for a moment Teilhard felt better.

In late May he applied to the local provincial ("to the R.P. John R. McMahan," he wrote, as if he were examining some odd species of American fauna, or perhaps the Gaelic word for "no"), asking his consent for a return visit. When the expected refusal came, he sat down miserably and wrote the French assistant, Bernard de Gorostarzu, in Rome—begging him to use his influence in his behalf.

Father McMahan's "No" stood firm. And staring at the return ticket he had purchased for July, Teilhard finally gave way to panic. In early June he wrote to Pierre Leroy, "It is just the way it was in China. . . . Everything I try to do seems mountainous to me!" And on June 5—without stopping to do more than write a goodbye note to Dr. Fejos—he took a Dutch ship home.

Leroy met him at the Paris station. Approaching him in the steam and ghostly light of St.-Lazare, he saw what seemed at first only a foggy memory of the happy traveler who had left for America four months earlier. Teilhard was gray-faced and in tears. His hands shook uncontrollably. At the sight of his old comrade, he almost fell into his arms. At first Leroy could not imagine what had happened. From Teilhard's confused explanation, he managed to piece together that his friend was so upset only because he had forgotten to lock his old metal footlocker and was afraid he had lost his papers. Leroy helped him gather his effects, took his bags, and brought him to *Études*. But when the supper bell rang, Teilhard protested he could not go down. Sitting at his desk with the door shut tight behind him, he dropped his head into his hands and shook with sobs.

Even then he could not articulate a real cause for his anguish. His old friend thrashed about for words of comfort. Remembering that Teilhard once told him how, when his sister Françoise was sad, he always reminded her that she was "looking at the crucifix from the wrong side," he repeated the remark. Teilhard looked up at him with such dumb anguish that he embraced him once again if only "to give him a little human warmth." Well after midnight Leroy went home to Versailles, leaving Teilhard as miserable as he found him.

The summer was wet in Paris and unseasonably cold. The trees wept onto the sidewalks; a melancholy chill hung in old houses like *Études*. Teilhard went out a few times to give private lectures, but he always felt as though there were a glass partition between him and his listeners. To Lucile Swan in America he wrote that he had found a doctor who assured him the depression was fundamentally of organic origin—though aggravated by his emotional state—and that it would soon pass away. But it did not pass. So, in that year when so many international conferences about the future of humanity were held both in and out of Paris, Teilhard occupied himself writing another essay about the possibility of progress.[3]

A few weeks after his return, the Collège de France again voted that he become one of the candidates for a science chair left empty by a member who had reached retirement age. Now Teilhard had a new excuse to write his general requesting permission to stand for the post. In the same letter he reminded Janssens of the Columbia lectures, and asked him once again about the unacknowledged revised copy of *The Phenomenon of Man* sent to Rome in 1947.

He wrote the letter without optimism, expecting it to end like all the others, on some cluttered Roman desk. He was really more absorbed in the composition of a larger essay he called "Comment Je Vois," which advanced the idea of a *mobile* "physics," "metaphysics," and "mysticism," in opposition to the *static* Aristotelian ones. An essay which ran a good twenty-five pages, it seemed bound to keep him busy well into the autumn.

But suddenly on July 10, 1948, he was stunned to receive a gently worded letter from his generalate, suggesting he come to Rome sometime in the early autumn to discuss his problems.

After waiting all those years for such a message, Teilhard was momentarily slow in grasping what it meant. But before he put the paper down, he realized full well the tremendous import of the thing he carried in his hand. The father general of his Order was actually *agreeing* that he come in person to "discuss" his philosophy, his books, the acceptance of the chair, the possibility of giving the Columbia lectures the next year—everything! . . . The whole direction of his life seemed turned around. He went blind with joy, taut with apprehension, anything but "calmly philosophical," as he protested that he was.

It did not even seem important to the sixty-seven-year-old man that it had taken him more than half his life to reach the time of possible rehabilitation. He did not stop to regret that if all did go well, he had so few years left to relish his success. All that mattered was that now, at last, he still might have a chance of leaving his message after him, and consequently of doing what he could to save the Christianity he still firmly believed in from the overweight of bureaucracy and immobility that so oppressed it.

After finishing "Comment Je Vois" on August 23, in a nearly empty Paris, he set out for his brother Joseph's in Auvergne to rest and gather his forces. The weather in Clermont was cool and cloudy, and the oaks just yellowing before the purple stretches of the *puys*. Most of the time he sat at the little table before the window in his room with its view of the skyline—Mont-Dore directly before him, the silhouette of the fourteenth-century abbey of La Chaise Dieu a little to the side—writing out a bibliography of his scientific papers and the twenty-four-page résumé of his work that was required if he was to stand for the Collège de France.

During that visit Teilhard called on his widowed sisters-in-law who lived in the nearby family houses—particularly Gabriel's widow, Caroline, at Murol. He took pleasure in the company of Joseph, "so sweet now even with the peasantry," his lingering melancholy over the loss of his son seeming to

have eased a little as he basked in the gaiety of his visiting
daughter and new son-in-law. Joseph was pleased to know
that Rome had finally taken notice of his brother (this time,
not in terms of censure); he was quite certain that once Pierre
visited the Holy City, wiser heads could talk him out of some
of his wild notions.

Just at the harvest festival time of wine and cakes, when
raisins blackened on rejected vines, Joseph took a business
trip to Paris. In his absence, Teilhard made a very deep retreat. He used the time to put himself in the Presence of God
and (perhaps a bit as a hedge against the visceral anguish of
anticipation) tried valiantly to abandon himself to the Divine
Will. That summer, his beloved Jersey contemporary the biblical scholar Joseph Huby died of a heart attack one night
when, by coincidence, he was passing through his own home
town; and death, too, was on Teilhard's mind.

When Joseph came back to Auvergne, the Jesuit spent
more time with the family. He walked with his brother the
dusty road around the square outbuildings behind the house
and sat before the fire in the grand salon in the evening. He
talked about his upcoming trip, and the beauty of the Holy
City he would visit. But as to what precisely he intended to
say to the Romans when he met them, he kept his counsel.

On September 14 Teilhard and his brother took the train
for Paris. The next day Mlle. Mortier called in at *Études*. In
that admirably bright, dry September, while he awaited word
from Rome of the exact date on which he was to leave,
Teilhard busied himself with arrangements for the journey.
There were papers to be gathered, conferences and visits relating to the appointment to the Collège de France he had to
make, and even a few lectures to be given. He sent a copy of
"Comment Je Vois" to de Lubac at Lyon and visited
UNESCO friends. He managed to see the Abbé Breuil, on a
home visit from his work in Africa, the Max de Begouëns,
and Professor Piveteau, while still keeping up his mask of
being "philosophical" about the outcome of his trip. He

often said that he was not particularly concerned about the question of the Collège chair, because he himself had less than three years to occupy it before he reached retirement age.

On September 21 Teilhard went to Versailles to talk to a group of chaplains from Catholic workingmen's associations about the need to combine the best in Marxism with the best of Christianity in an attempt to revitalize the Church.[4] When the Church was first established, Teilhard said, collective progress had not yet emerged as a human goal. But now that it had, it was the chaplains' job, as modern "analogues" of the Apostles, to open their vision to a changed and moving world. Not only was it necessary that Christianity be brought to scientists and philosophers living in a rarefied atmosphere; it was imperative that workers in their factories be prepared to play a role in bringing about the maturation of a more adult mankind.

In the ensuing question period, Teilhard was asked first whether, in his view, human life was growing more determined. "The very force of numbers," he responded, "limits liberty as we used to know it. But, simultaneously, cooperation with the moving forces of the whole brings us a new, higher, more directed liberty. . . ." "How do you place your perspective in the evolution of Church thinking?" someone asked. In the first centuries, Teilhard replied, theologians were occupied with Christ's relation with the Trinity; now, with the discovery of the immensity of the universe, the time had come for working out His relationship to the world. With mankind growing up, theology would have to grow as well if it was to keep man's view of Christ as large as his view of the world. As a matter of fact, Teilhard added, Christians, because they were gifted with the torch of faith, were privileged to move into the dark like scouts, to explore new human possibilities. "What about evil then?" someone inevitably asked. As far as individual wrongdoing was concerned, Teilhard saw little change in the old concept of the Christian's duty to fight temptation in himself. But as far as the larger problem of physical and moral evil went, he cautioned Christian thinkers to remember that the world was still unfinished. And, he continued, since Christians also had the weapon of prayer at their disposal, they were not nearly so helpless in dealing with evil on the grand scale as some imagined.

When the meeting was over, Teilhard wrote that rarely in his life had he found himself speaking before so completely sympathetic a group. Were it not for his apprehension about the problems he might face in Rome, he would have been completely happy. But nothing could ease his mind about that. In those nervous waiting days, most of his *Études* friends stood by him, delicately respecting his silences, and encouraging him to speak when they felt they honestly could do so.

The day before his departure, he fiddled uncomfortably through a luncheon given in his honor by Mme. de Margerie. Since Leroy was on retreat in the Midi, he marked more time by visiting Solange Lemaître and her friends. That night he finished packing early. Then he went downstairs to d'Ouince's office for more instructions as to how he should conduct himself in Rome—whom he should see, whom he should avoid, what he should say, what he should be careful not to say. For once, d'Ouince seemed almost more nervous than he.

The following afternoon, alone and carrying his precious green *cantine*, Teilhard set out by taxi for the Gare de Lyon. As he left the house, he turned again and waved to Jouve, who watched him from the door. He was now entirely unlike the confident young man who had waved goodbye to Valensin from a train window in Lyon a quarter of a century before. The arm he raised in salutation was now as stiff with apprehension as it was with rheumatism. And (as he later told a friend) at the sight, Jouve's mind went back to the afternoon that he and Teilhard had passed together a few days earlier among the papers of his confrere's room.

Teilhard had invited him to come and talk. They sat a long while speaking in banalities, and then went on to discuss an old paper Teilhard had made reference to. In one of the rapid alterations of sunlight and storm that are characteristic of Parisian autumns, the room suddenly went dark. Though Teilhard did not seem to notice, Jouve reached over and switched on the lamp. All at once Teilhard looked up at him, seemingly forgetful of the essay he was holding in his hand, and with a half-smile, said—as though they had been discussing nothing else that day—"But think, *mon vieux*. . . . A few days more, and I'll be off to stroke the tiger's whiskers."

# CHAPTER
# TWENTY-TWO

"One does not go to Rome for justice," it has been said, and wisely; "one goes to pray benevolence." Philosophically, even more than geographically, Rome has never been the city of Justinian. Though other Western capitals have passed through various democratizing revolutions in the last two thousand years, clerical and official Rome has remained (and to some degree still remains) the heir of the imperial Caesars, the last absolute monarchy on earth. Here, as in a vast museum—even after Vatican II—still to some extent survive the trappings of an ancient and autocratic life-style: palace cliques, ideological nepotism, and that cynical careerism for which certain men have always been ready to sacrifice many of the good things of this life.

But all of this with an important difference. Papal Rome has always had one quality that distinguishes it from other power centers and gives it its peculiar ambiance. This quality is the addition of the humanizing influence that has grown out of the practice of the Gospel counsel to compassion. In Rome, a cry from the heart may move the seven hills, while a legal brief is just a piece of paper.

Teilhard's mistake in going there as he did was that he went in search of justice. He had never fully understood how helpless he was against the prejudice of his superiors. He knew that he was personally persuasive: Women had always adored him for his good looks and gallantry, and men were fascinated by his originality and charm. He knew that he was absolutely honest in his devotion to the truth, and he could not imagine that others would not be the same. He knew, by report, a little of the city's lovely side—its companies of saintly souls leading lives of extraordinary gentleness and self-sacrifice in out-of-the-way convents. And if this had been the Rome that he came to treat with, he would not have had to worry.

But it was not. Teilhard had come to deal with a bureaucracy made of men who, like the elders of a provincial town, distrusted strangers and made a virtue out of fixity. It was a world of vested interests and long memories of interlocking vendettas, where a mostly Italian hierarchy of aged mandarins with medical fetishes about longevity and often boot-blacked hair repeated themselves on pontifical commissions, and, holding the consciences of millions in their hands, presumed their small skills equal to the task.

Into that alien city about midnight on October 4, 1948, Teilhard came, armed only with his old green footlocker full of essays and his irreformable French rationality. As he descended from the railway car, he was surprised to see, waiting at the gate, an old acquaintance: the saintly, gentle Belgian priest who had been sent to *Études* the year before to collect his papers for the Roman dossier. Though the Belgian had not changed his mind at all about Teilhard's ideas, he was too genuinely tenderhearted to support the thought of the old man coming into a strange city at that ungodly hour with no one to receive him and escort him to the generalate. So he had requested the key to the house from the father minister, to go to meet him.

At the sight of a familar face, Teilhard's own face broke into a sunburst smile. He rushed forward to greet his brother. The Belgian helped him with his baggage, hailed one of the small green-beetle taxis outside, and slid off with him into the heavy stillness of the Roman night.

Conversation in the cab came slowly. Though the Roman

priest was solicitous for Teilhard's comfort, their last meeting at *Études* had left an unbridgeable space of incomprehension between them. With some difficulty, they found topics of common interest: mutual friends in Louvain and Paris, the untimely passing of Joseph Huby the past summer, and the loss to biblical studies which that death presaged.

The taxi sped along the Via Nazionale and the Corso in clear moonlight. It crossed the Tiber at the little Victor Emmanuel bridge. To the right was the huge illuminated barrel-fort, Castel S. Angelo, with its footbridge of white marble angels twisted into attitudes of ecstasy, to which in other centuries popes so often fled from citizens and barbarians alike. Once past the bridge, the cab turned into the district of Borgo S. Spirito, in the heart of Vatican City, and drew up before the gloomy Jesuit barracks with its incongruous Monagasque glass canopy which Ledochowski had constructed in the 1920s just to the left of St. Peter's Square. The generalate stood just in front of the ancient palace of the Inquisition, whose jail-ringed courtyard was now a pool of shadow. Directly across the square were the Vatican apartments, but, as the pope was still vacationing at Castel Gandolfo, the windows were firmly shut.

When the Jesuits entered their house, they discovered that a few French priests Teilhard had met over the years, and even a Spaniard he had not seen since they were scholastics together in Jersey, had stayed up to greet him. As the cells in the generalate proper were all occupied, Teilhard was told he would be lodged in the "writers' wing"—a communicating building which housed the scriveners of long supportive articles on Vatican policy for *Civiltà Cattolica* and other important Church propaganda organs. Badly fatigued after his seventeen-hour train ride, he politely refused his guide's offer of refreshment, was conducted to his room, washed, said his prayers, and went to sleep.

The next morning he awoke to the glare of sunlight on whitewashed walls, his heart pounding with excitement. After his Mass, he made a courtesy call on his old interrogator Norbert de Boynes, now "admonitor" ("consultor in matters of conscience") to Father Janssens. De Boynes was heavier than Teilhard remembered, round and solid as a cupola from peace and pasta; he had not seen Teilhard since that day in Paris in 1939 when only the pleas of the staff of *Études* had restrained him from taking drastic action on the "Spiritualization of Matter" paper; and he greeted him with guarded cordiality. Immediately afterward, he sent him off to see the French Jesuit assistant, Bernard de Gorostarzu, who would be his liaison with the Jesuit Curia during the visit.

In his office Teilhard found Father de Gorostarzu fidgeting nervously but happily. A high-strung, hyperactive man, whose constant busyness earned him the nickname of "the Bee," he did not disguise his joy at having Teilhard in Rome with him at last. But after embracing him, he sat him down and rapidly explained the situation. The father general, he said, was terribly occupied and could not make any appointments for some days. They were all still waiting the return of two copies of the manuscript of *The Phenomenon* which had been sent out for criticism by different Jesuits and which would be arriving any day. When these "revisions" came, Teilhard could make the necessary changes, and the matter would receive final consideration. Meanwhile, de Gorostarzu offered to do all he could to keep him occupied, and to introduce him to the French community in Rome.

Teilhard had made the trip prepared to wait. "Here," he wrote a friend, "things move very much the way they did in China. One does not press too hard." He tried to bide his time. He stayed as close to home as possible, walking in the generalate garden, where the palpably loving southern light brought back memories of field adventures long ago. He made small talk with Jesuits he had not seen for many years who were passing through the house. He kept his peace.

A few days after his arrival, dressed in his cassock and his soup-dish hat, he made a ritual visit to St. Peter's, whose banklike vastness chilled him. There was, however, he wrote a friend, something breathtaking in the sense it gave of the universality and self-assuredness of Catholicism. Later, in the dark baroque pile of the Jesuit mother church, the Gesù, he knelt first before the tomb of Saint Ignatius and then in the little chapel of the Madonna della Strada, where so many eminent Jesuits had prayed, while moments of tender remembrance of his religious boyhood, of Aix, of Jersey, and of Hastings flooded in on him.

Very soon, though, his old vague sense of panic took hold of him again. The tangle of columns, cornices, and frescoes in the baroque churches, where angelic limbs and wings melted into one another in the shadows, left him with the vertigo of wandering in a Luna Park. The barbaric religious display of the city—its land-office market in religious souvenirs, its plethora of empty votive churches, its suffocatingly attitudinizing atmosphere of piety around him—were disquieting.

In the first few days of waiting, Father de Gorostarzu proved as good as his word. To keep up Teilhard's spirits, he squired him about, as much to keep him busy as (in Teilhard's opinion) to parade him before his critics and "show them what an inoffensive animal I am." They visited the little church of St.-Louis-des-Français with its three Correggios and its royal chapel still proudly displaying the fleur-de-lis on violet draperies. They went together to clerical dinners at the Procure St.-Sulpice in the same compound and to cocktail parties at the adjoining French Center, where Teilhard chatted easily with the new ambassador to the Vatican Wladimir d'Ormesson, a China friend named Gabriel Beauroy, and other acquaintances from Paris.

On October 8 the reports from Teilhard's censors still had not come. But on that day, he was told that Father Janssens was prepared to see him anyway—that very afternoon. His heart thudding in his ears, Teilhard hurried to the rendezvous.

At the door that opened on the interior garden, he stopped

suddenly. Before him, walking and reading his breviary, was
the general, a light-haired, rabbity creature with great, round
glasses and a fugitive smile. A canon lawyer whose specialty
had always been a source of strength and guidance, Janssens
followed Jesuit tradition as if it were the Decalogue, even to
the point of employing a lay brother whose major function
was to run upstairs and extend a bowl of holy water with
which he crossed himself as he came from dinner. Uncertain
of his private judgment, and unhappy in the employment of
power, he was timorous before the theological opinion-makers
of the city, and vacillated under pressure exercised on him by
his own men.

Charles Boyer of the Roman Academy of St. Thomas, the
pinch-faced Dutchman Sebastian Tromp, the giant, balding
Édouard Dhanis (whose intellectual tendencies as much as
physical appearance later prompted American seminarians to
call him "Mr. Clean"), the white-haired, studiously elegant,
up-from-Brookline Vincent McCormick (one of the last
American Roman Jesuits whom their brothers referred to as
the "Great White Fleet"), and Norbert de Boynes, his admonitor, all held leashes which could jerk him suddenly in
various directions.

And when it came to dealing with the Holy Office, Father
Janssens was quite nearly helpless. When any of his subjects
were criticized by its theologians, he simply *posted* soft letters
of protest to the Inquisition (a mere two-minute walk away),
begging that, if there were doctrinal irregularities in what
they taught, only "tendencies" and not individuals should be
denounced. Sometimes his letters lay for days unopened
under the sadly deprecating smile of Marchetti-Selvaggiani.

Teilhard, however, knew little of all this. All he had to go
on were d'Ouince's and Jouve's warnings, and the appearance
of the man before him. At the sound of Teilhard's footsteps,
Janssens turned quickly round, then blessed his nomad son
and invited him to join him in his walk.

That afternoon, the general was at his most beguiling. He

made it clear that he understood his subject's anguish. His "warmth and frankness," Teilhard wrote a friend after the meeting, "completely conquered me." Not only did he express sincere joy that the long-postponed meeting had come about at last; he even showed a certain interest in the things Teilhard had written.

But as the hour went on, Janssens began to explain some of his difficulties in dealing with Teilhard's problems. He was sure, he said, Teilhard would understand what complications would result from an immediate acquiescence to any of his three requests. There was plenty of time to think about the lectures in America. As to the question of standing for the Collège de France—he knew Teilhard would understand the scandal it could cause in certain quarters to have an evolutionist Jesuit speaking there; "the Villanova incident" alone had shown him that. As to the manuscript of *The Phenomenon of Man*—if, after all these years, it was the generalate itself which gave permission for publication, many people would consider it an official gesture of approval of Teilhard's theories by the Society itself.

Still, Janssens said, Teilhard must not be downcast. No one would come to any final verdict about his writings until those two overdue new criticisms had arrived. While he waited, the general offered him the hospitality of the house. He was welcome to stay on in Rome—even if he had to stay indefinitely.

The afternoon thus spent itself, with the two men sitting beneath a tree in the fading golden light that moved with shadows cast by the umbrella pines. As the darkness gathered, the general played idly with his rosary beads. In the end—in the same spirit of mutual good will—the conversation dissipated with the blowing leaves around their feet.

A week after that first audience, the first of the two criticisms of *The Phenomenon* arrived. It was formally written in Latin, and ten pages long. Its censor, a Louvain theologian whose name Teilhard was not supposed to know, was a Thomist of the old school, quite unable to think in any but

static terms. In those long days of waiting to see Janssens,
Teilhard had already finished twelve pages of an appendix to
the book, clarifying possibly "distressing" points. But as he
read through that first criticism, despair came over him in
waves. He added supplementary changes to the body of the
text, wrote ten new pages on the uniqueness of the human
psyche's God-directedness through socialization, and then
wrote several more explaining (or rather, excusing) the
book's lack of concentration on the place of moral evil in the
world. By the time he finished—even though he wrote to several friends he thought that the changes had "improved" the
manuscript—his mind was in a turmoil. It was only days away
from the date on which he was supposed to give his answer
about his candidacy for the Collège de France.

Adding to the pressure on Teilhard just then was the fact
that he was also being forced to entertain an uninvited visitor.
Mrs. Swan, who had come into an unexpectedly large amount
of money at her parents' death, had been traveling in Europe
and made a point of seeing Rome. Teilhard took time to walk
with her in the Pincio Gardens in the evening and along the
Tiber, and to call on American diplomats they knew from
China. Though Lucile found the encounters quite as difficult
as he did, she never stopped invading Teilhard's troubled pri-
vacy. For weeks she visited in one of the dark, high-ceilinged
generalate parlors lit by single overhanging light bulbs and
sought to evoke in the thin becassocked cleric before her the
spirit of the elegant adventurer of other days. To her dismay,
all she could find now was an aged priest, whose glances at
her were now painfully impersonal, who listened to her words
with half an ear, and started at the sound of bells. The dismal impression persisted until Teilhard gave her to understand that he was thinking of going home to Paris, where
Mrs. de Terra would be arriving the next month. Lucile departed Rome in mid-October.

It was still a little while, however, before he really left. Father Janssens did see him again, and they did talk. Every meet-

ing with his general left Teilhard with less hope. As time passed and no real answer came from the authorities, he began to feel he was losing his hold on himself again. He was awakening every morning now in a cold sweat, unable to breathe normally, his chest aching for the drop of cognac his doctors had prescribed to distend his arteries. The glances of the men about him, which at first seemed merely curious, now seemed to his distressed imagination almost hostile. To make things worse, he suddenly found himself "befriended" by an exasperatingly affable American priest from Vatican Radio, who popped in at odd hours, obviously fascinated by the progress of his drama. Once again, however, Teilhard's old compulsive courtesy made it impossible for him to throw his visitor out where he belonged.

Near the end of October Janssens summoned him a final time. The meeting took place in the general's office at five-thirty in the afternoon. From the first moment, Teilhard noted how nervous Janssens seemed, adjusting and readjust-ing his round glasses. The Church's major interest, he ex-plained, in a rambling discourse, was really in the afterlife, whereas everything Teilhard had written involved, if not the here and now, at least the future of the material world. All that he could really promise was that study of Teilhard's works would continue.

Leaving that Spartan office that afternooon in late Octo-ber, Teilhard finally admitted to himself that staying on in Rome would do no good. Even the arrival some days later of a second, more sympathetic criticism of his book made little difference. Janssens left the city that week, on some unex-plained business; the pope stayed in the country on vacation. Whenever Teilhard crossed the corridor from the writers' wing and saw St. Peter's dome, he remembered the view of Les Invalides he used to look at from his old room at *Études*, and felt ridiculously homesick.

Teilhard was only a poor foreigner lost in Caesar's city. He did not know the rules; he could not play the game. He was shocked and baffled by the lack of any sense of time he saw in everyone he met.

To make things worse, just at that moment an antievolutionist book by the powerful Sicilian Cardinal Ruffini appeared on the bookstalls of the Via della Conciliazione—a bad omen if there ever was one. Finally, at a party given to promote some new French religious books at the Centre St.-Louis-des-Français, Teilhard came face to face with his adversary of more than a quarter century, the Dominican Réginald Garrigou-Lagrange.

Teilhard had gone to the exhibition simply to be among his countrymen and to distract himself. But a short while after his arrival, Garrigou with his entourage appeared. For a moment the Dominican's dramatic figure seemed to attract all the attention in the room. But noting Teilhard among the guests, he smiled, adjusted his pince-nez, and came toward him quickly, radiating the sublime self-confidence that is the mark of the established Roman cleric. The priests shook hands, then stood together for a few moments, nodding across a gulf of seven hundred years, and chatted about Auvergne.

Since many other people at the gathering solicited the Dominican's attention, the encounter was a short one. Very soon, with a gesture meant to deprecate the burden of celebrity that he was forced to bear, Garrigou rolled off, still smiling, until his great white drapery was swallowed by the crowd. Surrounded by the pleasant clink of glasses and the hum of cocktail-party conversation, Teilhard felt his own face shut down in pain. He jerked aside and spoke to the French diplomat Gabriel Beauroy. "There," he said with a half-smile that was really not a smile at all, "goes the man who wants to burn me."

In the late afternoon of November 5, with all hope gone of standing for the dreamed-of place at the Collège de France, Teilhard climbed on the Simplon bound for Paris.

# CHAPTER
# TWENTY-THREE

At eight o'clock the next morning, the Simplon drew into the glass-covered cage of the Gare de Lyon. Across the crush of commuters pouring purposefully toward the Métro, Teilhard saw the defiant little figure of Mlle. Mortier, who hustled him into a cab and drove him to *Études*.

Once he had deposited his baggage, he hurried down to d'Ouince's study. His Roman reception, he reported, was not encouraging. With permission to stand for the Collège de France denied, and the American lectures undecided, he could only hope against all hope for the publication of *The Phenomenon*.

Sitting quietly before him, d'Ouince had the feeling he could have described the morning's interview before it happened. And when Mlle. Mortier came back to see Teilhard later, from the very start of the conversation she could sense a change in him. At last he had taken the measure of the mechanism with which he was wrestling, and he knew how powerless he was against it.

The next two months, Teilhard continued to mourn inwardly over the Church's growing loss of ground among the intellectuals he knew. But he limited his talks to groups of trusted friends—to the Union des Croyants, to whom he spoke about the difficulty of man's accommodating psychologically to his newly discovered vision of the abysses of time and space,[1] to the friends of the feminist psychologist Maryse Choisy, to whom he repeated his theories about the conditions necessary for the unification of humanity.[2]

In Paris he was loved and listened to. His "subterranean" activity among his admirers gave him a certain sense of purpose. But all the time, his real preoccupation continued to be the still unsettled fate of his beloved book. He wrote to the generalate about it; d'Ouince wrote to the generalate. To no avail. In early January, when Mme. de Margerie, during a semiprivate audience with the pope, had the temerity to bring up Teilhard's name only to be met by the unpapal growl: "That man is *not* a theologian!" he had his first sure clue as to its fate.

That same month *Osservatore Romano* reprinted a précis of a French criticism of the talk given to the Jocist chaplains at Versailles six months earlier, accompanying it with a "corrective note" and the comment that in no case should Teilhard's remarks be taken as reliable. Immediately afterward, Father Janssens wrote him, asking for an explanation of some of the terms he had used. Given the fact that that particular conference had been a very model of openness and clarity, it seemed only a question of time before he would be censured.

And so it was, on February 4, only a few days before the arrival of the first letter from the generalate. The answer was No. No, to everything: to the printing of the *Milieu* and *The Phenomenon*; to the Columbia lectures in America; to any further public theological or philosophical speculation on Teilhard's part.

It was as though someone had cracked a whip over his head. The night that he received the letter, he turned up at Mme. Lemaître's, pale and hollow-eyed. "My general doesn't *want* to understand!" he exclaimed. At the same time, he wrote to Mrs. Swan, "Those people in Rome are living on another planet!"

Though in the week that followed, Teilhard managed to

turn out for Torres-Bodet a paper on the biological roots of democracy,* he slipped into a kind of fugue. His despair, he said, was something like Sartre's *nausée*, but it was physical as well as psychological. For the first time in his life, he actually did not *want* to work, to lecture, to see his friends, or even to chat after supper with his brothers at *Études*. To several confidants he confessed a nostalgia for the peace and "mental freedom" he had experienced during his convalescence from his heart attack in 1947.

On the morning of February 25, 1949, when he gave the first of five projected lectures on "The Human Zoologic Group" at the Sorbonne, his respite came. As he walked, with Professor Charles Jacob and Mlle. Mortier, out of the auditorium into the bitter wind that lashed across the Rue St.-Jacques, his conversation seemed fuzzy and unfocused. He excused himself from a luncheon invitation and took a car back to *Études*. Within weeks he was back at the Rue Oudinot with galloping pleurisy, and by Easter, again at St.-Germain.

There, just for a while, he found his peace. The weather was soft, and the forest behind the house thick by day with the call of cuckoos and by night with the hooting of owls. For company he had among his fellow patients an elderly secular priest and two young Jesuits who were recovering from illnesses they had contracted when they were missionaries in China. It took a while for the shock of the winter's failure to wear away, but finally Teilhard began to write again—this time, the Galileo essay he had tossed over so long in his mind.[3]

He wrote it, for the most part, sitting on the terrace in the sun as though he had all the time in the world and nothing else to think of. Just as modern man's sixteenth-century ancestor, he began, had reacted with horror and disbelief to the

---

* Because man is rational, Teilhard felt, each human being has the natural need and, therefore, the inalienable right to opportunity for optimum personal growth—a situation possible only in a democracy. "L'essence de l'idée de démocratie," February 9, 1949.

demonstration that the earth was *not* the center of the universe, modern man, discovering the relentless infolding of his resisting self on all the other egos of the world, was struck with terror. To survive, much less succeed, he had to learn to overcome his natural resistance to the pull, to move with it, and follow joyfully toward the deeper individual personalization Teilhard believed that it presaged.

In those weeks he husbanded his strength, reading Sartre and Hemingway, entertaining visitors in the clinic garden, and taking short walks with Leroy. Despite all he could do against unwelcome encounters, he was, this time, unable to avoid meeting the still-touring Mrs. Swan, who arrived in June announcing she intended to stay in Paris for the summer. On the seventh of the month, when he went briefly into the city to lecture to a group of anthropologists, she was there; and when he finally returned to *Études*, she was there again.

Grateful for her years of dedication in China, and faintly guilty about having permitted her to form so ferocious an attachment to him, Teilhard over the next month gave her every moment he could spare. But his time was so taken up with appointments and visitors that she left for England by July. At her departure, he sent her a long letter asking that she not think of this most recent parting as a "goodbye" but as an "au revoir." "I want to tell you," he continued, "how much good you've done me this last year both in Paris and Rome . . . that we've been able to establish that the years in Peking were truly fruitful and we can count on one another to 'crown' our lives. . . ." He promised her his prayers "for your inner peace."

Just as Lucile left, Rhoda de Terra moved definitively back. She settled with her daughter Noël into the apartment of a friend on the tiny Rue de Poitiers, announcing not only that she proposed to take over all the practical errands Teilhard had neither time nor heart to do but that she would do so as long as he should live.

In August Teilhard went home to Les Moulins. The

weather there was dry, and it was almost too hot to move. There was no wind, and in the afternoon the sun beat down like metal. Like other Auvergnats, he searched the sky above the *puys* for signs of rain, and worried again about the threatened grape crop. From time to time his brother Joseph took him driving or out to lunch in a seventeenth-century castle belonging to some friends and buried deep in the forest of the Haute-Loire. He said his Mass ("for the more pious members of my family") on an eighteenth-century bombé fruitwood altar in the château's tiny chapel, received visitors, polished the rest of the conferences he had begun to give at the Sorbonne when his pleurisy struck (the ensemble of which he now thought would make a "good little book"), and spent two days entertaining the visiting George Barbour and his son. At last, he wrote, he felt "completely Auvergnat," delighting in the seven-month-old Olivier, Joseph's daughter Françoise's first child—"fat, strong, perpetually hilarious," and the apple of his grandfather's eye.

But even the safety of home was not enough to restore him after the February defeat. The magisterium of the Church, the head of his Order—all the hierarchy of that "phylum" he believed to be the most Christified in the evolving world—had told him his humanistic vision of the old faith was distorted, and in no uncertain terms. He began his retreat that summer, praying that if his understanding of reality were not true, he be "taken" before he did anything to spoil God's work in the world. But by the time the exercise was over he was again so sure of his position that, on September 8, he sent a "report" to the French Jesuit assistant, Bernard de Gorostarzu, begging that theologians give more of their attention to Saint Paul's concept of a cosmic Christ who suffused everything, "even Einsteinian physics." Old-fashioned Christians, he wrote, were content to await idly Christ's great return to glory; Marxists, on the other hand, worked to achieve the future of humanity. Why not, he asked (as he often had before), bind together the two imperatives with the idea of working to achieve the kingdom of God by achieving the fullest kind of humanity?[4]

To his surprise, when Teilhard returned to Paris in mid-September, he found the answer to his new proposals already waiting for him. Rome announced it found his new "neohumanistic apologetic for the 'gentiles'" at best only "faddish" and "inopportune." Her opinion of it reflected the unfavorable evaluation she had already begun to make of the mission of the worker-priests in France. The Roman letter, Teilhard wrote de Lubac, was "a real pearl." It said much the same thing as "my general said to me when I saw him a few years ago: the only value of the future is eternal life." But why, he continued, could not the Romans see that this reconciliation "of human faith in the world and a divine one in a transcendent God was *not* just another arbitrary tactic for making more conversions, but the *very condition of survival for the faith* of a growing number of Christians"? As Teilhard understood it, the Church no longer had a choice of saying "yes" or "no" to involvement in the material world. The question was already posed. . . . "And the ground wheels under our feet."

That autumn, while Lucile shipped off to the Far East, still searching for "peace of soul," Teilhard's year-old Galileo paper was printed in Louvain.[5] But Teilhard was now officially "jobless," instead of being a contributing guest at *Études,* and he filled his evenings speaking to groups on technical subjects. More and more, he depended on the efficiency and willingness of Mrs. de Terra to do his little chores.

All winter long he walked on eggshells, under the threat of being ordered out of France. That no such catastrophe occurred might well be attributed less to a lack of interest in Rome in his case than to the fact that at that time everyone in the city was busy preparing for the climax of Pius XII's pontificate: the Holy Year of 1950.

On balance, 1949 had been a bad year for Catholicism. The Mindszenty trial had taken place, as well as the Red take-over in China, and the proclamation of "an independent

Communist government" in the Soviet-occupied zone of East Germany. Pius, whose sleep was still troubled with nightmares of his confrontation with the Communist Spartacists who had invaded his nunciature in Munich in 1919,† hurled his thunderbolts of righteous anger at the atheist regimes behind the Iron Curtain and excommunicated Communists outside it, while publicly imploring the aid of the Virgin Mary in his crusade and cementing his relations with Cardinal Spellman and other Catholic leaders in America, which had recently constituted itself the "guardian of the Free World."

As early as May 1949 the pope had made it clear that 1950 would be Catholicism's year of triumph. That month, as the Common Father of all Christians, he mounted the papal throne to hear his Undersecretary of State, Monsignor Montini, read, in his name, the announcement that 1950 would be a "Holy Year," a year of great "return and reconciliation" when all men of good will could gather around him to renew their Christian fervor.

Pius XII was a curious kind of twentieth-century religious leader—simultaneously the most antimaterialist and the most "temporalist" of modern popes. Elected to the office because of his "political" rather than "pastoral" qualifications, he ruled the Church as though it were a mobile nation-state. A fixist in theological matters, he saw the world as static and the boundaries between "matter and spirit," "nature and supernature," "holy and profane" as unalterably set. Still, by a curious twist of logic, he seemed to feel it necessary to dignify the "profane" with blessing and to make himself a power on earth by extending the Church's juridical reign, using the tactics he had learned in his younger days in the Vatican diplomatic corps. A total autocrat, when he assumed the triple crown, he is reputed to have said (like Churchill speaking

† Testimony of one of his personal physicians. (See Falconi, Carlo, *The Popes in the Twentieth Century*, English translation [Boston: Little, Brown, 1967], p. 278.)

of the British colonial empire), "I may be the last pope to preserve everything, but I *shall* preserve everything!"

By the eleventh year of his pontificate, Pius had not failed to keep his promise. He was the firm and vocal advocate of all the attitudes his recent predecessors had cherished toward the papacy. He saw it as the voice of God instructing men, the capstone of a pyramidal Church, in which it was as much the hierarchy's function to teach "what the Church thought" as it was the lesser clerics' and laity's to listen and believe.

On Christmas Eve of 1949, while papal legates opened the sealed doors of three other basilicas, Pius XII used his silver hammer to open the ceremonial door of St. Peter's, closed since the last Holy Year of 1925, and with it, the "treasury of Divine Grace," applicable to the living as well as to the dead, for all those who would come to him as pilgrims.

Suddenly—incredibly—especially from America (where since the war the number of conversions to Catholicism had suddenly swung upward‡) it seemed that all roads did indeed lead back to Rome, to Pius, whose ethereal figure stood with eyes upturned behind his silver-framed glasses, his lovely hands outstretched in benediction. New saints were canonized; statues blessed; relics which had been shut up for years, exposed for veneration. All the old comfortable religious trappings for which Catholicism (to say nothing of mankind in general) had such nostalgia were invoked. Week after week, tall, and thin from fasting, the pope received national or professional delegations, heads of state, diplomats, boy scouts, journalists, film stars, members of world chambers of commerce, Catholic Action groups, doctors, workingmen, students, functionaries of the Banco di Roma, and even a Milanese pastry cook, who presented the pontiff with an enormous, exquisitely detailed cake replica of St. Peter's Basilica. For all his visitors, Pius had an appropriate instruction as well as a religious memento and his paternal blessing. Some of the things he blessed (or at least approved) that year seem bi-

‡ In 1949 120,000 such conversions are recorded for the United States alone.

zarre now—the approval he chose to give, for example, President Truman's testing of the H-bomb.

It was, of course, inevitable that Pius should take the occasion of the Holy Year to re-examine all things in the Church which differed from his own view of Her nature and Her mission. While his concern about the headcount of Catholics among the working classes restrained him from taking action against the worker-priests, all other French postwar innovations in ecumenism, new approaches to the apostolate, liturgical experimentation, and the study of philosophy became his targets.

The long-approaching storm at last broke over Fourvière. That mountain from which so many warriors of the intellect had come was now the symbol for the new and vital Christianity which had emerged out of the blood and shady politics of the Occupation, and a thorn in the flesh of the Spanish friars, Vichyite religious, and ex-Fascisti cardinals who called Rome home. In the postwar ecclesiastical squabbling, old political hurts mingled oddly with religious passions. As early as 1946, at Pius's first postwar consistory, when the anti-Nazi Archbishop Saliège of Toulouse went to Rome to receive his red hat, he was received as the great "defender of human rights" during the Resistance, at a reception given by the Gaullist ambassador Jacques Maritain (by then at loggerheads with Garrigou-Lagrange over "neo-" versus "classical" Thomism). When Saliège replied with a panegyric praising the adventurous strides French theological thought and practice had made during and after the war (making special mention of Lyon and Fourvière), the silence in the bureaucratic circles in Rome was deafening. The same year, a superficial, self-congratulatory essay on "New Directions in Religious Thought," written for *Études* by the liturgical aesthete Jean Daniélou, so much increased the alarm that two years later Édouard Dhanis came lumbering up to the scholasticate of Lyon to make an official visit of inspection. Though nothing worrisome happened at the time, from that moment on, the emotional climate of Fourvière had grown increasingly uncomfortable. By 1950 the scholasticate stood as an outpost ready for siege.

In Paris, at *Études*, where the link with Lyon remained strong, the tension mounted too. All year long the staff bent nearly double, trying to reconcile the blessed bacchanal below the Alps with reasonable religious behavior. But the pious enthusiasm fostered by the pope was difficult to cope with. "Miraculous statues" of "pilgrim Madonnas" continued to be supported from city to city by crowds of enthusiastic women with "Année Sainte" printed on their headscarves, to the despair of the traffic policemen. That year, an amused Raymond Jouve wrote to a friend that the history of the celebration would one day give psychiatrists a fascinating study of overcompensation in a mass inferiority complex.

There was little of the old camaraderie at *Études* that year. Near Christmas 1949 the frequent visitor to the house Père Leroy had set off on a French National Research Science fellowship for America. De Lubac, who was keeping as low a profile as possible, now rarely came to Paris. Doncœur developed a heart condition, and another priest had pleurisy. Eventually even Jouve (though he was only in his early fifties) showed signs of fragile health and was shuttling up and down the streets to the clinic on the Rue Oudinot for treatment of a hemorrhaging of the retina. As for Teilhard, most of his time was spent doing the little that he was still permitted to do privately, in an attempt to make some sense to his "gentile" friends out of a Christianity that had apparently sleepwalked out into deep space and was inexplicably supported there.

To various groups, he spoke about the necessity for discovering a ground for human love if man was to improve or to survive upon the planet[6]; about the problem of evil in terms of the fundamental arrangement of life that exacted a payment of blood and tears for every forward step[7]; and in insisting over and over that, to reach the fullness of his hu-

manity, man had to trust in the existence of a personal God.[8]
He understood too well how many people Camus spoke for
when he said in *Sisyphus* that if man believed the universe
could *love*, he could be resigned to it.

With the passing months, the tension in Teilhard's life increased. That spring his old counselor and friend Auguste
Valensin came all the way from Nice to warn him against his
careless tongue. When a letter from Rome to Cardinal Feltin
suggesting the themes emphasized in Lenten sermons at
Notre Dame were to be "violently anticommunist, moder-
ately antievolutionist, and strongly pro-Thomist" arrived at
the episcopal residence too late to forewarn the first preacher,
Michel Riquet (the Jesuit Resistance priest whose Dachau essays Teilhard had read at St.-Germain), he left the nave of
the cathedral echoing the cry that Christians, having emerged
from a "neolithic" spirituality, must now move forward and
think of God as the "Super-Soul of Cosmogenesis in which
we are plunged."

In March Teilhard contributed to a series in *Les Nouvelles
Littéraires* on the nature of life as a specific effect of corpuscular complexification—in other words, as the unraveling of
the one single stuff of the universe toward individuation in
ever more conscious states.[9] When the Roman censors refused to pass his *Human Zoologic Group*, he rewrote it. He
gave five lectures on the prehistory of the East at the Sorbonne, and traced "The Phases of a Living Planet"[10] for a
group at the Cité Universitaire from the feeble flush of life on
earth to the coming of man. In April he wrote a review of
Robert Broom's book on Australopithecines for *Études*,[11] and
a letter to Torres-Bodet on the complementary qualities of
the various races of humanity, noting in a letter to a friend,
"One talks quite openly now of being a 'maquisard' *inside* the
Church—a thing I've been for thirty years."

On May 25 he was finally elected to full membership in
the Academy of Sciences. The elevation, however, had the
side effect of starting a spate of luncheons and receptions in

his honor given by society matrons (who sometimes left him purple with embarrassment by climaxing their parties for him with operatic readings of his 1924 "Mass on the World") and by the people at *Études*. A wave of curiosity about him rose in the Paris press, much of it resulting from a long applauding article about him by the critic André Billy of the Académie Goncourt in the July 5 *Figaro Littéraire* which announced that in his papers—the *Milieu Divin*, the "Esprit de la Terre," the "Comment Je Crois"—this remarkable philosopher might even have sown the seeds for a "religion of the future." Before the month was over, an anonymous critical book called *The Redemptive Evolution of Père Teilhard de Chardin* was circulating through France.

That summer, when Teilhard discovered that his former admirer Maurice Trassaert was working for a government bureau in Laon, he wrote him trying to influence him to come back to the Jesuits. He failed. Then he set himself to working on an essay exploring "Two Forms of Religious Mysticism"—the flight from and suppression of matter, and his own alternative: a passing to God through matter.[12] He waited for an answer to his repeated requests to his general to publish his rewritten *Human Zoologic Group*. But that July Cardinal Ruffini republished his own views on evolution in *Osservatore Romano*, and so it came as no surprise to him to receive notice some days later, that Father Janssens "preferred" that he drop the project.

That summer there was no doubt left (Teilhard's special problems aside) that for his brothers at *Études*, for the Jesuits at Fourvière, and for French Dominicans such as Yves Congar and Chenu, real trouble was coming. There were even rumors that a full-scale "Syllabus of Errors," like the one Pius X wrote and directed against all the "errors" of the "new theology" in France, was about to be issued.

Long before the feast of St. Ignatius, at the end of July (the traditional date for Jesuits to receive notice of reassignment), five of Fourvière's most eminent theology professors—

Henri de Lubac, Pierre Ganne, an adventurous young thinker named Henri Bouillard, the concerned reviser of Teilhard's early essays, Alexandre Durand, and their venerable comrade in theology Émile Delaye—were all aware that they were about to be ordered to leave their professorial chairs. On July 31 the official notice came.

Twelve days later Pius dropped his bomb. It was not a "syllabus" but an encyclical called *Humani Generis*,[13] in which the pope called upon all "patriarchs, primates, archbishops, and other local ordinaries" not only in France but throughout the world, where now the methods and attitudes of the new French theology had begun to penetrate, to re-examine "disagreements and errors" then rampant in theological and philosophical thinking. They were, of course, to do it in the light of the doctrines postulated by the Council of Trent and the teaching of Thomas Aquinas.

Though human reason, he insisted, "by its natural capacities alone, *had*, absolutely speaking, the power to arrive at a true and certain knowledge of a personal God and the natural law," the effects of original sin could and did often darken and pervert it. "Imprudently" and "indiscreetly," he said, some teachers were assuming the truth of the "still unproved scientific theory of evolution," indulging in "reckless 'irenicism,'" questioning whether the old apologetics was still the best tool for the apostolate, and openly opting for new vocabulary or for modern scientific research methods. Among the problems that vexed the pope was the fact that theologians were still speculating over such questions as whether or not angels were personal beings, whether there were real distinctions between "matter" and "spirit," whether each human soul was separately and divinely infused at a given moment, whether or not the notion of "substance" was antiquated—all of which questions, he maintained, had been settled in the affirmative by Saint Thomas seven hundred years before.

The letter of complaint and the quasi-military obedience it exacted from the French episcopate spelled sudden death to almost all that had spearheaded the vital postwar French theology. Though it is difficult to see how the encyclical could have been more harsh, *Le Nouvel Observateur*[14] of the time declared that the pope's letter would have been worse had it not been for the intervention of "certain Church dignitaries, heads of some religious orders," and ambassadors to the Vatican from the anticommunist "Free World." At any rate, the result of the encyclical was the taming of a wind of the Spirit that would not come again for eight long years—and then only briefly at the initiative of a personally conservative old peasant pope with little time to live. Except for the warily watched priest-worker movement (and, to some extent, the progress in patristic studies) the too-short second spring of French theology was over. As the *Observateur*, closing its account of the affair dramatically but nonetheless justly remarked, however great the loss was to the Church, the battle had been a gallant one—and, giving a heroic example of obedience, the five deposed professors of Fourvière had departed with "tous les honneurs de la guerre."

# CHAPTER
## TWENTY-FOUR

When the storm broke over Fourvière in July, Teilhard was still in Paris, wearily entertaining the still-traveling Mrs. Swan, who found him even more distracted than when she saw him last. He was worried about the effect that the collapse of the "new theology" would have on the fate of his own message, edgy about dark rumors of the "syllabus" which was predicted to be coming, and playing in his mind with the idea of writing a long psychological essay in which he could explain his point of view in the light of its source and growth.[1]

In August, just as Mrs. Swan was leaving, Valensin, upset over the *Figaro* article, which, he felt, could not have appeared at a more dangerous time, wrote him a sympathetic note. As Teilhard had not yet met the author, and as the essays which it quoted were old and out of circulation, he could honestly reassure his friend that he was still "*en règle* (canonically speaking) with authority."

Teilhard had learned too well the lesson Valensin helped teach him twenty-five years earlier, when he had signed "purely as a mechanical gesture and not a sign of intellectual assent" his profession of faith in a literal Adam and Eve. And to his pain, he knew that he had learned it. At the same time, as he was answering Valensin's note he confided to a more comprehending confrère, "I'm aware I'm *not* so innocent as all that. . . ."

By the time the text of *Humani Generis* became available in Paris, Teilhard had gone to rest at Les Moulins. His reading of it seems to have elicited no immediate alarm. He even wrote to Mlle. Mortier, who sent it on to him, that he was totally in agreement with the theologians' desire to "protect dogma from evaporating into myth." What he deplored was the fact that they "had neither the vision nor the vocabulary to do it properly," thus giving the encyclical an air of "*simplisme* and anthropomorphism (e.g., the reassertion that Genesis 1 and 2 was 'historical' without being 'history')."

Another declaration out of Rome a few days later provoked more of a reaction from him. On August 15 Pius had announced that on November 1 of that year he would employ the infallibility conceded to the popes by the Vatican Council of 1867–70 to declare that the ancient tradition of the Assumption of the Virgin Mary into heaven was a "matter of faith" binding on all Catholics.

Not that Teilhard ever had any real intellectual discomfort with the Church's veneration of Our Lady. Ever since those mornings in his childhood when he prayed in the cold, dark crypt of Notre Dame du Port, the "Marial" had been a vital element in his religion. For years he had celebrated the Mass of the Assumption in the little open chapel on the *puys* of his brother's château in the hot and buzzing Auvergne summer, then watched his neighbors celebrate the day with picnics in the mountains and trumpet and organ concerts in the town. His only fear, on hearing the announcement of the coming definition, was that the pontiff's uninstructed scientific dilettantism might lead him to describe it in words that would strip it of all mystery and provide another formula that would challenge physics and biology ("a certain number of proteins escaping from our common time-space frame," or worse).

It was cooler than usual at Les Moulins that summer, but so dry, Teilhard wrote friends, that his brother Joseph spent much of his time "hitting the dial of the barometer in the hope that it would go down." George Barbour dropped by to see him again briefly toward the month's end and talked to him of Africa. When Barbour left, Teilhard wrote another friend, he began to be overwhelmed "answering SOS's that came by mail and word of mouth from every side" about the encyclical and the proposed definition of the dogma.

The following September, while other members of the family went off on pilgrimage to Lourdes, Teilhard stayed home, with just the servants and the grieving dog for company. He used his time and solitude walking the grounds, where he could sink his roots as deep as possible into the countryside of his childhood and the shadows of his past, or sitting at the desk before the window facing the *puys*, with pastel portraits of his long-dead brothers and sisters watching soberly from the walls oustide his open door, to finish his long-contemplated "spiritual biography."

The sounds and scents of the old house and the sight of the volcanic countryside outside awoke his sleeping memory. The shock of crackling branches under his feet echoed the snap of other branches he had crushed as a boy on the short cut to the village church behind the house; the atmosphere of old-fashioned piety all around him revived the memory of inner tension of a childhood when he had hung psychologically between the family's otherworldly practice and his own secret, irrational attraction to the tangible. He deliberately evoked the chill of terror he had felt at the sight of all things moldering around him, and recalled the peace, security, and dizziness of delight he found in his contemplation of iron or quartzite—the coldest, hardest matter he could find. And thus he rediscovered the beginning of that mysterious pull that had drawn him, all his life, through laboratories and dangerous explorations into "the last white spaces on the map," closer and closer to that beating heart from which the stars once burst.

When Teilhard returned to Paris in September, *Études* seemed desolate. Though neither the pope's letter nor the disciplinary arm of the Society had singled out any of the staff there for rebuke, a kind of thunder still hung in the air. De Lubac was now living on the Rue de Sèvres in Paris, having passionately thrown himself into a loving (if rather convoluted) meditation on "The Church Our Mother"; the brilliant Bouillard was in the Jesuit house on Grenelle, stoically finishing a study of Karl Barth; Durand and Delaye were exercising chaplaincies in Lyon; and Ganne was directing a youth center in Grenoble. At *Études* the house apologist, Robert Rouquette, wrestled with an obligatory approving article on *Humani Generis*.

Rouquette's article, which more or less only boiled down to an apology to the Catholic world for the "explosiveness" of the Gallic character, did little to bolster the sagging morale of French Christian intellectuals. But they pursued Teilhard in droves in search of comfort. Under the pressure of their supplications, he dropped his guard again and, as the next month began, sent a paper to de Gorostarzu in Rome asking that a distinction be made between "monogenism" and "monophylism," which he accompanied by a note reproaching *Humani Generis* for its attack on "that movement of thought uniquely attached to developing a Christology" worthy of the modern world. The action against Fourvière he called "a shame!" "Rome," he concluded, "has just shelled her own front lines."

Thereafter, he threw all discretion to the winds. He deliberately sought out André Billy, who had written the *Figaro* article about him, and bombarded him with papers. Since his only orders regarding the book *The Human Zoologic Group* were that he should not send it to a publisher, he had some hundred copies of the set of essays mimeographed for private distribution to "specialists"—particularly for members of the Institute of Human Paleontology and for other scientist friends. More and more he pressed Mlle. Mortier to duplicate new copies of his old *clandestins* for dissemination.

It was among his lay friends that he went to find his peace. Each afternoon, he stopped by to see Rhoda de Terra, who was then established with her daughter in a ground floor apartment in the nearby Cité Vaneau and was writing reports for an agency of the Marshall Plan. In exchange for her care of the worrisome details of his daily life, he introduced her to his circle of acquaintances, watching with some amusement as she played "la duchesse" in her "salon très St.-Germain."

It was not long, however, before Teilhard's newest theological imprudences caught up with him—and this time with a vengeance. Returning to Paris that autumn from an unsuccessful lecture trip to Belgium, where, he wrote with some pain, he did not manage to see anything of his old friend Pierre Charles—"not even the tip of his nose!"—he found not only that his Jesuit superiors had been agitated by his tireless diffusion of his ideas but that there were now rumors that a large number of French bishops were about to make a new complaint about him in Rome. Nothing was said to him directly, but he suddenly felt in so much peril that, despite his age and doubtful health, he knew he had to leave for Africa as soon as possible. The Abbé Breuil still worked there with Marshal Smuts, so Teilhard wrote to him at once, asking that he speak to the South African paleontologists on his behalf.

The climax of the Holy Year, Pius XII's ceremonial declaration of the dogma of the Assumption on November 1, proved a great success with Catholics. But throughout the world ecumenists worried that his invocation of infallibility would be a new roadblock to Christian union. In France the wounds inflicted by *Humani Generis* were not allowed to heal. Pressures on the worker-priests to prove they were not Marxist-influenced grew from day to day. Their adoption of the point of view of the workers, their joining unions and agitating for better working conditions, even their use of the unlovely speech and manner of the poor, their defiance of the Vatican by demonstrating against the testing of the American H-bomb exposed them to fire from Rome—especially from Cardinals Piazza and Ottaviani. That same month, following a stiff letter from the Jesuit father general, three of de Lubac's books, one of Bouillard's, two by the gallant de Montcheuil, and even one by the more pliant Daniélou were removed from Jesuit libraries, only to reappear there mysteriously within weeks. When at the end of the month d'Ouince received an invitation to go to Rome to address a conference of bishops and superiors of religious orders, he was not sure whether he was called there to be rebuked or to be honored.

While he was away, Teilhard concentrated all his gifts of persuasion on getting off to Africa. In November 1950 he wrote Dr. Fejos in America, asking quite bluntly whether or not the Viking Fund would sponsor him on a trip there. Given the relative obscurity that still surrounded the stratigraphical and systematic disposition of the Australopithecines, he suggested, his experience in China might be very useful.

While waiting for the answer, Teilhard kept his head low and only spoke privately to meetings of close friends, such as the Union des Croyants, to whom he talked about the "Taste for Life" in early December.[2] On Christmas Day, while the pope was sealing up the ceremonial door again, thus officially ending what Teilhard called "this devil of a Jubilee Year," he sat beneath Rhoda's glittering Christmas tree talking to the visiting geologist Wong Wen-hao about the old days at the Survey in Peking.

A few days later he wrote to the Viking Fund again, enclosing a duplicate of his petition of November, "in case the mail had gone astray"; and when, after a few more weeks went by, he was still without an answer, he grew so frantic that—answer or no answer—he went down to the Union Castle steamship line and booked a berth on a ship leaving for South Africa in July.

Try as he might, he now seemed incapable of keeping out of trouble. In January 1951 an ex-Dominican named Denys Gorce invited him to join a schismatic Catholic group in Switzerland; and, though Teilhard wrote back an angry letter of refusal, Gorce continued publishing his own version of the Jesuit's philosophy. At the same time, the public press decided to make Teilhard's cause its own, and it took all of d'Ouince's persuasiveness to secure his friend the right of censorship over an interview he had given to a writer from *Les Nouvelles Littéraires*. Finally, the rightist religious paper *France Catholique* began a series about the types of religious deviation reproved by *Humani Generis*, and chose as the subject of the first of the articles Teilhard's philosophy.

In January he began giving a course of five technical lectures on the "Phyletic Structure of the Human Group" at the Sorbonne, and this time, despite the havoc worry always worked on his health, he finished the assignment. Still, he was looking more exhausted every day. And when, around February 1, he received Fejos's approval of the African project, he almost wept with joy.

The troubles of the Holy Year hung on in the new year. And not for Teilhard alone. One night before the end of February, as the men of *Études* sat down to dinner in the refectory, Père d'Ouince rose to read them a letter from the general addressed to all the Jesuits of the world. It struck a note that startled them. Around the room, heads snapped up, jaws dropped, and forks lay idly by their plates as the unbelieving listeners tried to take the message in. It was a moment before they realized that what they were hearing was a rebuke stronger than the one *Humani Generis* had leveled at some of their brothers months earlier—and much more shattering because it came from the one person they depended on to plead their cause.

Although the letter sighed over the "fatherly pain" that it had cost Janssens to remove the five professors from their chairs in Fourvière in anticipation of the encyclical, it made it clear that he was shocked to see that so many in the Church's "spiritual militia" had not renewed their hearts to bow to its demands. In case some Jesuits might not have fully understood the document, the letter carefully listed again all the

"errors" *Humani Generis* condemned, and added a few of
Janssens's own choosing for good measure. Finally, lest there
be any doubt about where the reproof was aimed, the letter
was pointedly written in French.

When Auguste Valensin visited Paris a few weeks later, he
spent time with Teilhard. But even with the deep mutual
affection that still bound the priests to one another, they discovered how large was the psychological gap that the years
had opened between them. Valensin now saw in Teilhard's
singleminded, burning vision only "a sort of superior con-
cordism"; Teilhard was bemused by his friend's "duality of attitude—a childlike faith coupled with a sophisticated and almost complete intellectual skepticism." ("In his place," he
sighed, "I would have given up believing long ago.") For
Teilhard, that one way of seeing reality (and his need to communicate it to others) was his life. His much-discussed
"naïveté" was really often honesty to the point of pain.

In his request for aid from Dr. Fejos, Teilhard had specifi-
cally asked for a letter assuring American officials that he intended to return to France when his work was done. But
now his plans for the "brief" trip to Africa and America
began to stretch out in his imagination. He behaved as
though he expected to come back, but, all things considered,
he wondered why he dared plan to see France again. With
Jouve's and Mlle. Mortier's help, therefore, he spent the end
of winter scavenging among his effects for old copies of his
widely scattered early essays in order to assemble a complete
collection of his work. What he would do with it when it was
finished, he dared not even think.

In March the Vatican announced that the ancient Easter
Vigil ritual for Holy Saturday would be revived in France. It
was observed without much interest by most of the men at
*Études,* except for Daniélou, who, with Doncœur and a few
disciples, went off to Troussure, where he celebrated a fourth-
century ritual in which, according to Teilhard, he "divided a
'galette' beneath a cup of nonconsecrated wine, if you

please!" All this publicity over so surface a "revolution" as a liturgical change, when what was really needed was a change *en profondeur*, was hard for him to grasp. "What a need we have for real reform!" he wrote; "not just of manners—but in our very idea of God Himself!"

Teilhard spent the remainder of the spring boning up on African anthropological data and giving at least one talk to a group of Catholic laymen. In April he spoke with young Claude Cuénot,* son of his late colleague Lucien Cuénot, the great biologist of Nancy. In May he barely managed to avert a new disaster when Mlle. Mortier, who had been traveling in Italy, tried to help his cause by leaving a copy of his "Cœur de la Matière" with Père de Gorostarzu.

The Roman reaction to that paper was so violent that for a moment it seemed almost certain he would be formally censured. Thanks to the intervention of Jacques Groussault, the Paris provincial, however, the only measure taken against him was another warning to cut down on giving private counseling while he waited out the time before his departure. That month he wrote to George Barbour, inviting him to join him in Africa. "On the advice of my doctors," he added, "since they dislike the idea of my traveling alone, Rhoda de Terra, who is going home anyway, is managing to escort me—something I realize represents an appreciable psychological safeguard. . . . A bit humiliating though, to feel less able to travel alone as one grows older. . . ."

Since Fejos was then traveling in Europe, Teilhard dined with him on June 29 and discussed his plans in more detail. By that time, thanks mainly to Mrs. de Terra's efficient handling of his schedule, he had his shots, his papers, his reservations, his tickets, and his carefully worked-out itinerary. His bags and medicines were packed.

There remained but one more troubling problem. What was to be done with the collection of *clandestins* that Jouve

---

* Claude Cuénot, Docteur ès lettres, a member of the board of the Fondation Teilhard de Chardin and Teilhard's first biographer.

and Mlle. Mortier had helped him to gather that year? Teilhard was aware of the fragility of his health. If he should die in Africa or in America, what, he asked himself, would become of all his work? To his Jesuit superiors, his papers were examples of misguided, if not pernicious, thinking; and if his Jesuit vow of poverty (to say nothing of his vow of obedience) meant he had to leave his essays to the Order, everything on which he had spent his life working could be blotted out by one stroke of a Roman pen.

As early as 1948 Paul Rivet had suggested that he make a kind of "will" and leave his papers formally in some sure place until the world was ready to receive them. Since then, he often idly talked of such a possibility, without ever planning how to do it. The thought of taking such an action was abhorrent to him. He did not want to seem disloyal to the Society which he loved deeply. He wanted to die within it with dignity and grace. Though he might well be too single-minded a man to have been able to live well the kind of discipline to which he had submitted himself, once he had given his word he found it difficult to take back.

For Raymond Jouve, the problem was a simpler one. Unlike the subtle d'Ouince, whose complicated maneuvering had often baffled even his admirers, Jouve was a man of cool and practical intelligence. Providentially that July he was substituting for the absent d'Ouince as superior of *Études*. Three days before Teilhard's proposed departure, therefore, he went to him to ask for a decision as to the disposition of his papers. He found Teilhard sitting in his room, surrounded by his baggage, seemingly paralyzed with indecision. Seeing he had no choice but to take the case in hand himself, he put Teilhard's moral quandary (as a purely hypothetical problem) to a canon lawyer who happened to be visiting the house. As the canonist saw it, two possible courses of action were open to Teilhard: to consider the essays the property of the Society, or to follow what his conscience told him was his real vocation and make provision for the preservation of his papers

after his death.† Both decisions, said the canonist, were
equally legitimate.

That was all Jouve (and later Teilhard) needed to hear.
Now there could be no question of putting off action to protect Teilhard's work. A faithful and dependable lay person
should be found at once and made his legatee. Mlle. Mortier
was the most likely candidate.

When the lady arrived at *Études* for her weekly visit with
Teilhard the following Monday, Père Jouve passed her near
the porter's box, just as she was coming in. Although he was
occupied escorting other visitors to the door, he seemed to her
unusually excited. Then, just as Brother Cochet telephoned
Teilhard to come down, Jouve came back and stood with her
a moment in the hall. He whispered urgently, "Mademoiselle,
you know that Père Teilhard is leaving for the Transvaal. He
may never come back. Since it is impossible for us to publish
any of his papers, if they come to us, they will be lost. . . .
Please, when you see him, ask him to bequeath them to you
for safekeeping."

Walking alone toward the back parlor, Mlle. Mortier did
not even try to think of a reply. She felt a little numb. Like
most people who live their lives only on the fringe of great
events, she was not prepared for the responsibility. Now suddenly someone was telling her calmly and firmly that she was
about to be made the legatee of a body of work whose destruction she, at least, believed would have been an irreplaceable loss to her Church and to humanity.

† "Probabilism": one of many systems recognized in Roman Catholic moral
theology as entirely acceptable. "*According to this system, anyone may follow
the opinion which favors liberty, as long as it is well founded,* even though *a
contrary opinion may be more probable.*" (Heribert Jones, O.F.M., Cap.,
*Moral Theology* [Westminster, Md.: Newman Press, 1959], p. 45.) Although
this view is at least as old as Aristotle, it was given its final theologico-
philosophical formulation by the Dominican Bartholomeus de Medina in
1557, and later was adopted by the Jesuits, who "made it one of the most
prominent ideas of their moral system." (René Fulop-Miller, *The Power and
Secret of the Jesuits* [New York: George Braziller, 1956], p. 187.) For the
classical arguments against the system, see Pascal on Probabilism in his
*Pensées*, numbers 907–23.

Teilhard came down to join her within moments. He still seemed unresigned to the possibility that he might not return to France, but he continued to move mechanically in the quietly desperate state in which Jouve had found him the night before. He simply asked for paper, sat down with it before him, and scratched out a brief note saying that in the event of his death, he wanted all his essays to go to Mlle. Mortier. "And in the case that you are indisposed, who else?" he queried brusquely. "Jean Piveteau, André George, François Richaud . . . ?" she gasped. He wrote the names and put the paper in her hand.

To discuss more of the details of the bequest with Mlle. Mortier was much too difficult for him. Sensing her distress, he murmured something about seeing her again in Paris when the Africa assignment was completed. He closed the session quickly; he had other work to do that day, and so had she. So with a quick *au revoir*, he sent the gentle little lady, still stunned (though inwardly apotheosized by glory), out into the sunny street, head-on into the crowd of noontime shoppers from the Bon Marché.

Teilhard and Mlle. Mortier did not meet again that summer. But the afternoon before he left Paris, he dropped in at Mme. Lemaître's spare apartment with its white walls and its little Burmese Buddha to say goodbye. Comtesse Béatrice d'Hauteville was with her. Both ladies were alternately mournful and indignant at the way Teilhard was being treated. Again, he gave no sign of great emotion. Of his imminent departure, he only shrugged and said, "I have pledged my fidelity. I must accept the verdict. I must go."

When he had gone, "taking the sunlight with him," as Mme. Lemaître picturesquely put it, when the glasses were washed and put away, both ladies remembered other times when they had spoken to Teilhard about his attachment to his Order, and he murmured just in passing and with the faintest flicker of a smile, "If I'd had it to do over, I wonder if I'd still have been a Jesuit!"

# V

# BY
# BABYLON'S
# WATERS

# CHAPTER
# TWENTY-FIVE

On June 12, 1951, after a short trip to England, where they visited London, then put Noël on the *Île de France* for New York, Teilhard and Mrs. de Terra set out on the *Carnavon Castle* for South Africa.

Once on shipboard, Teilhard breathed easier. Sailing southward under a night sky where the Great Bear yielded to the Southern Cross, he mulled over another essay, in which he contrasted Hoyle's theory of the explosion of the galaxies from the primal mass with his own concept of the gathering implosion in the universe of the last phenomenon to develop out of evolution—its psychic energies.[1]

On July 15 he docked at Cape Town. That night he took the train north across the Transvaal to Johannesburg with its "white slag dumps from the gold fields to the north and blooming residential quarter to the south." Barbour was waiting for him and Mrs. de Terra. They breakfasted with him and a local anthropologist. That afternoon they took tea with the handsomely goateed chief of the National Bureau of Archaeology, Dr. "Peter" van Riet Lowe, and for the next few days, while Rhoda shopped for shirts to replace those missing from his suitcase since Le Havre, Teilhard plunged into the printed material on the South African excavations provided him on his arrival.

Since his doctors had warned him against overexertion, Teilhard was happily surprised at how well he felt once he was in the field again, and delighted to note that Johannesburg's six-hundred-foot elevation caused him no difficulty in breathing. His new colleagues feted him and deferred to Mrs. de Terra (even though she seemed to some of them "something of a mixed blessing . . . fluttering about him too much like a hen"). "I knew . . . she was his courier and amanuensis," sniffed one scientist, "but I didn't realize she had virtually constituted herself his companion!"

On August 3, over Mrs. de Terra's vigorous protests, Teilhard and van Riet Lowe drove forty miles over asphalt roads to see the site at Sterkfontein where Broom had found his 1939 Australopithecus. The trip, which was planned in easy stages, went off without a hitch, leaving Teilhard refreshed and eager to dine with his flamboyant host that night in town.

He was particularly curious about van Riet Lowe's pet project—the excavations at Makapansgat, 150 miles to the north. In that valley, where, one hundred years before, the native chieftain Makapan perished in his stand against the Boers, a team from the National Bureau of Archaeology had already been working for four years. In one cave they unearthed a block of rubble containing layers of broken bones and Stone Age hand axes, and in another, the "Cave of the Hearths," they gathered a sufficient amount of carbonized material to indicate that very early man had lived there. By the time Teilhard arrived, van Riet Lowe's team had begun an excavation in a new bluff overlooking the valley that was yielding Levalloisian flaked tools such as the ones Teilhard had become familiar with in China.

After lunching with Dart in Johannesburg, Teilhard moved north to the gardeny little city of Pretoria to see the late Robert Broom's Transvaal Museum. Since Broom's successor, J. T. Robinson, was then in England, an assistant showed him through the fossil bone collection. It was, as he expected, a staggering one, containing parts of possibly thirty different individuals, including the Australopithecus of Sterkfontein, the big-jawed Paranthropus found in Kromdraai in 1938, and the more human-looking mandible from another kind of creature labeled Telanthropus, which Broom's young successor had recently unearthed at Swartkrans.

On August 7 van Riet Lowe joined Teilhard in Pretoria, and the next day he drove him over smooth but dusty roads to Makapansgat. Back in the middle of a working dig, Teilhard soon recaptured his old enthusiasm for field work. He traveled by jeep up to the edge of an old ridge track on the cliff above the cave where the work was going on, and had himself lowered by rope to the entrance to examine things more closely. In late August he made a visit to Kimberley and the diamond-mine country, where diggers in the "blue pipes" still occasionally turned up fossils, and another to Taungs, where "Dart's Baby" had turned up thirty years before.

When September came, Dr. Barbour flew back home. But Teilhard stayed on in Africa. His work was all but finished, and he had what he needed to make his Wenner-Gren report. But without having the faintest idea how he might turn his situation around, he was still emotionally unequipped to push himself farther away from France. A few weeks later, when Mlle. Mortier notified him of the appointment of André Ravier, a liberal, progressive man of fifty, as the new Lyon provincial (made, he did not doubt, "to make last year's bitter pill of Fourvière easier to swallow"), Teilhard wrote him at once to feel out his position. He congratulated Ravier on his new post and graphically described his work in Africa, leaving the question that afflicted him so bitterly—when and how he might think of getting home—unspoken.

It was not hard to read between the lines. Ravier answered by return mail, putting Teilhard's unhappy situation in the kindest light he could. He warned that, given the anxiety his case still caused in Rome, if Teilhard did try to come back to France just then, the provincial would have no choice but to shunt him off to a retreat house and a life of strict surveillance. For the moment, he announced regretfully, Teilhard's only recourse was to find himself an unchallengeably "scientific" job in America, and stay with it as long as necessary. As far as he himself was concerned, though, Ravier indicated, Teilhard was free to continue with his philosophical writing so long as he did not attempt to propagate it. He even indicated he would be happy to read anything Teilhard might write, so that they could "think along together." Meantime, he suggested, it would be a good idea for Teilhard to write the general directly, reassuring him of his fidelity and telling him his plans, in order to make his submission to Rome more formal.

Now that Teilhard had confirmation of his exile, his coming to terms with it was thoroughly traumatic. Though it was, of course, comforting to know his new provincial stood behind him, he now had the problem of finding a long-term job in America. On September 23, when he wrote his preliminary (and favorable) report on the African dig, he did so as carefully as possible, the idea of applying for a permanent position with the Fund prominent in his mind. Knowing how similar his thinking was to Fejos's, he trusted the director of the Fund (as well as Providence) to see that he was accepted.

A few weeks later he took a ship from the busy, bush-ringed seaport of Durban down to Cape Town. As rough weather delayed his sailing some weeks, he had time to revisit nearby Hopefield and to compose the letter Ravier had suggested that he send the general in Rome.

He wrote this document as "candidly" as possible, promising never again, without permission, to propagate the philosophical ideas "without which I could not breathe, adore, or believe." Since Rome found his vision "incomplete or premature," he promised to devote himself henceforth to the kind of work that would give "a purely scientific cast to the end of my career—and my life." All he could do about his private thoughts, he said, was ask his superiors to accept him as he was—"with all the congenital qualities (or weaknesses) that I can no more change than I could change my age or the

color of my eyes." After sending Ravier a copy for his approval, he pocketed the original to hold for mailing from
New York.

On October 18 he left Africa and made a stop in Argen-
tina, where he took a cruise ship on the last lap to New York.
The ship docked on November 26, 1951. Even before looking
for a place to check his bags, Teilhard rushed to the Wenner-
Gren Foundation to see Fejos. To his immense relief, the im-
perious Hungarian received him with an absolutely "touching
warmth," told him that "dreamers" such as he was, were precisely what American anthropology most needed, bestowed
on him the title of "research associate" specializing in African
exploration and project-funding, and led him to a quiet little
eyrie on the top floor of the building, where he was invited to
settle in and "think great thoughts."

While he was still at sea and still uncertain of his professional future, Teilhard had written to Father John LaFarge,
asking to be given "shelter" at America House. Since the
place was being overhauled just then, LaFarge had phoned
the father minister of the Jesuits of St. Ignatius Loyola parish
on Park Avenue and asked if he could take him in. The father
minister acquiesced.

Though Teilhard had hoped to stay with "intellectuals"
such as LaFarge and the *America* staff, the new arrangement
turned out even better for him. Besides being closer to the
Wenner-Gren, St. Ignatius was a perfect place in which to
disappear. An enormous, busy complex set among the posh
apartment houses and exclusive co-ops of New York's "silk
stocking district," with a great church in what could be called
"American Railroad Station Splendid" style, a rectory, residential brownstones, and two highly rated schools, Regis and
Loyola, it had for its superior one Father Justin Hanley, a big,
gentle man more interested in the progress of the sixteen-
month-old Korean War than in any visitor's clouded history.
The genial Father Hanley received Teilhard almost noncha-
lantly; and the sixty-odd priests of the community—some

teachers, some executives in Jesuit enterprises around town—
were too preoccupied with their various duties to bother
much with him. In that place of *va et vient*, "Father de
Chardin," as he was usually called, passed almost unnoticed.
If he ever did come to anyone's attention, it was only as a
faintly disturbing foreign presence with a confusing reputation, whose history was irrelevant to the residents.

Those early months in New York, Teilhard lived very
much as he had in China before Leroy had joined him. His
attachment to St. Ignatius parish house (like Chabanel) was
the visible sign of his connection with his Order, and he
obeyed its rules to the letter, even to the point of making
some species of "manifestation of conscience" every month to
its superior. He rose for his daily meditation before five, said
his Mass, made his thanksgiving, caught a quick breakfast in
the refectory, and left the house. He entered the Foundation
about eight, with a special key Fejos had had made for him,
wrote there until noon, when he took a light lunch in a coffee
shop, then bused a few blocks to the apartment where Mrs.
de Terra and her daughter lived ("presque la Cité Vaneau!")
to take the nap his doctors had prescribed.*

Usually he stayed on to dinner there, sometimes with his
hostess only, sometimes with her and her daughter, sometimes in the company of old friends such as Fejos or new acquaintances made through the Foundation, for whom Mrs.
de Terra (to whose middle years he brought a whole new social life among the scholarly or celebrated) acted as his hostess. He spent a little time with the sculptor Malvina Hoffman
(quite exhausted then after the long illness and the death of a
beloved sister) or with Ida Treat, who came down from
Poughkeepsie, or with friends from the Museum of Natural
History. But, however interesting the conversation, Teilhard
always tried to get back to St. Ignatius just before the door
was locked at 10:00 P.M., often, as he came out of his evening

---

* "I spend half my day at Rhoda's." (Letter to Solange Lemaître, September
21, 1952.)

visit to chapel, just in time to smile wanly over the wit of a hearty Irish priest who delighted in greeting him with some variation of a joke about which of them had a monkey for an uncle.

In those days, he wrote the Abbé Breuil, Mrs. de Terra was his "great *calmante*." Without her support, he said, he doubted "I would be able to surmount my nervousness and worry." She kept an eye out for his health, arranged his social calendar, deposited him and picked him up at many of his appointments, took care of nuisance errands, introduced him to her literary cousins the Roger Strauses, and—except for polite inquiries about the opening career of Pierre Leroy and the health of Raymond Jouve (whose eyesight had now failed to the point that Teilhard suggested buying him a radio)— avoided prying into his relation with his Order. Sometimes she could not restrain her curiosity about his zealously guarded inner life. But her repeated requests to be allowed to attend his private Mass made him so patently uncomfortable that Mrs. de Terra finally gave up.†

Once a month, Teilhard went to lunch or dinner with the Jesuits of St. Ignatius ("les cops," as he sometimes ruefully referred to them). After the lunch he always spent some time in the recreation room, with its radio, pool table, and high-backed wooden rocking chairs, standing among the fathers like a smiling ghost, making himself as agreeable as possible and trying to avoid a confrontation with the self-appointed antievolutionist apologist "Defender of the Faith," Francis LeBuffe.‡

Most Sundays, however, he lunched among the odd collection of relatives and friends that Mrs. Straus's widowed father

† To a French Jesuit, Teilhard, conscious of his debt to Mrs. de Terra, once remarked in some distress, "Rhoda keeps asking me to let her hear my Mass, but I don't want to let her. She would not understand."
‡ Father Francis LeBuffe (1885–1954), sodality director and founder of the American branch of the Catholic Evidence Guild of street-corner speakers, responsible for a great number of New York conversions to Catholicism at that period.

used to gather in his midtown apartment. A curious gothic figure in clerical black, disguising his amusement, Teilhard sat decorously before the fine china and cut crystal, bracketed on one side by the voluptuous, dark-haired, negligéed actress. Linda Darnell (the current wife of Mrs. Straus's brother) and on the other by protective Rhoda. Genteelly sipping gin and making transatlantic phone calls, Miss Darnell absent-mindedly caressed a scruffy, mangy marmoset which perched on her white shoulder and surveyed the gathering with fearsome, disapproving eyes. In that eccentric mix of personalities Teilhard was at his ease, and he usually chatted animatedly until the coffee came, then retired to his host's bedroom for his nap.[2]

Near Christmas 1951 Père d'Ouince wrote that he had been ordered to reassign the room he had always held for Teilhard at *Études*, even when he was in China. By return mail the exile calmly directed the disposition of the last of his effects. The first winter away from home passed with merciful speed. In January Teilhard was mostly occupied with paper work at the Foundation, where, among other projects, he offered his hearty recommendation for a grant for a brilliant young geologist whom he had met in England on his way to Africa, Kenneth Oakley, to try his fluorine dating technique on the Australopithecine sites of Africa. In February he went to Washington to visit friends from Georgetown and Catholic universities. In March he slushed through the late snow to the Academy of Sciences to talk on African prehistory for his old friend Dr. Harry L. Shapiro of the American Museum of Natural History and Columbia University. As weeks went by, his old eyes watched for the first sign of green in the dark, neglected tangle of Central Park that he could see on entering and leaving the Foundation.

Suddenly one morning he awoke in his overheated rectory room to bright sunlight on the windowsill and the gurgling of a pigeon just outside. Spring had come at last. He telephoned Childs Frick out on Long Island, and went to spend the week with him amid the bursting blossoms of his great estate at Roslyn. On Easter Sunday, after he said his private Mass, he went, at Rhoda's suggestion, to hear Monsignor Sheen preach at St. Patrick's.

Spring brought a revival of his social life. His long-ago Aurora University companion Emmanuel de Breuvery (considerably different now in silhouette and character from the quick, khaki-clad visitor whom Teilhard had shown around Peking in 1943) joined the French mission to the United Nations as economic adviser and drew Teilhard back into diplomatic circles he enjoyed. There followed pleasant encounters with old friends he had known in China, evenings with Guillaume Georges-Picot, the Henri Hoppenots, and the Francis Lacostes (through whom, at one particularly graceful Périgordean feast, he met and chatted amiably with the Soviet ambassador Jacob Malik), and afternoons with celebrities such as the socialist politician Jules Moch. In late spring Teilhard gave lectures at Yale and Harvard, where the Hallam Moviuses gave a reception in his honor. When he came back to New York, he went out to Scarsdale with Rhoda to see the dogwood, and accompanied her to Connecticut to visit a Franco-American Benedictine convent, built in the shell of an old brass factory, where he sat patiently through an impeccable piping of Sunday Vespers. "A film about that convent," he commented in a letter to his brother Joseph, "played in Paris just last year."*

In the same note, he remarked on Joseph's announcement of a forthcoming ceremony at his boyhood school at Mongré: "It's the last place, perhaps, that I would ever want to see again. . . . It leaves me with a feeling of revulsion . . . a vague sense of somehow (even with the best will in the world) having been played upon and misled by my educators. . . . Without the consequence of this 'error,'" he, however, admitted, "God knows if I would have known the passionately exciting and fortunate kind of life I've had."

---

* *Come to the Stable*, with Loretta Young and Celeste Holm (Fox, 1949).

The Wenner-Gren symposium of June 9–20 was a disappointment to him. To a philosopher for whom man was essentially a "cosmic rather than aesthetic or moral or even solely a religious phenomenon"—a creature whose nature could be really understood only when it was "historically reconstructed through physics, chemistry, biology, and geology" —the narrow outlook of the scholar-specialists who attended was discouraging. In his retreat at the Strauses' country house in Purchase, Teilhard tried to put it from his mind. In early June, with Mrs. de Terra in tow, he set out to see his old friends Professors Camp and Chaney at the University of California.

After a kaleidoscopic trip through the carnival of placards, bunting, and straw hats of the Chicago Republican Presidential Convention that nominated Eisenhower over the ultraconservative Robert Taft, he climbed eight thousand feet to George Simpson's adobe hideaway at the border of the San Juan Basin. Then he traveled on to the West Coast.

In San Francisco he went from his hotel each morning to visit Camp and Chaney at the eucalyptus-blooming university grounds in nearby Berkeley. Thanks to the intervention of the then-departing Dr. Chaney, he was given a privately guided tour of the university's complex of cyclotrons. That walk among the atom-smashing engines, planted in a miniature city of the scholars and technicians who attended them, he wrote Leroy, gave him every bit of the "shock" that he expected. Before the immensity and complexity of the cyclotrons, he felt he "lost his footing" in the "human"—at least as he had known it up to then. They seemed the work of a "new kind of humanity just coming into being . . . a coming together of complex theory and technology, all in the service of a single work" from which, he wrote, "only God knows what we can expect."[3]

In August, after a stopover in Glacier Park in Montana, Teilhard turned back east and spent the end of his vacation with another pair of Mrs. de Terra's cousins in their summer

house on an island off Bar Harbor. There, ringed by the
reflecting water, shuffling through pine needles on lonely
walks, he gathered his thoughts in silence. Twelve months
had passed, as bare of meaning as they had been crowded
with events. He had been faithful to his promise. He had kept
absolutely mute before the barrage of criticisms of his
thought in rightist publications. And his silence left him in
worse repute than ever.

So much of his old life was disappearing. Henri Cosme, the
patron of his China days, had died that summer; René Grousset was seriously ill; d'Ouince, to whom he had once written
"wherever you are the superior I shall feel I have a home,"
had just requested to be relieved of his position as director of
*Études* and was transferred to a larger Jesuit house on the
Rue de Sèvres.

Though there never was, perhaps, a man more fundamentally of a single piece than Teilhard, in those years in
New York he knew that he was living a double, triple, quad-
ruple kind of life. It was as though he had decided he had to
manufacture from his many-faceted personality as many
different *personae* as he needed to survive. To the Park Avenue Jesuits, he was the odd but observant religious whose job
kept him away most of the day; to Fejos and the staff of the
Wenner-Gren, the worldly scientist and philosopher whose
insight gave a new propulsion to so many of the director's
dreams; to Mrs. de Terra and her friends, the frail, dependent
but somehow grand old man of the aristocratic manner and
the deep-set eyes that seemed forever fixed on something just
beyond their gaze, vaguely murmuring "très gentil" at everything, impressive or banal, that they brought to his attention.[4]

Whenever any of his friends did accidentally catch glimpses
of the real Teilhard, they started, as though they had touched
a live electric wire. Mrs. Movius, for instance, who with her
husband had first met Teilhard on the Burma trip of 1938,
stumbled upon him suddenly one morning when he was visiting her home in Cambridge. She glimpsed a cleric in her

kitchen talking passionately to her husband about Divine Love. "Excuse me," she murmured quickly and backed out of the room, only to realize a few minutes later that her husband's strange companion was that old field companion she had been entertaining as guest all weekend. "For a moment," she said, "I simply did not recognize him."

That September Teilhard sustained a blow that quite unmasked him. A letter from Leroy told him that the irreplaceable Raymond Jouve—who in his days as father minister of *Études* in 1947 had rushed with cassock flapping down the Rue Monsieur when Teilhard had his heart attack—had been himself the victim of a heart attack, and was now recuperating at the small hospital on Oudinot where Teilhard was taken that June morning five years earlier. Teilhard dashed off a poignant letter to Ravier complaining that his enforced silence only made the permanence of his exile more certain, and implicitly pleading to be allowed to come back home. Painfully aware of the violent opposition to the spread of his ideas in France, Ravier could only reassure his subject of his personal admiration and repeat his invitation for Teilhard to share his philosophical and theological thought with him.

When he received Ravier's reply, Teilhard began another essay.[5] His intention in writing it was to put his superior in touch with the present development of his thought, which was, as it had been in 1948, essentially a cry for reconciliation between religion and the aspirations of modern man; its focus was a reinterpretation of the meaning of the cross.

From Labor Day, when he returned to work at the Wenner-Gren, until near month's end, Teilhard left notes for the new essay on backs of envelopes or any paper handy in his office at the Foundation. Once again he undertook to wrestle against the mystery of evil. Christianity, he patiently explained, was by its very nature vowed to, crowned by, and essentially identified with the Cross, the effective instrument of Jesus' redemptive passion and death. But since this symbol had, for centuries, been interpreted by theologians as a denial of the goodness of matter (the matrix of human suffering), and since more recently it had been seized on only as the symbol of "reparation and expiation" for human folly, how, he asked, was mankind, awake now to the biological movement of the earth, to understand it?

Only when the Church accepted evolution's part in the Divine Plan, he reasoned, and saw the Cross as the symbol of this agonizing process, could she restore true value to that sign. Evolution, by its nature, was a movement that exacted struggle. And, after evolution reached the level of reflection, it cried out for a recognizable "amorizing" sign to inspire and drive it forward, against all the arguments that tempted it to shut down before the discouragingly demanding task of self-achievement still before it.

Properly understood, only the example of a crucified God, forced by the very nature of his fierce love to penetrate to the death—to the agony of his broken flesh and the blind terror of human despair—could give mankind the courage to attempt the next step forward. Only the concept of a Christ who was crucified not simply "to carry the sins of a guilty world" but "to carry the weight of an evolving world" could convert the "sign of contradiction" into the seal of strength. Once church doctrine reinterpreted the Cross in this light, Teilhard concluded, the symbol would stand again where it belonged: at the place where faith and advancing human values met. And only then could it effectively become the criterion by which man would judge himself, rise or fall, stop where he was, or edge painfully forward on the long road before him.

Teilhard mailed off the essay to Ravier as soon as it was finished. Then, in a letter to Mlle. Mortier dated September 18, he noted with surprise that coincidentally he had completed it on the feast in the Latin calendar of the Exaltation of the Holy Cross.

On September 29, while his mind still dwelt on these ideas, Teilhard heard from Père Leroy: Raymond Jouve's illness had recently turned critical; surgery was required, and he was moved to the Hôpital de Bon Secours. There on September 24, with the same simplicity and lack of drama that had characterized him all his life, he had died.

"Jouve's passing," Teilhard wrote to a friend, "leaves an awful void in me. He was one of the few Jesuits I ever knew to whom I could say anything, certain of being understood." The next few weeks seemed shadowed by the loss. Despite the love Teilhard had borne his old ally, despite his recollection of so many irrelevant details of things they had done together, he was bewildered to discover how quickly memories of Jouve had faded from his mind. He could not recall the nuances of his voice or the play of expression across that wry, mischievous face. Those autumn afternoons Teilhard stayed late and accomplished less than usual in his little eyrie at the Wenner-Gren; and as he walked up past the lighted shop windows of Madison Avenue toward Mrs. de Terra's for dinner, at the change from daylight-saving to standard time, the darkness seemed to come too early. He could feel the winter rushing in.

# CHAPTER
# TWENTY-SIX

There were, however, that autumn of 1952, some periods of brightness. St. Ignatius had a new superior: Father Robert Gannon, an ex-rector of Fordham University, a passionate clubman, and a ruddy little leprechaun of Irish charm, who paraded Teilhard before the prestigious Century Club one evening that September at a special dinner in his honor. For one moment it almost seemed the Frenchman was about to be an honored guest at St. Ignatius. But soon, during the monthly manifestations of conscience that he so conscientiously made, Teilhard began slipping into what Father Gannon still calls "his dreams." The *quasi-amitié* cooled.

The troubles that the exile had in finding an American priest other than John LaFarge whom he could talk to in those days makes an unhappy story. In general the American Catholic Church of the early 1950s produced a type of cleric unlike any seen before or since. It was the heyday of the anticommunist reaction, and most of the lower clergy (with, Teilhard pointed out, the staff of *America* magazine—"to the glory of the Order"—a notable exception) stood staunchly and vocally behind McCarran and McCarthy. From the time of World War II, where the religious revival had its roots, the Roman Church had been enjoying the largest harvest of conversions in that country in its history, and more and more "Americanism" and "Catholicism" had begun to find common ground. By the early fifties, backed up by political pronunciations by the Pacelli pope, American priests came to see the battle against Communism as part of their sacred ministry. Simultaneously, groups of Catholic laymen, often calling themselves by religio-military names such as the "Blue Army" ("blue of Mary's color," as distinct from the Communists' red) began practicing anticommunism almost as an act of piety to the Virgin. As new religious and political coalitions came into being, the white Protestant majority in America recognized, in what they had lately regarded as an alien immigrant intrusion, an increasingly respectable ally against "the common foe."

The popular culture reflected this recognition. The film industry, for example, which from its earliest days had thought of the Catholic Church primarily in terms of an interfering, moralizing pressure group, began during the war to recognize the commercial vein to be exploited in its exotic attitudes and life-styles. Films such as The Song of Bernadette, Going My Way, and The Bells of St. Mary's drew long lines to box offices. At the same time, the popular imagination had begun to look for demonstrations of presence of "the supernatural" in life as well as art. An epidemic of unsubstantiated "miracles," entirely unsupported by the hierarchy but details of which were soberly reported to the press, was still spreading across the land. The "miracles" of "the Lourdes-Fatima contagion," as Teilhard called it, ranged from the appearance of the Blessed Virgin to some children in the Bronx in 1945 (the site of the "apparitions" was still much frequented by the curious or credulous in the fifties), to the phenomenon of a plaster statue of Saint Anne which "wept" in upper New York State, to a "Lady in Blue and White" who drew crowds of sick and praying people, leaving money on the grass, after her "manifestation" to other children in Philadelphia's Fairmont Park in 1953. Whether he regarded the phenomenon as a residual demonstration of the old human craving for the miraculous or as "the reflective being's inability to accept the idea of living in a 'closed universe,'" religious simplism which

drew even so many other quite rational souls to convert to the
Church was the sort of thing with which Teilhard's mind
could not cope. As for the dread Stalinism (as distinct
from socialism or even communism), Teilhard had long ago
judged it for what it was—the "nationalistic and totalitarian"
distortion of that "biophysical totalization" that he believed
to be in process on the earth—a movement whose expan-
sionistic pride and greed, whose underlying opposition to the
deeper "humanization" that Teilhard dreamed of, made it the
mortal enemy of all he hoped for for man. If all of this were
not enough, as a cultivated man Teilhard found "communism" an implacable enemy to conversation. "It is so easy to
be 'anti'!" he wearily wrote a friend; "it dispenses one from
thinking."

In late autumn 1952, just when his isolation began to feel
most heavy, Emmanuel de Breuvery, by this time separated
from the French United Nations mission and looking for a
permanent job with the UN Secretariat, moved in with him at
St. Ignatius. Though de Breuvery's highly structured "classical
and *enfantine*" spirituality precluded the growth of a real inti-
macy such as Teilhard had shared with Pierre Leroy in China,
and though his unnerving experiences under Communist
house arrest in Shanghai, where he had remained until 1951,
made him considerably less sanguine about socialistic revolutions than Teilhard was, he was at least by birth and temperament a Frenchman and well-informed about the state of the
religious world in France. In contrast to the only other
priestly companionship available to Teilhard at the time, de
Breuvery's friendship was a gift from heaven. "You can't
imagine," he wrote a friend soon after de Breuvery's arrival,
"what it is to me to have someone like him to talk to, here in
this country where to ninety per cent of the clergy, religion is
nothing more than simple anticommunism."

Suddenly Teilhard's social life began again. In late October, when Malvina Hoffman, now almost constantly ill with
headaches and back pains, looked down at the audience in

the Plaza Hotel, where she had been invited to be decorated with the Légion d'Honneur for her contribution to art, it encouraged her to see him smiling up at her from a seat in the front row. Miss Hoffman's physical pain made her acutely sensitive to Teilhard's nervous distress, and soon after the ceremony she arranged a dinner party to introduce him to her own French doctor, the perceptive and sympathetic Albert Simard, with whom Teilhard got on at once.

When the Madeleine Renaud–Jean-Louis Barrault company performed in New York, he joined a distant cousin, the French consul Jean de Lagarde, at a party in the artists' honor held at an East Side restaurant. Meanwhile, he and de Breuvery spent many early evenings that month discussing the perils and the pleasures of the latter's entry into the international political arena at the UN. Though de Breuvery already had in his favor an old acquaintance with Dag Hammarskjöld (whom he had known since they were delegates together at an international economic conference in Paris), there was among Hammarskjöld's subordinates a considerable amount of resistance to the idea of a priest making a place for himself at the Secretariat. To the economist's surprise, however, the strange psychological climate around him worked to his advantage. With so many powerful anticommunist pressure groups scrutinizing the United Nations for spies and fellow travelers, he was happily surprised to find that even the Roman collar Cardinal Spellman insisted he wear proved to some a reassuring symbol. After a month or so of sticky maneuvering, he received a temporary contract in the UN's economic development section in October 1952.

For a while, de Breuvery's accounts of his adventures on the job provided new interest for Teilhard. He worried his friend over the opposition he had to outmaneuver even in his own UN department, or smiled over light gossip about the dashed hopes of romantic typists who discovered, after weeks of secret euphoria, that the handsome young men following them were only FBI agents at work.

When Fejos came back from Europe a month earlier, Teilhard had heard for the first time that the Wenner-Gren had decided to send him back to Africa in the summer of 1953 on an inspection tour of the Foundation's projects on that continent. At the office, therefore, most of his working hours were taken up with business related to "Operation Africa," making decisions on grants to be given to researchers in Africa for work in the Sahara, to Desmond Clark of the Livingston Museum in Northern Rhodesia, to van Riet Lowe for his excavation at Makapansgat, and to Robinson for his museum in Pretoria, and considering a new grant to an English adventurer named Louis Leakey, who, with his anthropologist wife, was sifting a hand ax pit in Olduvai Gorge in Tanganyika. In November a Board of Directors meeting considered the details of his trip and possibilities of his seeing Kenya, Angola, and South Africa and scheduled a second meeting to be held in London for that summer to polish the details.

Though Teilhard fussed over the possibility that the current Mau-Mau uprising still might "make the continent explode from Kenya to the Cape" and force him to cancel his trip entirely, the thought that he might go to London was enough to make his head reel. On November 20, not without some trepidation, he wrote to Père Ravier, informing him of the projected meeting, inquiring about the possibility of taking the occasion to cross to France for a few weeks. Meanwhile, he wrote two essays which he hoped would "break the glass that separates anthropology from biology": one, defining "hominization" in terms of biological speciation[1]; and a second, identifying "socialization" as the form that the biological process of "speciation" took in man.[2] The main point of both essays, was that, unlike the other species, whose individuals stayed fixed, disappeared, or adapted to the circumstances in evolution's flamboyant play, the human group from its beginnings had been converging and tightening on itself in search for absolute fulfillment.

In November Teilhard wrote to several people letters mourning Adlai Stevenson's defeat at the hands of the "honest, simple Ike" and his dangerous "second-rate bouche trou" Richard Nixon. The new administration, he feared, was moving into the White House "with a threatening school of Republican sharks" in its wake, and he expected it to effect the "resurgence of capitalism" at its worst—the triumph of the passion for gold, with all human considerations pushed into the background—instead of looking to man's true self-interest.

In December Ravier's answer to Teilhard's request to visit home arrived. It was a reply Teilhard might well have expected, solely on the basis of the fact that he had only been away a year. But even had he been in exile longer, it should have been apparent to him that the summer of 1953 would be a most inopportune moment for a return to France. The worker-priest movement was just then in deepest trouble. For years the Vatican had watched with apprehension the development of the late Cardinal Suhard's beloved missionary enterprise, and now it seemed about to lose its patience. By 1953 the Holy Office files spilled over with complaints and denunciations from faithful bourgeois Catholics who saw the priests only as Communist tools. In May of 1952 many of them had marched in the demonstration against the reorganization of the NATO forces under General Ridgeway, and two young priests were badly beaten by the police. They had already drawn more fire on themselves by protesting the choice of Barcelona, "that symbolic city [where] so many militant workers await death for having broken the conspiracy of silence,"[3] as the site for the upcoming Eucharistic Congress, and later on they sent representatives to the reportedly Communist-inspired Peace Congress in Vienna. The novel *Les Saints Vont en l'Enfer,* was a long-popular best seller; and the secular press by then had turned the priests into celebrities. At the very moment when Teilhard was asking for a home leave, a horrified Holy See was already considering declaring the movement "more dangerous than useful" and ordering that the number of priests engaged as workers (of whom quite a few were Jesuits) must be contained at its present complement of eighty-five. It was hardly the moment for one in Ravier's position to invite new problems; he suggested that it might be better for Teilhard to wait to visit home until the summer of 1954.

However difficult Ravier's refusal was for him to accept, Teilhard did the best he could to bow to it. In observing New York's Christmas-shopping fever ("a curiously innocent combination of spirituality and commerce . . . with its carol-bawling loudspeakers, flesh and blood Santas on street corners, and glittering yellow line of trees stretching up Park Avenue"), he found momentary half-fascinated, half-appalled distraction.

The week before Christmas he noticed in surprise that even Mrs. de Terra was behaving oddly. Determined to "cheer him up" as best she could, she decided to provide him with "a real American Christmas with all the trimmings," stood a decorated tree in her parlor, and hung a special Christmas stocking for him at her fireplace. Teilhard's effort to accommodate her mood ("très gentil!") left him exhausted. "I did my best to please her," he wrote a friend, "but I'm afraid I'm still too much the undemonstrative Auvergnat to carry off the way I would have liked. I kept remembering what the most intelligent of my uncles used to say in the face of such sentimental exhibitions: 'They make me gag!' "[4]

In the last days of December, Teilhard went off to a conference in Philadelphia for Operation Africa, then passed New Year's Day with the Strauses in the blizzardy, stripped woods near Purchase. On his return to the city, where the Wenner-Gren board awarded him five thousand dollars for his summer trip, he went out often in the evening with de Breuvery to dinner with his cousin the consul Jean de Lagarde, or to the Henri Hoppenots, where he ran into Mme. Lemaître's friend Louis Massignon, "sparkling and full of wit as ever." At St.

Ignatius he could find little American religious readings with which to feed his faith. He was distressed to find even in the newly published *Journals* of the Resistance hero-priest Raymond-Léopold Bruckberger ("a talented aesthete-and-hero-choirboy") a strict warning to young Americans about the dangers of France's now nearly defunct "new theology." Almost masochistically he stood rooted in a Madison Avenue shop, flipping through a book on "the boy Jesus," with a picture of a huge-eyed, hungry-looking child staring from the frontispiece.

Other news from home was far from cheerful. Tension about the worker-priests continued to mount. Even the scientist-priests such as Lejay and Dubarle, with whom Teilhard had shared so much in the years before *Humani Generis*, were now removed from research and given teaching posts. Without d'Ouince, *Études* "seemed to have lost its soul." The Young Christian Workers, in whom the Dominicans had always put such hope, were no longer rethinking their religion on a scale consistent with the new size science gave the universe; they seemed to close their prayer life down over a devotion to a comrade Christ gazing placidly down on them in the jeweled light of yesterday's cathedrals. It was as though, Teilhard complained, the Church was deliberately starving herself to death out of her own antimaterialism. She seemed to be suffering the same sort of suffocation as did the Christianity of the first generation, when it found it must break out of the closed world of Israel into the "pagan" world. Christianity's only chance to grow, he wrote, lay in her being born again among the "gentiles" (non-Christians), because only the gentiles had retained their taste for the earth.

Much of what was on his mind, unhappily, he could not tell even de Breuvery, and day by day his desperation deepened. Now even the Sonyril sleeping tablets he had asked to be sent to him from France were almost useless. While his brother Jesuits at St. Ignatius slept their innocent sleep, Teilhard stood before his window late at night, staring at the slow hypnotic flow of traffic up and down Park Avenue while astonishingly vivid memories of happy moments in his past rose up to mock him.

By February Teilhard's anxiety had neared hysteria. With Mrs. de Terra at his side almost everywhere he went, with de Breuvery's support, and with the encouragement of Dr. Fejos and the people of the Wenner-Gren, he was almost never alone. Still Teilhard had never in his life felt quite so lost. Even the preparations for the projected summer trip seemed suddenly too much. He fussed about the Mau-Mau; he worried that another yellow fever shot might trigger his old heart trouble. His doctor, in whom he confided absolutely, was unable to reassure him. To the Jesuit geologist Christian Burdo back in France, he cried out in a letter, "I feel I'm coming apart inside!"

Though in the two years since he had come to America Teilhard had visited Mrs. Swan, who lived only a taxi ride away, about once a week in an attempt to "work out a constructive friendship" with her and to "disperse the seeds of bitterness" that still existed between them, that month the thought of facing the obligatory emotional scene that always closed their meetings was too much for him to face. Still, Lucile was one of the few people in New York who remembered the happy days in China when he still hoped for his future, and he needed to remember those good days. On one occasion when the sympathetic Dr. Simard saw how vain were all his efforts to calm Teilhard, he called Mrs. Swan (whom he knew through Malvina Hoffman) and asked her to hurry to his office. "Father Teilhard is here; please come," he begged. On her arrival, Lucile found Teilhard sitting in a chair before the doctor staring at his hands. He did not speak; he did not raise his head. All that Simard said to Lucile was, "Tell Father Teilhard someone loves him." She obeyed and left.

On the sixteenth of the month Teilhard dashed off a letter to Ravier which he admitted had "neither head nor tail," complaining of the crippling anguish that possessed him. Throwing all caution to the winds, he begged again for the impossible—just a few months home in France that summer before setting off for Africa.

He knew too well what the response would be: Sail straight to South Africa and do the job, then return directly to America. This was obviously the will of Providence for him. Still, to reassure himself against the uncomprehending gossip generated by his dependence on Mrs. de Terra, he decided to ask his superior in writing for official permission for "a woman friend of canonical age" to go to Africa to care for him. Ravier agreed.

Suddenly just before Easter the snow turned into rain and it was spring. Rhoda recovered from a minor operation that was worrying them both; Teilhard spent Holy Week with the Fricks amid the magnolias of Roslyn; and the raw edges of his nerves began to heal.

"I'm still not completely over my difficulties of last winter . . ." he wrote his brother Joseph April 9, "but at last I think I'm coming out of it." He and Mrs. de Terra dined with Malvina Hoffman; and later he chatted with Maritain ("looking very grand in full academic robes") when he sat on the platform at Columbia to hear Governor Dewey eulogize the visiting Georges Bidault. At a luncheon for Prince Norodom Sihanouk, he ran into Jacques Rueff, a former governor of the Bank of France, who was thinking of arranging a 1954 "conference on human problems 'From the Atom to Man,'" at which he hoped to put thinkers such as Niels Bohr from the prelife sciences in touch with biologists, psychologists, and men of letters of equal stature in their fields.

Soon Teilhard began to write again. Several of his friends in France had recently sent clippings from various scientific articles: a piece by the eminent Louis de Broglie in the *Revue d'Histoire des Sciences*, a tribute to Einstein in the popular weekly *Paris-Match*, and one by Paul Chauchard in another learned journal, all of which spurred Teilhard to make his own comment. Ever since his first brush with Einsteinian thought, he had tried to design an "energetics" for his personal cosmology. In *The Phenomenon of Man* finished in 1941, he had divided energy into two categories, that energy he called "tangential" (the measurable energy which had long been under scrutiny in laboratories) and the energy he called "radial" (the as-yet unmeasured and unexplained drive of evolution that caused beings to complexify and rise on the ladder of creation toward a specific end). Now, nearly fifteen years later, he was sad to see that science still confined itself to examining only energy's "tangential" aspect.

In a new essay called "The Energy of Evolution,"[5] he repeated his old theory. Since everyone admitted that all the universe, from the atom to man, was "corpuscular" (granular) in nature, he wrote, and since it was plain that the "inner reserve" (or functional capacity) of each "corpuscle" always increased as it complexified, it seemed incredible to him that the old barrier between the life sciences and the prelife sciences still stood. If, instead of viewing the atom only "geometrically" (in terms of measurements of its parts), scientists began to examine it "biologically" (in terms of that functional capacity), many of their problems would be gone. Since all the universe was a single stuff and every property of nature that manifested itself at any point in its development (as in the glow-discharge of radium*) was present to some degree in all created things, matter, besides being polarized mechanically particle-to-particle, was also psychically polarized from above. And though the cosmos in obedience to the law of entropy continued to be diminished physically with the loss of heat from each "tangential" action, each new complexification which this "tangential" action brought about without it, actually increased its total "radial" (or psychic) content.

---

* "Every being radiates; every mass is modified by its own velocity; every movement is veiled in immobility when sufficiently slowed down." *The Phenomenon of Man* (Harper & Row), p. 55.

Though Teilhard did not do any better than his colleagues in explaining *why* matter, whose natural state is one of complete disorganization, kept on associating into ever larger and more complex "corpuscles" and progressing upward to ever less probable states of being, his essay at least focused attention on that point. To him, this "radial energy" was itself the fundamental "energy" of evolution and the most important field of investigation open to researchers of the future. Only when science had settled on a "unified theory of energetics," he declared, would it be capable of presenting a comprehensible and "livable" universe to man. And only when religion encouraged such investigation and integrated its conclusions into its doctrinal statements would it be able to present to modern man articulations of the old dogmas of the creation and redemption awesome enough to bring him to his knees again.

That June, after reading an article about the first observations from the telescope on Mount Palomar, he wrote another paper urging the Church to widen her intellectual horizon.[6] Since he believed that the production of intelligence was the inevitable consequence and purpose of stellar evolution, he was sure that in a universe of such immensity, other planets where conditions hospitable to the birth of life and intelligence obtained must already exist. This possibility was, he felt, one so pressing that the Church could no more close its eyes to it than it could to heliocentricity. Nor was there even any danger that the widening of astronomical perspectives would diminish man's importance in his own eyes. As Teilhard wrote in a letter to a Jesuit friend, the greatest personal reward he found in considering the data in the Palomar article was that it reinforced "my feeling for the value of 'the Human.'"

Everything about that spring was pleasant for Teilhard. He and Rhoda lunched with the visiting Moviuses at Malvina Hoffman's. He enjoyed such small diversions as the Wednesday afternoon walks he took with her and her cousin Mrs.

Straus, while the ladies practiced French. The walks were usually prolonged by visits to the Central Park zoo, where he talked amiably about the animals just as he had when he walked in the gardens of the Forbidden City, or by afternoon tea in the park cafeteria. From those sunshiny days, the only disturbing memory Mrs. Straus still holds concerns one afternoon when, in rising from a tea table, Teilhard fumbled with his breviary and a garish prayer card fluttered out. As Mrs. Straus describes it,[7] it was an image of a Jesus with "a pale effeminate face" proffering a penny valentine "Sacred Heart" to the beholder—a Saint Sulpician image very like one she remembered seeing on the bureau of her French governess when she was a child. Teilhard's attachment to this clumsy attempt to represent the unrepresentable lay in the fact that it reminded him of the profundity on which his whole philosophy was based. As he bent to pick up the card, his eyes met Mrs. Straus's. She saw the wall go up, and for a moment Teilhard blushed. He shoved the card back inside the book and changed the subject.

On July 5, with Mrs. de Terra managing the details, Teilhard set out once again to South Africa. By July 14, as the volcanic hulk of St. Helena broke the smooth horizon line, he finished "The Convergence of the Universe." After a short stay in Cape Town, where he examined a Neanderthal skull piece which had turned up six months earlier at Seldanha Bay, he pushed on to Johannesburg to study Dart's newest work and visited Makapansgat, which, having just yielded "a beautiful lower jaw" of Australopithecus, was beginning to show a succession of culture layers that promised to be as rich as those at Choukoutien had been.

Toward the end of August, still unhappy that Leakey's dig had been closed down because of Mau-Mau trouble, Teilhard took a plane to Desmond Clark's museum in Northern Rhodesia. Clark drove him 250 miles north, through land that seemed unchanged since Dr. Livingstone's time, to Twin Rivers near Lusaka, where he had dug in vertical, hole-shaped fissures in the karstic crystalline limestone deposits with Kenneth Oakley the previous winter. Though their yield was still quite small, Teilhard remarked that since the fissures had acted as traps for successive layers of breccia, they constituted an intriguing promise to the geologists. In the last day of his visit, Clark and his family took Teilhard and Mrs. de Terra picnicking on one of the long, comfortable *bateau-mouche*-like boats that glide on the Zambesi, where crocodiles and hippos still lounge along the banks, to admire the breathtaking mile-long roaring curtain of Victoria Falls. Soon afterward Teilhard set out for South Africa again, then left for home.

As before, he took a boat to Buenos Aires, and then another back to New York. The shipboard leisure gave him time to make his annual retreat. "Less and less," he wrote a friend, "do I see any difference now between research and adoration." At night, pacing a deck where the sky hung so close it seemed that one could pluck down the stars by handfuls, he composed another essay on the resonance of his theandric Christ throughout the universe. He finished it on the feast of Christ the King, "somewhere below the equator."[8]

Despite Teilhard's feeling that he owed much of the trip's success to the tact and energy of Mrs. de Terra ("I cannot tell you what a help Rhoda has been to me, from every point of view," he wrote another Jesuit†), he returned to New York —for all his physical fragility—revitalized and happy. He was satisfied that he had put together a good team of collaborators in Africa, and that in devising a network of excavations in Hopefield, Makapansgat, Northern Rhodesia, Nyasaland, the Omo region of Ethiopia, and (if something could be worked out with the obstreperous "ultranationalistic" Portuguese) some place in Angola, he had helped mount a prac-

† She was "a marvelous diplomat and liaison agent in all that concerns coping with people interested in the projects of the Foundation. Since she knows everyone I have to deal with, both here and in the U.S., she has helped a great deal with her psychological insights. And you know how much my candor needs to be directed when it comes to this area." August 5, 1953.

tical five-point "plan of attack" on the problem of human origins there. He was reasonably certain that there were two axes where evolution had worked its way to pre- and para-hominians: one in Asia and the other in Africa. But judging from the completeness of the African series, it was only in Africa, he decided, that the hominid succeeded in moving past the Neanderthal stage without miscarrying and emerging into *Homo sapiens*.[9]

Counting on the fact that Ravier would hold to his suggestion that he might return to France the following summer, Teilhard took the transfer of the brilliant young Jacques Sommet from his teaching chair at Chantilly to the rectorship of the still-shattered theologate at Fourvière as a good augury. He seized the occasion to write Ravier of his pleasure in the appointment, and, in the process, to restate his desire to go home. Since Ravier was then traveling in the Middle East, Teilhard knew he must wait for confirmation on his invitation of the previous year. While he waited, Teilhard began writing letters to prepare the way for his return, restraining writers who were too quick to publish books or articles on him, and leaking to more reliable French contacts what information he felt would help. Even now, he wrote friends, he dreamed of trying to write a new and "publishable" book on man, perhaps one that would simultaneously answer the pessimistic *The Next Million Years* by Charles Galton Darwin[10] and the stoic, skeptical *Ce Que Je Crois* just written by the French biologist Jean Rostand.[11] Anticipation of the visit home lit up the last months of 1953 for him, and soon after his return from Cape Town to New York, he was not only writing Père Leroy and his Cousin Marguerite Teillard-Chambon about seeing them in France the next summer; he was writing his brother Joseph about spending the following August with him at Les Moulins, just as he did each summer from 1946 to 1950.

Just before the year came to an end, however, a certain shadow fell across his mind. On November 19 Kenneth

Oakley, who had been working with fossil-dating methods back in England, wrote him that the famous "Piltdown Man," in whose "discovery" Teilhard had innocently collaborated in 1913, had turned out to be a fraud. "You were hoodwinked," Oakley wrote, "about the whole affair!" Using the fluorine dating method, Oakley and J. S. Weiner had just established that the Piltdown skullpiece Dawson presented to the Geological Society in 1912 (though even then it had been put to question) was only a few hundred years old at best. Using an ordinary dental tool to drill into the lower piece and noticing the fresh smell of burning, the researchers concluded that it was nothing but the jaw of a modern ape. Teilhard's famous "interlocking canine" was fairly young as well. Like the ape molars of the jaw, it now appeared to have been carefully filed to fit against the human teeth above and painted Van Dyck brown. Though the debunking of Piltdown erased a rankling problem in the story of human development and so was a landmark accomplishment in paleontology, it was a considerable embarrassment to Teilhard.

The role of the dupe is difficult to play with dignity; and Teilhard carried it as best he could. He congratulated Oakley elaborately and patiently on his discovery, and answered his long stream of letters asking for details of Teilhard's part in the adventure. While Teilhard did not admit it to his New York friends, the incident cut him quite deeply. To Abbé Breuil, he wrote (perhaps a little overcharitably), "I still have trouble believing that Dawson himself perpetrated the fraud. Fantastic though it seems, I would prefer to think that someone else innocently threw the bone fragments from a neighborhood cottage into the ditch. . . . Nevertheless, I must admit to you that this new discovery, splendid though it is, spoils one of the happiest memories of my early scientific career."

# CHAPTER
# TWENTY-SEVEN

On a bright December morning in 1953 Auguste Valensin died of an arterial embolism at Nice. The following February Pierre Charles died at Louvain. Though, as the postwar breach between the French and the "Belgo-Romanos," as Teilhard ruefully called them, had widened, Charles had in the last decade pointedly avoided his old friend, in Teilhard's mind only the roguish boy with whom he shared his heady thoughts on Jersey had ever really existed.* In a letter from New York to his cousin Marguerite, he wrote that he was crushed under an "avalanche" of deaths. "First . . . our wonderful Valensin, and now my other friend as well. I have lost the two people who taught me how to think."

At home that year in France, a tragic drama was in progress. After a decade of dissension, the controversy of the worker-priests had finally come to climax. By the end of the winter, this last remaining fruit of the spiritual revival that had greeted Teilhard when he arrived home after the war was finally cut down. As early as the previous August 29 Cardinal Pizzardo had sent a confidential circular to the heads of all religious orders commanding them to recall their subjects gradually from the movement. On September 26 French superiors and bishops were summoned to the palace of the Archbishop of Paris to hear the papal nuncio, Paul Marella, convey Rome's notice that the experiment must be termi-

---

* "*Lui*, intégriste?" Teilhard always repeated in disbelief across the years when Charles's rightist tendencies were commented on.

nated. Though on November 4, 1953, Cardinals Gerlier, Liénart, and Feltin had gone to Rome to make a last-ditch plea to save the movement, the trip was all in vain. The pope made it totally clear that, although he would agree to the institution of a new and carefully controlled organization of "missionaries to the Marxist masses," whose members would live so as "not to jeopardize the traditional forms of the Church," he could not consider continuing the movement in its present form. Before they left, the visitors were photographed with the pope at his insistence.

As requested by the memo of August 29, therefore, Father Janssens, who only four years earlier had declared that "the principal object of the Jesuit Order was the apostolate of the working class," on November 28, 1953, recalled his subjects from the mission. In February 1954 the Dominican master general, Emmanuel Suarez, too, recalled his men and accompanied the order with a demand for the resignation of three French Dominican provincials and for the removal to positions where their influence would be minimal of the theologians Chenu, Congar, Feret, and Boisselet.

Teilhard's reaction was more sadness than surprise. He called the event "a second Fourvière" which, because of the simple obedience of its victims, had probably been "just as disconcerting as Fourvière had been to the authorities." Memories of the attitudes that saw "work as a punishment, and research as something which one blesses without believing in it . . ." that he had seen on his visit to Rome in 1948 returned to him. The same old Vatican authorities were in power, still holding to the same opinions, though they were probably astonished now "to see that their missionaries sent among Marxists, instead of making converts, were themselves often converted. . . ."

Despite the volatility of the religious situation in France, Teilhard remained determined to get Ravier's permission for a return home that summer. On January 26 he wrote to him again for confirmation. He had already begun writing his an-

swer to the recent books by Galton Darwin and Rostand, a
sixty-five-page painstaking scientific representation of his conviction of man's uniqueness among animals, under the title
"Les Singularités de l'Espèce Humaine."[1]

The reply confirming his permission came in February.
Mrs. de Terra agreed to sail over with him on the *Flandres* on
June 4, but planned to return to New York in early August;
therefore Teilhard suggested to Père Leroy, who was planning
to resume his scientific work in Chicago in September, that
they return together.

He waited, alternately overjoyed and terrified. Before him
lay the prospect of breathing space in the Parisian air—the
only place, he often said, that he did not feel spiritually
suffocated. At the same time, he knew that if during this trip
he should fail again to win permission to "commute" between New York and Paris, he would never have another
chance at it.

In New York everything seemed to be coming apart around
him. The New York Jesuits had decided to remodel the rectory at St. Ignatius, "forcing," in Teilhard's words, "the
charming Father Gannon to throw seven [visiting] fathers
out of the house into the street within ten days." Through
Roger Straus, Teilhard found temporary quarters at the Lotus
Club, "a chic and quite cloistered men's club" a few blocks
from the Wenner-Gren and not far from a Dominican
church on Lexington Avenue where he could say daily Mass.
Coincidentally, the new location put him in even closer prox-
imity to Mrs. Swan, who had a bleak little apartment in the
East Sixties. Though he never stopped longing to make peace
with her, now with the desolation of old age stretched out before her like a tunnel, she almost violently rejected all his
overtures of friendship, and all her conversations with Teilhard somehow ended with her attacking everything to do
with Mrs. de Terra, from her "possessiveness," to her relative
youth, to her comfortable financial circumstances, and even
to her choice of hats.

After one completely impossible encounter in late March, Teilhard crossed the street to a liquor shop and scratched out on an order blank an almost desperate note to her, telling her again how unhappy he was to think he was the cause of her malaise. "Don't let me be!" he begged. "You know that I have found peace—the real peace of God's Presence. And there's nothing in the world I want more deeply for you, too, than this peace. . . . But," he added cautiously, "if you think it would be easier for you not to see me, let me know."

The next few months were full of planning and of packing. Rhoda, in high spirits, talked incessantly about her own "religious experiences," a topic which always embarrassed Teilhard, raised as he was in a Catholic mystical tradition which suspects all "enthusiasm" and fruitless "consolation." It bewildered him that Rhoda always seemed to be most vocally religious and most interested in prying into his own prayer life "when her health was at its best." Still he was grateful she felt so well, and on June 3 he set out with her for France.

The boat train pulled into St.-Lazare on the evening of the eighth. While Mrs. de Terra taxied off in the fading summer light to a little apartment an old friend had found her in the Passage de la Visitation, Teilhard set out again for *Études*.

Though a new superior, Père Jean Villain, was in charge, and though many of his old friends were already on vacation, Teilhard rejoiced to be once more in a "maison des amis." His friends had found a room for him among those left empty by the vacationing fathers. Père Chaillet was visiting the house; d'Ouince, superior now of the larger Jesuit residence on the Rue de Sèvres, was a short walk away; Lejay had waited for his coming; and de Lubac, who had returned from Nice, where he had been gathering material for a commemorative book on Valensin, dropped in to see him every morning. Immediately on Teilhard's arrival, young François Russo, with whom Teilhard had been corresponding regularly since he went to America, arranged for him to give a conference on

Africa under the sponsorship of a Catholic intellectual group in the Salle des Sociétés Savantes.

Scarcely a week after the news of his projected talk was out, everything turned sour. D'Ouince came in to see him one bright morning, pale and troubled. He had a message relayed straight from Rome which said that when the generalate heard of the projected conference, its reaction was to ask that he go back to America at once.

Go back at once? The warning was too sudden and unexpected. How could the Romans panic about a text they had not even seen? Would it appease them if he postponed the conference? But that was impossible since the announcements had already been made. No, he had to go ahead and give the conference. Then, when it was over, he could go down to Lyon and enlist Ravier's support for a prolongation of his stay.

Though immediately after d'Ouince's visit Teilhard had gone to a ship's agent and changed his booking to return with Mrs. de Terra on August 5, he was too embarrassed even to tell Leroy about it. His time was spent in socializing quietly, taking tea with Miss Hoffman (who was also summering in France) at Rhoda de Terra's flat, keeping up with his scientific contacts, and visiting the museum. To Jean Piveteau, with whom he was discussing plans for a Sorbonne-sponsored paleontology symposium which was to be held the following April, he gave the long "Singularités" paper (without the religious coda he had written when he thought that there was hope that he could publish it himself) to be printed in the *Annales de Paléontologie*.

On June 28 he steeled himself to give the lecture. He was acutely conscious of the hostility in the room and the presence of unfriendly Jesuits, all dressed "en clergyman." †
Though he had carefully designed his talk never to pass the bounds of the scientific, and though it was meticulously

† In France the soutane was required for all Catholic priests until 1962; the Roman collar and black suit was the dress of Protestant clergymen.

thought out, the effort of talking before that audience was too much for his nerves. His delivery was dull and lackluster, and when he finished, he did not wait to talk with his admirers.

Out on the Rue Danton, Leroy chatted with a lady auditor. Suddenly in the lighted doorway, he saw the silhouette of Teilhard, beside himself, quite "furious." Oblivious of everyone else, the scientist rushed over to his friend and asked him to drive him back to *Études* at once.

A few days later, with Leroy chauffeuring a big, shiny, black Citroën D-11, he made a trip to Lyon. As soon as possible he called on Ravier and, sitting tensely in his office on Montée Fourvière with the great windows open to the sky, asked him, as a kind of test, to convey to Rome his wish to be allowed to stay in France at least long enough to answer Rostand briefly. Ravier agreed, and putting his problems momentarily from his mind, Teilhard ended a "luminous" day chatting with Sommet, Victor Fontoynont, and the visiting de Lubac and showing slides of Africa to the admiring scholastics.

On July 5 (in the company of Mrs. de Terra, who had come to Lyon to be with him) he and Leroy drove over to Auvergne to visit Sarcenat. On the terrace of the barony where he had played so many boyhood summers, he chatted briefly with his brother Victor's widow, Marguerite. Then he led his two friends wordlessly inside across the dark wood floors from room to room, his opaque gaze glancing off one object after another as though trying to recover something he had misplaced. Only in the bedroom, where his mother's big blue chair had stood between the oleograph of the Sacred Heart and the plaster Infant Jesus, did he address his companions. "This," he seemed to muse aloud, "is the room where I was born."

From Sarcenat the trio went down to Lascaux in the Dordogne to see its famous cave paintings. For a half hour Teilhard passed breathlessly through caves still magic with the dreams of the awakening human imagination, the exquisite renderings in yellow, red, and black of wounded stags and galloping horses, and of bisons so powerfully conceived that a Picasso might approve them. Then, to please Mrs. de Terra, he asked Leroy to drive to George Sand's château near La Châtre. Though Teilhard napped most of the journey to the writer's shrine, he was bright and witty on the way to Paris through the château country of the Loire.

Back at *Études* everyone tried to be cordial. De Lubac and d'Ouince returned; Russo rushed in and out. But Teilhard's depression grew. When Claude Cuénot visited him on July 7, he thought he could detect something like near-cynicism under Teilhard's kindly graceful manner. The old priest was so upset that month that finally one rainy afternoon, rereading a coda he had added to "Le Cœur de la Matière" on "Le Féminin" he began to weep uncontrollably at the memory of all the reproachful "Beatrices" he knew he had hurt unwittingly during his lifetime.

Rome's reply to Ravier's "test" letter was forwarded to him near the month's end. Before he finished it, he knew his cause was lost. It was "No" again to everything—to the extension of his visit, to the new *Ce Que Je Crois* he wanted to write in answer to Rostand. "Now I understand," Teilhard wrote Ravier, "and I know how to obey." As if the answer sent to Ravier were not enough, on July 31 Teilhard received a letter addressed to him personally and directing him to go back to America. Père d'Ouince has recorded, as an example of Teilhard's soldierly obedience, his visit to his friend that morning. Scarcely had he crossed the threshold of the room when Teilhard came toward him smiling, arms extended in the old familiar gesture of greeting. "How good of you to visit me today," he said. "What a beautiful feast of St. Ignatius!"[2]

How much real submission, how much patience, how much passion, or even how much downright irony lay behind Teilhard's remark is impossible to guess. Whatever else he felt, he surely knew that he had missed his final chance at spreading his mission in his lifetime. This time the blow was mortal. This time, he could not count on strategy, influence, or even time to help him. He was seventy-three and under an irrevocable sentence to labor in a foreign attic until death.

After one stop in England to visit Kenneth Oakley, he sailed with Mrs. de Terra for America. Both the Strauses were waiting on the dock. They drove him up to Purchase, where he made what he called his deepest and "most orthodox" retreat since 1948 and one from which he emerged fortified and resigned to his fate. Despite the "chaotic" impression the weeks at home had left on him, he wrote friends, he now felt more determined than ever to consecrate the remainder of his life to absolute fidelity to the Church that silenced him, as his function in bringing about the kingdom of the "universal Christ" he wished to preach.

The remodeling of the St. Ignatius rectory was not expected to be completed until spring at least, and Teilhard and de Breuvery had to find a more permanent place to live. Mrs. de Terra discovered for them a pair of connecting rooms on the sixth floor of the Hotel Fourteen, at that time a respectable middle-class apartment-hotel much used by the French community.

In September on his way out to Chicago, Père Leroy spent a few days at the hotel. In mid-October, Teilhard went to the seminar on "The Unity of Human Knowledge" at Averell Harriman's Arden House, amid the gold and purple sycamores of the Catskills, with a group of physicists (Niels Bohr, John von Neumann), naturalists (Huxley), philosophers (Gilson), and theologians (Henry van Dusen). But it was only to see once more, to his chagrin, how impossible it was for humanists and scientists to reach accord. In December he declined Jean Piveteau's invitation to attend the next April's more promising Sorbonne paleontology symposium in Paris, but he did manage to send a paper.[3]

All fall and winter, Teilhard seemed gentler and more thoughtful than anyone remembered having seen him before.

He shared de Breuvery's worry about whether or not he would be well enough to pass the physical examination required to accept a permanent United Nations contract, but now Teilhard showed so little of his old intellectual fire that the younger priest sought other occupations to fill the time he might have spent with him. De Breuvery formed a small group to study Scripture; he renewed his old interest in horseback riding; he developed a stronger interest in French films playing in New York. " 'En haut! En avant!' " he sighed to a friend about Teilhard; "that's all he ever talks about! One begins to be bored."

But Teilhard's new self-control can be easily interpreted another way—as witness to the vehemence of the prayer that he was making. Mrs. Straus has described coming upon him unawares while he paced her Purchase garden with his breviary in his hands. "It was a bleak and windy day," she wrote. "The old elm at the end of the garden was bare, its black branches gesticulating wildly in the gale." Through the closed french windows she suddenly saw "a tall figure, black coattails flapping, a supernatural apparition with an open prayerbook held in long hands—a pious scarecrow circling the house. Like the elm, it seemed conjured from the elements, untamed as the wind itself, dark as a storm-tossed sky. . . ."[4]

Near Christmas, Leroy passed through New York again and stopped to see Teilhard. The winter was at its ugliest. In three days a two-inch snow had turned into a dirty ooze. Leroy found his friend as sad as he had ever seen him. As they slogged across the slushy streets to a nearby coffee shop for lunch, Teilhard remarked, as though musing to himself, "Right now in my life it's 'ten minutes before midnight.' " Leroy turned and stared at him. Because he could sense the struggle underneath the calm, he asked, "How do you feel?" To which Teilhard replied, to his surprise, "Oh, I'm much less anxious than I used to be. . . . Would you believe it? I really feel that now I'm always living in God's presence."

As his depression deepened, Teilhard now found sleep a

more and more elusive thing. His hotel room seemed smaller
and more dismal daily. If he still rose sleepless in the night as
he had done at St. Ignatius, it could not be to look into the
street. Outside his window was nothing but the air shaft and
the Copacabana wall, lit by the reflection of neon lights from
uncertain sources—a light show only faintly reminiscent of
what he had seen those gun-lit nights in the Aisne basin,
when his mind went back to other times and lights, all the
way to his childhood and the two multicolored lights flashing
in the Clermont railroad station, that led away to strange exotic places.[5]

In January Teilhard wrote Msgr. de Solages to congratulate
him on a newly published book about the prophecies of
Isaiah and on his plan to undertake a second book, on metaphysics. As for himself, Teilhard confessed he had never been
able to deal with analysis of reality by deduction. "Only a
type of physics, proceeding *per ascensum*, a function of general laws of energetics, rather than a function of pure
thought" had ever made real sense to him. "For what it's
worth, though," Teilhard volunteered, "I'm thinking of examining . . . my Weltanschauung again." Although unpublishable, of course, he hoped his essay might "help to
bring about the appearance of the 'trans-Christian' God we
have all been waiting for. . . . Toynbee is right," he said,
"when he remarks that we have already passed out of the
'Christian era.'" But he objected to the word "post-Chris-
tian" to describe them. "'Trans-Christian' would be a better
word," he said. "And I am convinced that only when the
Church sets out to re-examine the relationship between
Christ and a universe now grown fantastically immense and
organic will she take up her conquering march again." In fact,
he continued, the Church could only survive when in her
theology she subdistinguished in the "human nature" of the
Incarnate Word a "cosmic" (relating to the universe) as well
as a "terrestrial" (purely historic) aspect. Until that time, neither Christian faith nor charity would be stretched to the full

breadth of their potentialities. "The situation is simultaneously tragic and magnificently clear. . . . If only Rome
would start to doubt herself at last, a little!"

March brought a sudden unseasonal return of winter, and
an almost daily fall of snow or rain. Waiting for spring,
Teilhard wrote (for Ravier's eyes alone) a repetition of his interpretation of the function of the scientist and working man
in bringing about the Kingdom.[6]

For months, he had been living with a strange sense of
things coming to climax. To Mme. Lemaître, to Msgr. de
Solages, to Père Ravier, and to many others, he wrote about
the feeling. It seemed to him, he said, that Christianity was
reliving, at a distance of sixteen hundred years, a psychological conflict as profound as the one it had endured at the
time of the great Arian heresy and a crisis that cried out as
desperately for solution.

In other words, in the fourth century it had taken a landmark council to lay upon the cornerstone of the perfect di-
vinity (as well as the humanity) of Christ the foundation for
Western theology in the next two millennia. Now, at another
stage of human development, another equally significant
council was required—not just another small prophetic council to momentarily uncover all the Church's struggling, stifled
problems, but a "new Nicaea" which, in its exploration of the
"cosmic" aspect of the God-Man, would lay the groundwork
for advances in every area of theological thinking, thus set-
tling the various arguments between sacred and profane
knowledge which had arisen over the last five hundred years,
and preparing theologians to come to grips with present and
future problems.

Teilhard had not the slightest doubt that such a council
had to come. And when it did, he felt religious faith would,
for the first time perhaps, become an explicit motive for
human progress. Despite the fact that the Church had removed him from the field of combat, "never," he wrote Mlle.
Mortier, "have I felt as deeply linked to her as I do now."

"And never," he wrote another friend, "have I felt more certain that, once the re-examination I'm proposing has been made, hers will be the religion of the future."

On the face of it, at that point Teilhard's remarks seemed only wild imagining. In Rome, thanks to the ministrations of his brigade of doctors, Pius XII had recovered his faltering health and was busy bemoaning the slippage in the number of religious vocations in Europe, denouncing Perónist anticlericalism, and planning to institute that year a feast day for St. Joseph the Worker—presumably to give the working class (deprived of their priest comrades) a model for the virtues with which they should bear their difficult lot.

That month Teilhard finished the philosophical papers he had mentioned in his letter to de Solages. But now he wrote "only for posterity." He sent copies of his essays to Ravier and to the archives kept for him in Paris by Père Russo and Mlle. Mortier. Still, during the Lenten season he was unusually restless, and suddenly he seemed to yearn for some sort of affirmation for his work. If only, he remarked to several people, God would put some seal of approbation on his life, even though he himself would never live to see his work published. How splendid if, for instance, he should die on Good Friday, the day when Christians commemorate Jesus' death, or better still, on Easter.

Good Friday 1955 came, cool and cloudy, with weather typical of the city between seasons. Teilhard used part of the day to write to Ravier, an almost weary repetition of his lifelong contention that "Evil is not 'catastrophic' (the fruit of some cosmic accident), but the inevitable side effect of the process of the comos unifying into God." The day came and went, leaving him as it had found him.

He passed his Holy Saturday much as he usually did. He and de Breuvery made their confessions to one another in the morning, and followed their old custom of postponing their Easter Mass from Saturday to Sunday. That year for the first time de Breuvery, who had spent the previous Sunday afternoon with Teilhard and Miss Hoffman at Rhoda's apartment, decided to spend Easter in the Connecticut monastery Teilhard had visited three years earlier, in order to say his Mass in its piney, golden chapel full of chant. Before he left, he moved the portable altar with the aluminoid-looking collapsible chalice he had borrowed from *Études* years earlier, on which he and his old friend so often served at each other's morning Mass, into Teilhard's room.

When Teilhard came home to his hotel that night, he was, therefore, alone. The weather had suddenly turned warm, making the dismal, tan-walled room seem smaller and stuffier than usual. Outside the window was the gaping darkness of the air shaft and the wall.

As Teilhard flashed on the light, he still did not feel very well. He played with the idea of calling Roger Straus to cancel the next day's project of traveling to the country in favor of resting in the city under the care of Mrs. de Terra. Afterwards, in the scattered dark, whether he tossed in bed or rose to take more notes for his unpublishable papers, he could not but have been bitterly aware of what lay before him now. There would only be more days when he would not feel well enough to leave the city, more empty time to fill with writing essays hardly anyone would read, and—since field work had become more difficult—more paper work in his claustrophobic office in the Wenner-Gren.

All he really had to say of his situation, he had said a few weeks earlier in "Le Christique," one of the most explicit analyses of his feelings he had ever written.

"How is it possible," he had sighed then, that " 'descending from the mountain' and despite the glory that I carry in my eyes, I am so little changed for the better, so lacking in peace, so incapable of passing on to others through my conduct, the vision of the marvelous unity in which I feel myself immersed? . . .

"As I look about me, how is it I find myself entirely alone of my kind? . . .

"Why am I the only one who sees?"[7]

And so the struggle of a lifetime seemed only to have come to this—a tiny room to wait in, and a wall. Like the monk of the Auvergnat legend, Teilhard seemed to have followed his Bird of Paradise across the world only to lose himself in the adventure. Like the imagined seeker in an essay he had written the previous New Year's, he found himself now standing in his mind before a barrier that blocked out any sign of what, behind it, justified more effort.

But was that wall outside his hotel-room window really just the rain-stained, impermeable mass it seemed? Or was it, like the volcanic stone of Auvergne, lit with a brilliance from within?

# EPILOGUE

The week after Low Sunday, Père Ravier returned to Lyon from Alsace. In the old convent where he had gone for his retreat he first heard on the radio the news of Teilhard's death. At Fourvière, a letter from Père Leroy, was waiting.* It was dated April 13, 1955.

*Reverend and dear Father Provincial,*

*Our dear Father Teilhard has left us. You must have received Father de Breuvery's telegram on Monday morning. . . . The accident occurred on Easter Sunday at six o'clock in the evening. . . . The Father passed a most pleasant day: High Mass at St. Patrick's Cathedral in the morning and a walk in the afternoon. The weather was radiant; and he was quite happy about how he spent the time.*

*At six o'clock he found himself with friends, speaking quietly with the other guests. He was standing, when suddenly he fell to the ground as though stricken from behind. At the end of a few minutes, he seemed to regain consciousness. "Where am I? . . ." he asked. "What happened?" A lady who rushed to help and press a pillow beneath his head then tried to calm him. "You're with us," she said. "You recognize me, don't you?" "Yes," he said, "but what happened?" —He could not remember anything.*

*His hostess telephoned his doctor; but he was away. Another physician, who arrived a few minutes later, at once realized the end was near. A call was placed to Father de Breuvery; but he was out of town. A priest from St. Ignatius High School, Father Martin Geraghty . . . arrived. But by then, Father Teilhard had already given up his soul.*

*He had made his confession the day before and celebrated [private] Easter Mass. He died of a cerebral hemorrhage. . . .*

* Père Leroy had flown to New York from Chicago the day after Teilhard's death.

# Notes

# I. THE BURNING BUSH

### CHAPTER ONE
1. "Le cœur de la matière," Les Moulins, 1950.

### CHAPTER FOUR
1. March 22, 1917.
2. "Nostalgie du front," September 1917.
3. "La grande monade," September 1917.
4. November 1917.
5. January 1918.

### CHAPTER SIX
1. April 1922.
2. "La paléontologie et l'apparition de l'homme," *Revue de philosophie*, March–April 1923.

### CHAPTER SEVEN
1. "La Messe sur le monde," summer 1923.
2. Tientsin, March 25, 1924.

### CHAPTER EIGHT
1. "Le paradoxe transformiste," finally published in *Revue des questions scientifiques*, January 1927.
2. Paris, May 6, 1925.
3. December 1924.
4. "Les fondements et le fond de l'idée d'évolution," Gulf of Bengal, Ascension Day 1926.

# II. THE CHINA YEARS

### CHAPTER NINE
1. Essays printed as *L'exigence idéaliste et le fait de l'évolution* (Paris: Bavain, 1927–28).
2. February 12, 1929.

## Chapter Ten

1. "Que faut-il penser du transformisme?" Peking, June–July 1929.

## Chapter Eleven

1. Claude Aragonnès, *La loi du faible* (Paris: Calmann-Levy, 1925).
2. "Esprit de la terre," in the Pacific, March 1931.
3. Maynard Owen Williams, "From the Mediterranean to the Yellow Sea by Motor," *National Geographic*, November 1932.
4. "Christologie et évolution," Tientsin, Christmas 1933.

## Chapter Twelve

1. March 1918.
2. "L'évolution de la chasteté," Peking, February 1934.
3. Peking, December 1934.
4. "La découverte du passé," September 1935.

## Chapter Thirteen

1. "Esquisse d'univers personnel," May 4, 1936.
2. "Quelques réflexions sur la conversion du monde," Peking, October 9, 1936.
3. Published in *Études*, October 1937.
4. "L'énergie humaine," Marseille–Shanghai, August 6–September 8, 1937.

## Chapter Fourteen

1. "Le phénomène spirituel," Pacific Ocean, March 1937.

# III.  THE WAR

## Chapter Fifteen

1. *Le phénomène humain* (Paris: Éditions du Seuil, 1955). *The Phenomenon of Man*, trans. Bernard Wall (London: William Collins Sons & Co., Ltd.; New York: Harper & Row, 1959).

## Chapter Sixteen

1. "Sur les basses possibles d'un credo humain commun," Peking, March 30, 1941.
2. "Nostalgie du front," 1917.

## Chapter Seventeen

1. "La place de l'homme dans l'univers: Réflexions sur la complexité," published in Peking, November 15, 1942.
2. "Réflexions sur le bonheur," Peking, December 28, 1943.

## Chapter Eighteen

1. Peking, finished June 20, 1944.
2. Jean Decoux, *A la barre de l'Indochine*, (Paris: Plon, 1949).
3. Henry Shaw, Jr., *The United States Marines in North China: 1945–49*, Historical Branch, G-3 Division Headquarters, United States Marine Corps, Washington, D.C.
4. "Un grand événement qui se dessine: La planetisation humaine," Peking, December 25, 1945.

# IV. JUDGMENT

## Chapter Nineteen

1. An English edition appeared under the title *France Pagan?: The Mission of Abbé Godin* (New York: Sheed & Ward, 1949).
2. John Petrie (translator), *The Worker-Priests* (New York: Macmillan, 1954).
3. "Quelques réflexions sur le retentissement spirituel de la bombe atomique," *Études*, September 1946.
4. "Le Christianisme et la science," *Esprit*, August–September 1946.
5. Paris, December 15, 1946.
6. "Hérédité et progrès," *Études*, April 1947.
7. "Esquisse d'un dialectique de l'esprit," Paris, November 25, 1946.
8. "Un colloque scientifique sur l'évolution," *Études*, April 1947.

## Chapter Twenty

1. "La foi en la paix," January 1947.
2. "Place de la technique dans une biologie générale de l'humanité," Paris, January 16, 1947.
3. "La foi en l'homme," Paris, February 1947.
4. "Quelques réflexions sur les droits de l'homme," Paris, March 22, 1947.
5. "La valeur religieuse de la recherche," St.-Germain-en-Laye, August 1947.
6. "Le rebondissement humain de l'évolutio et ses conséquences," St.-Germain-en-Lave, September 23, 1947.
7. "Réflexions sur le péché originel," Paris, November 15, 1947.
8. "Agitation ou genèse? Y-a-til dans l'univers un axe principal d'évolution?" Paris, December 20, 1947.

## Chapter Twenty-one

1. Paris, February 1948.
2. *Autour da ma foi* (Paris: Aubier, 1948).
3. "Les directions et les conditions de l'avenir," Paris, June 30, 1948.
4. "Ce que la science nous apprend de l'evolution: Conséquences pour notre apostolat," Paris, September 21, 1948.

### Chapter Twenty-three

1. "La peur existentielle," Paris, January 25, 1949.
2. This essay was published in *Psyché* in February 1950.
3. "Une nouvelle question de Galilée," St.-Gemain-en-Laye, May 1949.
4. "Le cœur du problème," Les Moulins, September 8, 1949.
5. *Revue des questions scientifiques,* October 20, 1949.
6. "Sur l'existence probable, en avant de nous, d'un ultrahumain," Paris, January 6, 1950.
7. Teilhard's introduction, called "L'énergie spirituelle de la souffrance," to the life of his sister Guiguite, written by Monique Givelet, January 8, 1950.
8. "Comment concevoir et espérer que se réalise sur terre l'unanimisation humaine," Paris, January 18, 1950.
9. "Qu'est-ce que la vie?" March 2, 1950.
10. Paris, April 27, 1950.
11. June 1950.
12. "Pour y voir clair: Réflexions sur deux formes inverses d'esprit," July 25, 1950.
13. New York: Paulist Press, 1950.
14. Then *L'observateur politique, économique, et littéraire,* August 31, 1950.

### Chapter Twenty-four

1. "Le cœur de la matière," Les Moulins, September 1950.
2. "Le goût de vivre," Paris, December 9, 1950.

## V. BY BABYLON'S WATERS

### Chapter Twenty-five

1. "Convergence de l'univers," Cape Town, July 23, 1951.
2. Dorothea Straus, *Showcases* (Boston: Houghton Mifflin, 1975).
3. "En regardant un cyclotron: Réflexions sur le reploiement sur soi de l'énergie humaine," *Recherches et débats* (Paris: Fayard), No. 4 (April 1953), pp. 123–30.
4. Straus, op. cit.
5. "Ce que le monde attend en ce moment de l'Église de Dieu: une généralisation et un approfondissement du sens de la croix," finished at the Straus estate in Purchase, New York, September 14, 1952.

### Chapter Twenty-six

1. "Hominisation et spéciation," *Revue scientifique,* December 1952.
2. "La fin de l'espèce," *Psyche* (New York), December 9, 1952.

3. Petrie, op. cit., p. 24.
4. December 24, 1952.
5. "L'énergie de l'évolution," New York, May 24, 1953.
6. "Une suite au problème des origines humaines—la multiplicité des mondes habités," New York, June 15, 1953.
7. Straus, op. cit.
8. "Le Dieu de l'évolution," October 25, 1953.
9. "Sur la probabilité d'une bifurcation précoce du phylum humain au voisinage immédiat de ses origines," New York, November 23, 1953.
10. Garden City: Doubleday & Co., 1953.
11. Paris: Grasset, 1953.

## Chapter Twenty-seven

1. Finished in New York on March 25, 1954.
2. René d'Ouince, *Un Prophète en procès* (Paris: Aubier, 1970).
3. "Une défense de l'orthogénèse," New York, January 1955.
4. Straus, op. cit.
5. "Nostalgie du front," 1917.
6. "Recherche, travail, et adoration," New York, March 1955.
7. "Barrière de la mort et co-réflexion, ou De l'éveil imminent de la conscience humaine au sens de son irréversion," New York, January 1–5, 1955.

# Notes to the Paperback Edition

(Italic figures refer to lines on designated pages)

| | |
|---|---|
| *14, 27* | Jacques Levron, *Contes et legendes d'Auvergne* (Paris: Fernand Nathan, 1948). |
| *20, 16–30* | Unpublished family memoirs by Joseph Teilhard de Chardin, "Et sousvenirs qui moult s'avance" (title derived from a 13th century saying). |
| *21, 21* | Alice Teillard-Chambon to the authors. |
| *21, 22–35* | Adrien Dansette, *Histoire religieuse de la France contemporaine* (Paris: Flammarion, 1948). |
| *22, 10–19* | Unpublished family memoir by Joseph Teilhard de Chardin, *Sarcenat.* |
| *23, 7* | Ibid. |
| *25, 18* | Prize lists, now in the possession of the Assumptionist Fathers, present directors of Mongré. |
| *25, 19–22* | Letter from Teilhard to his parents on the occasion of his entry into the "Cinquième" at Mongré. |
| *26, 13–14* | Teilhard's notebook, now in the possession of his family; also, Joseph Teilhard de Chardin, *"Et sousvenirs . . ."* |
| *26, 29 to 27, 15* | Dansette, *Histoire religieuse.* |
| *27, 34* | To his parents, January 4, 1906, collected in *Lettres d'Egypte* (Paris: Aubier, 1963). |
| *27, 36* | Monique Givelet, *Marguerite-Marie Teilhard de Chardin* (Paris: Editions du Seuil, 1951). |
| *28, 1–36* | Joseph Teilhard de Chardin, *Sarcenat.* |
| *20–31* | Dansette, *Histoire religieuse.* |
| *30, 13* | Pope Leo XIII, *Aeterni Patris*, August 4, 1879 (Reprinted by Paulist Press, New York, N.Y. 1951). |
| *31, 18* | *Jesuit Catalogue of the Province of Lyon*, 1903. |
| *31–32* | "Le coeur de la matière," Les Moulins, 1950. |
| *32–33* | Souvenirs of Jersey, individual "Hommages" and obituaries collected in the Jesuit Archives of Les Fontaines, Chantilly; additional material, Henri de Lubac, S.J., and Joseph LeCler, S.J., to the authors. |
| *32, 25 to 33, 3* | "Le coeur de la matière," letters from Teilhard to his parents, September 5, 1905, and subsequent dates. *Lettres d'Egypte. 1905–1908* (Paris: Editions Montaigne, 1963). |
| *33, 5–30* | "Le coeur de la matière." |
| *34, 10* | *Annuario Pontificio 1910* (Rome: Vatican Press). |

**34, 11–22**    *Documenta Romana Beatificanis et Canonisationis Servis Dei Pii Papae X* (Rome: Vatican Press, 1950); Emile Poulat, *Intégrisme et catholicisme intégral. Un réseau secret international antimoderniste: La 'Sapinière' (1909–1921)* (Paris: Casterman, 1969).

**35, 19**    Henri de Lubac, S.J. (ed.), *Auguste Valensin: textes et documents inédits* (Paris: Aubier-Montaigne, 1961).

**35, 29**    "Le coeur de la matière."

**36, 1–20**    Letter from Teilhard to his father (hereafter, all letters from Teilhard identified as "to" and the recipient's name), July 1, 1909, *Lettres d'Hastings et de Paris, 1908–14*, Introduction by Henri de Lubac, annotation by Auguste Demoment and Henri de Lubac (Paris: Aubier-Montaigne, 1965).

**36, 26 to**    J. S. Weiner, *The Piltdown Forgery* (London, Oxford University
**37, 3**    Press, 1955); also, letter from Charles Dawson to Arthur Smith Woodward, February 10, 1911. Archives of the British Museum (Natural History) (unpublished).

**37, 16**    Auguste Demoment, S.J., "De Sarcenat and Lao-gnen-dang," *Decouverte (Bulletin trimestriel des Petites Soeurs des Pauvres* (Rennes: Automne 1975); letter to his parents, June 17, 1911 (*Lettres d'Hastings*).

**37, 17—33**    To his parents, August 1, 1911 (*Lettres d'Hastings*); also, Joseph Teilhard de Chardin, "Sarcenat."

**39, 3**    Marthe Vaufrey to the authors.

**39, 6 ff.**    Description of ambience of Boule's quarters at Museum, Jean Piveteau to the authors.

**39, 22**    Teilhard's tribute to Boule on the occasion of his jubilee, *L'Anthropologie*, 1937–47 (Paris).

**40, 11**    Gilbert Guilleminault (ed.), *Avant 14* (Paris: Denoël, 1965).

**41, 22**    To his parents, October 30, 1912 (*Lettres d'Hastings*).

**41, 23 ff.**    Alice Teilhard de Chardin and Joseph Teilhard de Chardin to the authors.

**41, 32**    To his parents, December 23, 1912 (*Lettres d'Hastings*).

**42, 7**    To his parents, February 5, 1912 (*Lettres d'Hastings*).

**42, 22**    Denise de Sonneville-Bordes, *La Préhistoire moderne; l'age de la pierre taillée* (Périgueux: Pierre Fanlac, 1972).

**43, 2**    Letter to his parents, June 16, 1913 (*Lettres d'Hastings*).

**43, 7–25**    Weiner, *The Piltdown Forgery*.

**43, 12**    To his parents, June 3, 1912 (*Lettres d'Hastings*).

**43, 28**    To his parents, August 15, 1913 (*Lettres d'Hastings*).

**43, 31–33**    To his parents, September 10, 1913 (*Lettres d'Hastings*).

**44, 2**    Teilhard's letter to Dr. Kenneth S. Oakley, reconstructing his memory of the event, November 28, 1953; Archives, British Museum (Natural History).

**44, 13**    To his parents, November 14, 1913 (*Lettres d'Hastings*).

**45, 8**    To his parents, August 9, 1914 (*Lettres d'Hastings*).

**45, 35**    To his mother, September 24, 1914 (*Lettres d'Hastings*).

**448 ff.**    André Maurois, *Histoire de France*, vol. VI (New York: Editions de la Maison Française, Inc., 1948); also, letters to his parents, February 9, 1915 to Christmas Eve, 1915.

| | |
|---|---|
| 49, 11 | Letters to Marguerite Teillard-Chambon, December 13, 1914 to January 8, 1916, *Genèse d'une Pensée* (Paris, Grasset, 1961). |
| 49, 36 | Teilhard's original notebook which was in the possession of Alice Teillard Chambon at the time it was read by the authors. |
| 50, 5 | To Marguerite (*Genèse d'une pensée*). |
| 50, 36 | Joseph Teilhard de Chardin to the authors. |
| 51, 8 | Alice Teillard-Chambon to the authors. |
| 51, 20–27 | To Marguerite, April 9, and June 25, 1916 (*Genèse d'une pensée*). |
| 52, 21 | To Marguerite, January 6, 1917 (*Genèse d'une pensée*). |
| 53, 21 | To Marguerite, September 23, 1917 (*Genèse d'une pensée*). |
| 54, 7 | Paul Galland, *Histoire de la Grand Guerre* (Paris: G. Durassie & Cie, 1965). |
| 54, 11 | *Jesuit Catalogues of the Province of Lyon*, 1914, 1916. |
| 54–55 | To Marguerite (varia), 1916–18 (*Genèse d'une pensée*); also, Joseph Teilhard de Chardin, "*Et Sousvenirs....*" |
| 55–57 | To Marguerite, July 15, 1918 and January 1, 1919 (*Genèse d'une pensée*); also, Joseph Teilhard de Chardin to the authors. |
| 58, 26 | Alice Teillard-Chambon to the authors. |
| 58, 31 to 59, 19 | To Marguerite, April 4, 1919 (*Genèse d'une pensée*). |
| 61, 6 to 62, 7 | Henri de Lubac (ed.), *Auguste Valensin: Textes et documents inédits* (Paris: Aubier, 1961). |
| 62, 8 ff. | Gabriel David Astruc, *Pavillion des fantômes* (Paris: Grasset, 1929); also, Maurice Sachs, *Decade of Illusion, Paris: 1918–28* (New York: Knopf, 1933) and Gertrude Stein, *The Autobiography of Alice B. Toklas* (Reprinted, New York: Vintage Books, 1961). |
| 64, 19 | "Chute, rédemption et géocentricité," July 20, 1920. |
| 64–65 | *Acta Apostolicae Sedis*, vol. XVII. (Rome); obituaries and memoirs of the Society of Jesus conserved in the Library of *Etudes*, Paris; also, Dansette, *Histoire religieuse*. |
| 65, 31 ff. | "Wladimir Ledochowski, Obituary," *Acta Romana S.J.*, 1942; also testimony of various American, French and Italian Jesuits to the authors. |
| 66, 1–13 | *Auguste Valensin: Textes et documents inédits*. |
| 66, 13 | Letter of Father General Wladimir Ledochowski, July 15, 1920, entitled "Doctrina de actii fidei a R. Petro Rousselot p.m. proposita prohibetur," *Acta Romana S.J.*, 1920. |
| 66, 22 | Letter to Valensin, February 28, 1920, in Henri de Lubac (ed.), *Pierre Teilhard de Chardin: Lettres intimes à Auguste Valensin, Bruno de Solages, Henri de Lubac, André Ravire, 1919–1955* (Paris: Aubier-Montaigne, 2nd ed., 1974). |
| 67, 10 | To Valensin, August 11, 1920 (*Lettres intimes*). |
| 67, 20 | To Arthur Smith Woodward, August 1920, Archives, British Museum (Natural History) (unpublished). |
| 69, 7 | To Valensin, July 4, 1920 (*Lettres intimes*). |
| 70, 2 | Edouard LeRoy, *Etude de philosophie et critique religieuse: Dogme et critique* (Paris: Bloud, 1907). |
| 70, 17 to 71, 16 | Jean Piveteau, "Les debuts de l'oeuvre scientifique du Père Teilhard de Chardin," *Europe*, March–April 1965; also Piveteau to the authors. |

**71, 26 to**
**73, 18**
General description by René d'Ouince, S.J., to the authors; quotation is from a letter to Valensin, Holy Saturday 1922 (*Lettres intimes*); subsidiary sources are *Jesuit Catalogue of the Province of Champagne*, 1922.

**74, 14**
To Valensin, May 14, 1922 (*Lettres intimes*).

**75, 36**
To Valensin, December 17, 1922 (*Lettres intimes*).

**76, 8**
The others include Marguerite, May 11, 1923, *Ecrits du temps de la Guerre* (Paris: Grasset, 1965).

**77, 8**
To the Abbé Henri Breuil, May 25, 1923 (unpublished).

**77–78**
John B. Powell, *My Twenty-Five Years in China* (New York: Macmillan, 1945); Arthur N. Holcombe, *The Spirit of the Chinese Revolution* (New York: Knopf, 1930); James E. Sheridan, *Chinese Warlord: The Career of Feng Yu-hsiang* (Stanford University Press, 1966); Barbara W. Tuchman, *Stilwell and the American Experience in China, 1911–45* (New York: Macmillan, 1971); John K. Fairbank, *The United States and China* (Harvard University Press, 1958).

**79, 9**
"Le R.P. Emile Licent S.J.," *Bulletin des études indochinoises*, Nouve. serie. 41, 1966.

**79, 24**
To Breuil, December 12, 1923 (unpublished).

**80, 2–26**
Mrs. Bernard Read, William Drummond, and Mrs. O. Edmund Clubb to the authors; also, Arlington and Lewisohn, *In Search of Old Peking* (Peking: Henri Vetch, 1935); Nigel Cameron & Brian Brake, *Peking: A Tale of Three Cities* (New York: Harper, 1965); also, Mary Ferguson, *The China Medical Board and Peking Union Medical College: A Fruitful Collaboration* (New York: China Medical Board, 1970), and Ann Bridge, *Peking Picnic* (Boston: Little Brown, 1932).

**81, 12 to**
**83, 23**
Henri Bernard, "A la suite d'un explorateur au debut du XXme siècle: Le P. Licent et ses voyages dans la Chine du nord," *Etudes*, 1926; Emile Licent, *Hoang-ho, Pai-ho: comptes-rendus de seize années (1923–1939) de sejour et d'exploration dans le bassin du fleuve Jaune, du Pai-ho études autres tributaires de golfe de Pei Tcheuly*, Vols. 1–2 (Tientsin: Mission de Sienhsien, 1935–1936); also, letters to Abbé Christophe Gaudefroy and Breuil, August 15 to October 23, 1923 (unpublished).

**83, 24**
To Breuil, August 19, 1923 (unpublished).

**83, 30**
To Joseph Teilhard de Chardin, February 1924 (unpublished).

**84, 18–22**
*Acta Apostolicae Sedis*, vol. XIV (Rome).

**84, 22–25**
*Ibid*, vol. XV.

**84, 24**
Dansette, *Histoire religieuse*; letter to Gaudefroy, March 1, 1924, in *Lettres à l'Abbé Gaudefroy* (Paris: Fayard, 1973).

**84, 34**
July 13, 1924.

**85, 18**
De Lubac to the authors.

**85, 23**
Treat to the authors.

**86, 22**
November 13, 1924.

**87, 6**
Rene Fulop-Muller, *The Power and Secret of the Jesuits* (New York: Viking, 1930).

**88, 7**
Costa's description from his obituary notice in the Library of *Etudes*, Paris; route Teilhard and Valensin would have taken to the Provincialate traced by de Lubac for the authors.

| | |
|---|---|
| 91, 21 | To his parents, March 1925 (unpublished). |
| 91, 32 | *Acta Apostolicae Sedis*, Vol. XVI (Rome). |
| 91, 33 *ff.* | Obituary of Father General Ledochowski, *Acta Romana Societatis Jesu*; also, James Brodrick, S.J., and various other Jesuits to the authors. |
| 93, 2 | May 16, 1925. |
| 93, 11 | Treat to the authors. |
| 93, 36 | Ledochowski quotation repeated in letter to Valensin, June 12, 1925. |
| 94, 8 | D'Ouince to the authors. |
| 95, 7 | To Valensin, August 22, 1925. |
| 95, 18 | Recalled by Paul Rivet. Tribute to Teilhard given at *Débats de l'Assemblée nationale constituante*, March 15, 1946. |
| 99, 1–25 | O. Edmund Clubb, *Twentieth Century China* (New York: Columbia University Press, 1964). |
| 100, 27 | Lionel Max Chassin, *The Communist Conquest of China* (Cambridge: Harvard University Press, 1965). |
| 101, 14 | Mrs. Bernard Read, William Drummond, Mr. and Mrs. John Carter Vincent to the authors. |
| 101, 22 | To Joseph Teilhard de Chardin, October 26, 1926 (unpublished), and to Gaudefroy, November 12, 1926 (typescript). |
| 102, 3 | To Valensin, December 31, 1926 (*Lettres intimes*). |
| 102, 30 | To Treat, November 28, 1926, in *Letters to Two Friends* (New York: New American Library, 1968). |
| 103, 30 | To Edouard LeRoy, January 25, 1927 (unpublished). |
| 104, 17 | Ibid. |
| 106, 7 | Joseph Dopp, S.J., to the authors. |
| 106, 22 | To Valensin, June 28, 1928 (*Lettres intimes*). |
| 107, 28 | Ambassador Abdulrahmin Abby Farah to the authors; also, Ida Treat, "With the Slave Traders in Abyssinia," *Travel*, June 1931, and Henri de Monfreid, *Pears, Arms, and Hashish: Pages from the Life of a Red Sea Navigator* (London: Gollancz, 1930). |
| 108, 20 | De Monfreid to the authors. |
| 109, 5 | To his mother, January 1929 (unpublished). |
| 110, 14 | Month illegible, probably March 1929 (unpublished). |
| 111–113 | Davidson Black (ed.), with Teilhard de Chardin, C. C. Young, and W. C. Pei, *Fossil Man in China: The Choukoutien Cave Deposits with Synopsis of our Present Knowledge of the Late Cenozoic in China* (Peking: Geological Survey of China, 1933); also, Dora Hood, *Davidson Black: A Biography* (Toronto University Press, 1964). |
| 113, 16 | Mrs. Olga Hempel Gowan to the authors. |
| 113, 33 | To Gaudefroy, February 7, 1930 (typescript). |
| 113, 34 to 114, 9 | Mrs. Bernard Read to the authors. |
| 114, 14 | Gen. Worton (by telephone) to the authors. |
| 114, 26 | To Valensin, December 30, 1929 (*Lettres intimes*). |

| | |
|---|---|
| 115, 34 | John Carter Vincent and Read to the authors; quotation from de Monfreid is from his memoir of his adventure with Teilhard, printed in the Teilhard memorial issue of La Table Ronde, June 1955. |
| 116, 9 | George Barbour and Lucile Swan to the authors. |
| 118, 2 | February 7, 1930 (unpublished). |
| 118, 3 to 119, 20 | Vincent, Read, Swan, and Ida Pruitt to the authors. |
| 119, 21 | Roy Chapman Andrews. *New Conquest of Asia: A Narrative of the Exploits of the Central Asian Expedition in Mongolia and China: 1921–1930* (New York: American Museum of Natural History, 1932); also, Andrews, *Under a Lucky Star: A Lifetime of Adventure* (New York: Viking, 1943). |
| 121, 24 | Junius Bird to the authors. |
| 121, 32 | Georges Duhamel, *America the Menace: Scenes from the Life of the Future,* trans. Charles M. Thompson (Boston: Houghton Mifflin, 1931). |
| 122, 16 to 125, 18 | A. Raymond, "Resultats scientifiques d'un voyage en Asie Centrale, "Paris, *Revue de géologie physique,* 1938; also, George LeFevre, *Expedition Citroën Centre-Asie; la croisière jaune; troisième mission Georges-Marie Haardt* (Paris: Plon, 1933). |
| 126, 10 | To Edouard LeRoy, Dec. 21, 1931 (unpublished). |
| 126, 28 | Dansette, *Histoire religieuse.* |
| 126, 3 | Malvina Hoffman, *Yesterday Is Tomorrow: A Personal History* (New York: Crown, 1965); Hoffman, *Heads and Tales* (New York: Scribner's, 1936). |
| 127, 31 | To Swan, July 1933 (unpublished). |
| 128, 17 | To de Lubac, December 9, 1933 (*Lettres intimes*). |
| 129, 19 | Hood, *Davidson Black: A Biography.* |
| 130, 7 | To Swan, March 1934 (unpublished); also, Olga Hempel Gowan to the authors. |
| 130, 32 | George Barbour to the authors; also Barbour, *In the Field with Teilhard de Chardin* (New York: Herder & Herder, 1965). |
| 131, 7 | To Swan, May 23, 1934 (unpublished). |
| 113, 16 ff. | Swan, Pruitt, Drummond, Mrs. Vincent to the authors; letters to Swan, June 1933, November 1933, March 1934 (unpublished). |
| 134, 10 ff. | Swan, Pruitt, Drummond to the authors. |
| 134, 24 | To Swan, November 1933 (unpublished). |
| 134, 34 | To Swan, March 1934 (unpublished). |
| 134, 35 to 135, 18 | Swan, Pruitt, and Mrs. Vincent to the authors. |
| 135, 28 | To Valensin, November 11, 1934 (*Lettres intimes*). |
| 136, 20 | Swan to the authors; also letter to Swan, December 31, 1935, describing the events of the previous year (unpublished). |
| 136, 29 | To Swan, March 1935 (unpublished); also, Swan to the authors. |
| 137, 29 | *Jesuit Catalogues of the Province of Lyon,* 1904, 1911; *Jesuit Catalogue of the Province of France,* 1936; d'Ouince and LeCler to the authors. |
| 138, 8 | D'Ouince to the authors. |

| | |
|---|---|
| 139, 4 | D'Ouince and Joseph Teilhard de Chardin to the authors. |
| 139, 20 | Givelet, *Marguerite-Marie Teilhard de Chardin*; letter to Swan, August 13, 1935 (unpublished). |
| 139–140 | Helmut de Terra, *Memories of Teilhard de Chardin* (New York: Harper, 1964); also Pierre Teilhard de Chardin, "Chronique des alluvions pléistocènes de Java," *Anthropologie*, vol. XLV; letters to Swan and to his sister Marguerite-Marie (Guigite) (unpublished). |
| 140, 31 *ff.* | To his parents, September 10, 1935 (unpublished). |
| 141, 20 | To Swan, June 1935 (unpublished). |
| 141, 32 | January 26, 1936, in *Lettres à Léontine Zanta* (Paris: Desclée de Brouwer, 1965). |
| 142, 20 | Givelet, *Marguerite-Marie Teilhard de Chardin*. |
| 143, 23 | Drummond to the authors. |
| 144, 2 | Edgar Snow, *Red Star over China* (Garden City: Doubleday, 1938). |
| 144, 17 | Reported in *New York Times*, January 4, 1937. |
| 145, 3 | Read and Claire Taschdjian to the authors. |
| 145, 4–23 | Drummond to the authors. |
| 146, 9 | Villanova news story reported in *New York Times*, March 23, 1937. |
| 147, 2 | To Swan, May 1937 (unpublished). |
| 148, 6 | Reference to Treat in letter to Swan, June 27, 1937 (unpublished). |
| 152, 2 | Archives of Jesuit Missions, New York City, 1970. |
| 152, 10 | To Swan, December 20, 1937 (unpublished). |
| 153–154 | Teilhard's evaluation of the de Terras was made in a letter to Swan, April 4, 1937, while he was visiting them in Philadelphia during the Villanova celebration. |
| 154, 31 | To R. de Terra, June 22, 1938 (*Letters to Two Friends*); Barbour, *In the Field*. |
| 155, 14 | Leroy to the authors. |
| 155, 36 | Gowan to the authors. |
| 156, 30 | D'Ouince and LeCler to the authors. |
| 157, 6 | René d'Ouince, *Un prophète en procès: Teilhard de Chardin* (Paris: Aubier, 1970). |
| 157, 8 *ff.* | To Swan, January 10, 1939 (unpublished). |
| 157, 18 | Joseph Teilhard de Chardin and Régis Teilhard de Chardin to the authors. |
| 157, 32 | Treat to the authors; letter to Swan, January 1937 (unpublished). |
| 158–159 | Carlo Falconi, *The Popes in the Twentieth Century* (Boston: Little, Brown, 1967). |
| 160, 26 | *Ibid*; also, *Annuario Pontificio*, 1940; individual obituaries from the Library of *Etudes*, Paris. |
| 160, 21 | D'Ouince to the authors; also, letter to R. de Terra, May 7, 1939 (*Letters to Two Friends*). |
| 160, 28 | D'Ouince to the authors. |
| 161 to 162, 7 | Swan to the authors. |
| 163, 2 | To Joseph Teilhard de Chardin, December 11, 1939, excerpted in *Nouvelles lettres de voyage* (Paris: Grasset, 1957). |

| | |
|---|---|
| 172, 9 | This and preceding paragraph, *Le Coeur de la matière*. |
| 173, 32 | Jean-Paul Sartre, *Huis clos*, ed. Jacques Hardre and George B. Daniel (London: Methuen, 1964). |
| 176–177 | Leroy to the authors; also, letter to Breuil, December 15, 1939 (unpublished). |
| 178, 2–30 | *Nouvelle Revue Française*, vols. 27–28, 1939. |
| 179, 1–26 | Leroy to the authors. |
| 180, 7 | Description from letter to Swan, July 1940 (unpublished). |
| 180, 8 to 181, 2 | Leroy to the authors. |
| 181, 8 | Swan to the authors. |
| 181, 24 | Irena Wiley to the authors. |
| 182, 12 | Leroy, Raphael, and Burchart (by telephone) to the authors. |
| 182, 13 to 183, 2 | Leroy, Raphael, and Taschdjian to the authors; also, letters to Raphael written in that period (unpublished). |
| 183, 17 | To Joseph Teilhard de Chardin, October 3, 1930 (unpublished). |
| 184, 9 | Leroy to the authors; also, letters of July 20, 1940, and July 26, 1940 to Marguerite Teillard-Chambon, and September 28, 1940 to Max de Begouën (abridged in *Lettres de voyage*). |
| 185, 2 | Leroy to the authors. |
| 185, 7–8 | "Alea jacta est." From a letter to Breuil, April 18, 1941 (unpublished). |
| 185, 34 | Swan to the authors. |
| 186–187 | Swan and Drummond to the authors; letter to Swan, August 8, 1941 (unpublished). |
| 188, 32 | Leroy to the authors. |
| 190–191 | Burchart to the authors. |
| 191–192 | Mary Ferguson, Leroy, and William Foley to the authors; also, Henry Shaw, Jr. *The United States Marines in North China: 1945–49*, Historical Branch, G-3 Division Headquarters, USMC (Washington, D.C.). |
| 193, 20 to 194, 7 | Robert D. Murphy, *Diplomat among Warriors* (Garden City: Doubleday, 1964); also, Robert Aron, *Histoire de Vichy, 1940–44* (Paris: Fayard, 1954). |
| 194, 21 | Leroy to the authors. |
| 194, 22 to 196, 28 | Claude Rivière, *En Chine avec Teilhard* (Paris: Seuil, 1968); also, Emmanuel de Breuvery, S.J., to the authors. |
| 197, 13 | Roland de Margerie and Leroy to the authors; also, Rivière, *En Chine avec Teilhard*. |
| 198, 25 | "La place de l'homme dans l'univers: Réflexions sur la complexité," Peking, November 15, 1942. |
| 198, 26 to 199, 14 | Jennie de Margerie and Leroy to the authors; also, Rivière, *En Chine avec Teilhard*. |
| 199–201 | Leroy and Raphael to the authors; also, Georges Magloire and Hubert Cuypers, *Présence de Pierre Teilhard de Chardin: L'homme, la pensée* (Paris: Editions universitaires, 1961). |
| 201, 12 | Ferguson and Leroy to the authors. |
| 201, 33 | Leroy, Raphael, and Taschdjian to the authors; also, letter to J. de Margerie, March 24, 1943 (unpublished). |

| | |
|---|---|
| 201, 33 to<br>202, 34 | Leroy and Comtesse Raoul de Sercey to the authors. |
| 202, 34 | Leroy and de Breuvery to the authors. |
| 203, 7 | Admiral Jean Decoux, *A la barre de l'Indochine* (Paris: Plon, 1949). |
| 203, 9–31 | Raphael and Ferguson to the authors; also, Decoux, *A la barre*. |
| 203, 32 to<br>204 | Raphael to the authors; also, Magloire and Cuypers, *Presence de Pierre Teilhard de Chardin*. |
| 205, 11 | Ferguson and Leroy to the authors. |
| 205, 18 | Raphael and R. de Margerie to the authors. |
| 206, 3–31 | Leroy and Taschdjian to the authors. |
| 207–209 | Leroy and Raphael to the authors. |
| 209, 9 | Decoux, *A la barre*; also: Aron, *Histoire de Vichy*. |
| 210, 15 to<br>211, 17 | Raphael and Leroy to the authors. |
| 211–214 | Raphael, Ferguson, Leroy, and Gen. Carl S. Day to the authors. |
| 214, 18 | To Joseph Teilhard de Chardin, December 10, 1949 (unpublished); Raphael and Leroy to the authors. |
| 214, 19 | Tuchman, *Stilwell and the American Experience in China*; also, Chassin, *The Communist Conquest of China*. |
| 216, 19–29 | To Swan, March 5, 1946 (unpublished). |
| 217–218 | To Raphael, March 17, 1946, March 26, 1946 (unpublished); Joseph Teilhard de Chardin, Leroy, and Raphael to the authors. |
| 221, 20 | D'Ouince and Gaston Fessard, S.J., to the authors. |
| 222, 12 | Michel Riquet, S.J., *Chrétiens de France dans l'Europe enchaînée* (Paris: Editions S.O.S., 1971); also, Paul Dupire to the authors. |
| 222, 13 to<br>223, 9 | D'Ouince, de Lubac, and Fessard to the authors. |
| 223, 15 | Paul Philibert, O.P., to the authors. |
| 223, 16 to<br>224, 34 ff. | Robert Aron, *Histoire de l'épuration: De l'indulgence aux massacres, Novembre 1942–Septembre 1944* (Paris: Fayard, 1967); Riquet, *Chrétiens de France dans l'Europe enchaînée*; *France Pagan?: The Mission of Abbé Godin* (New York: Sheed & Ward, 1949); John Petrie (trans.), *The Worker-Priests* (New York: Macmillan, 1954); F. Boulard, *Essor ou declin du clergé français?* (Paris: Les Editions du Cerf, 1950); Adrien Dansette, *Destin du catholicisme français, 1926–56* (Paris: Flammarion, 1957). |
| 224–225 | D'Ouince to the authors. |
| 226, 8–10 | To R. de Terra, May 26, 1946 (*Letters to Two Friends*). |
| 226, 11 to<br>227, 2 | Jeanne Mortier to the authors. |
| 227, 3–19 | Leroy to the authors. |
| 228, 2 | To Swan, June 8, 1946 (unpublished). |
| 228, 29 | To de Lubac, June 26, 1946 (*Lettres intimes*). |
| 229, 32 | To Swan, June 8, 1946 (unpublished). |
| 230, 8–30 | Carlo Falconi, *The Silence of Pius XII* (Boston: Little, Brown, 1970). |

| | |
|---|---|
| 230, 20 to 231, 16 | To Breuil, April 4, 1947 (unpublished); *Annuaire pontifical catholique* (Paris, 1948); Falconi, *Popes in the Twentieth Century*; also, Francis Cardinal Brennan and Monsignor Alberto Giovanetti to the authors. |
| 232, 13–34 | Robert Broom, *Finding the Missing Link* (London: Watts & Co., 1950). |
| 233, 1–7 | To Baron Alberto Blanc, January 26, 1947 (unpublished). |
| 233, 9–25 | D'Ouince and LeCler and Françoise du Passage to the authors. |
| 234, 3 | To Swan, July 1946 (unpublished). |
| 234, 25 to 235 | De Lubac to the authors. |
| 237, 12 | Letter from Swan to Teilhard, October 11, 1946. |
| 239 | "Equipe Science et Conscience," debate between Teilhard et Gabriel Marcel (stenographic notes), Paris, January 21, 1947. |
| 239–240 | Edmund Lamalle, S.J., to the authors; also, d'Ouince to the authors, and *Un Prophète en proces*. |
| 240, 29 | Memoir of Teilhard by Solange LeMaître, read at the annual meeting of the Amis de Teilhard de Chardin, Paris, 1965. |
| 241 to 242, 17 | D'Ouince and Fessard to the authors. |
| 242, 30 | Letter of Brother Déodat Pénnéréth to the authors, August 1973; also, Leroy and Raphael to the authors. |
| 243, 1–36 | Leroy and Mortier to the authors. |
| 243, 13 | To Breuil, July 15, 1947 (unpublished). |
| 244, 3–36 | Joseph Teilhard de Chardin to the authors; also, Letter to R. de Terra, August 6, 1947. |
| 245–246 | De Lubac, d'Ouince, Leroy, and Raphael to the authors; also, letter to Swan, August 1947 (unpublished). |
| 247, 12 | Swan to the authors. |
| 247, 24 | To Breuil, September 23, 1947 (unpublished); to Jesuit Father General Ledochowski, September 25, 1947 (unpublished). |
| 248, 24 | Aron, *Histoire de l'épuration* and Rivière, *En Chine avec Teilhard de Chardin*; also, Leroy to the authors. |
| 250, 34 | To R. de Terra, January 3, 1948, *Letters to Two Friends*. |
| 251, 7–20 | To Raphael, January 2, 1948 (unpublished). |
| 251, 21 ff. | To Monsignor Bruno de Solages, January 7, 1948 (*Lettres intimes*). |
| 252, 4–22 | To Leroy, March 1, 1948, published with some excisions in *Lettres familières de Père Teilhard de Chardin, mon ami* (Paris: Centurion, 1976). |
| 252, 28 | Fathers John LaFarge, Robert Graham, and other American Jesuits. |
| 253, 11 | To Mortier, March 2, 1948 (unpublished). |
| 253, 23 | To Leroy, March 1, 1948, *Lettres familières*. |
| 253, 36 to 254, 28 | John W. Dodds. *The Several Lives of Paul Fejos* (New York: The Wenner-Gren Foundation, 1973); also, Lita Fejos Osmundsen to the authors, and wire recording of Teilhard's conference in English, made available to the authors by the Wenner-Gren Foundation. |
| 254, 30 | To Leroy, April 15, 1948. |
| 255, 8 | Lita Fejos Osmundsen to the authors. |

| 255, 21 | To d'Ouince, May 1, 1948 (unpublished). |
|---|---|
| 255, 26 | Unpublished diaries of Malvina Hoffman, made available to the authors by Mrs. Charles Hoffman; also, Malvina Hoffman, *Yesterday Is Tomorrow*, and Gulborg Groning to the authors. |
| 244, 36 | To d'Ouince, April 25, 1948 (unpublished). |
| 256, 4 | Correctly "R.P. John McMahan." From a letter to d'Ouince, May 1, 1948 (unpublished). |
| 256, 14 | May 24, 1948, *Lettres familières*. |
| 256, 12 to 257, 4 | Leroy to the authors; letter to Swan, June 18, 1948 (unpublished). |
| 257, 34 | To de Lubac, September 18, 1948 (*Lettres intimes*). In the same volume, de Lubac gives the date of the General's letter: July 10, 1948. |
| 258, 10 | To Swan, July 30, 1948 (unpublished). |
| 259, 7 *ff.* | To Mortier, August 24 and 31, 1948 (unpublished). |
| 258, 35 | To Swan, July 31, 1948 (unpublished). |
| 259, 1–23 | Joseph Teilhard de Chardin to the authors; obituary of Joseph Huby, S.J., from the Library of *Etudes*, Paris; letter to R. de Terra, September 15, 1948 (*Letters to Two Friends*). |
| 260, 1–18 | Mortier and d'Ouince to the authors. |
| 260–261 | From the stenographic notes taken at the JOCIST chaplains' meeting at Versailles, from the archives of the Fondation Teilhard de Chardin, Paris. |
| 261–262 | D'Ouince to the authors. |
| 264–265 | Edmund Lamalle, S.J., Teilhard's sometime guide in Rome, to the authors. |
| 265, 23 to 266, 11 | To d'Ouince, October 7, 1948 (unpublished). |
| 266, 26 | Leroy to the authors; also, letter to d'Ouince, October 7, 1948 (unpublished). |
| 266, 29 to 267, 18 | To Leroy, October 15, 1948 (*Lettres familières*). |
| 267, 30 | To d'Ouince, October 7, 1948 (unpublished). |
| 267, 31 *ff.* | Obituary of Jean-Baptiste Janssens, S.J., *Acta Romana S.J.*, 1963; Brodrick and other Jesuits to the authors. |
| 268, 13–22 | Fathers Brodrick and James Hennessey, S.J., to the authors. |
| 268, 31 to 269, 31 | To Leroy, October 15, 1948 (*Lettres familières*); to Joseph Teilhard de Chardin, October 19, 1948 (unpublished); also, d'Ouince to the authors; description of conversation is contained in letter to Mortier, October 8, 1948 (unpublished). |
| 270, 1–14 | To Mortier, October 20, 1948 (unpublished). |
| 270, 14 | Letters to Père d'Ouince, October 24, 1948 (unpublished); to Père Leroy, October 30, 1948, *Lettres familières*. |
| 270, 15–34 | Swan to the authors. |
| 271, 1–36 | Lamalle and J. Edward Coffey, S.J., to the authors. |
| 272, 3–32 | Ambassador and Mme Jules-Gabriel Beauroy to the authors. |
| 273, 1–11 | Mortier to the authors. |
| 273, 12–18 | Mortier and d'Ouince to the authors. |

| | |
|---|---|
| 273, 19 to 274, 1 | Comtesse Beatrice d'Hauteville and Mortier to the authors. |
| 274, 4–13 | J. de Margerie, d'Ouince, and Leroy to the aauthors. |
| 274, 18 | *Osservatore Romano*, January 30, 1949. |
| 274, 23 | Teilhard's response to this charge is contained in a letter to the Jesuit Father General on August 1, 1949 (unpublished). |
| 274, 14–30 | To Swan, February 1949. |
| 274, 30–35 | D'Hauteville to the authors; also, letter to Swan, February 2, 1949. |
| 275, 3–9 | To R. de Terra, March 1, 1949 (*Letters to Two Friends*). |
| 275, 10–19 | Mortier to the authors. |
| 276, 9 | To R. de Terra, April 27 and August 25, 1949 (*Letters to Two Friends*). |
| 276, 17–29 | Swan to the authors; also, letter to Swan, July 5, 1949. |
| 276, 30–35 | Mortier to the authors. |
| 277, 18 | To Mortier, August 15, 1949 (unpublished). |
| 278, 2–20 | To de Lubac, October 29, 1949 (*Lettres familières*). |
| 278, 34 | Dansette, *Destin du catholicisme français*. |
| 279, 21 ff. | *Les Temps modernes*, Paris, vols. 2–3, 1946; *Documentation catholique: chronique de la presse* (Paris: Maison de la Bonne Presse), vol. 43, 1946. |
| 280, 15 | *New York Times*, December 25, 1949. |
| 280, 16 ff. | Falconi, *The Popes in the Modern World*. |
| 280, 19 | *New York Times*, May 27, 1949. |
| 280, 26 | *Observatore Romano*, June 2, 1950. |
| 280, 32 | *New York Times*, April 19, 1950. |
| 281, 20–30 | *New York Times*, May 18, 1946; *Temps Modernes*, vols. 2–3, 1946. |
| 281, 31 to 282, 3 | Dhanis incident later recollected by Teilhard in a letter to Leroy, December 7, 1950 (*Lettres familières*). |
| 282, 15 | Unpublished postscript by Raymond Jouve, S.J., written on a letter from Teilhard to Leroy, April 17, 1950 (*Lettres familières*). |
| 282, 25 | To Leroy, April 17, 1950 (*Lettres familières*). |
| 283, 4 | To Leroy, March 4, 1950 (*Lettres familières*). |
| 283, 5 | Ibid. |
| 283, 34 | To Père Leroy, June 25, 1950 (*Lettres familières*). |
| 284, 4 | J. de Margerie to the authors. |
| 284, 13–33 | To Leroy, June 25, 1950 (*Lettres familières*). |
| 285, 4 ff. | *Humani Generis*, August 12, 1950 (English translation: National Catholic Welfare Conference, Washington). |
| 287, 11–18 | To Valensin, August 8, 1950 (*Lettres intimes*). |
| 288, 1–10 | To Mortier, September 4, 1950 (unpublished). |
| 288, 18 | *New York Times*, August 16, 1950. |
| 288, 26 | Joseph and Antoinette Teilhard de Chardin to the authors. In 1974, when the authors last visited Clermont, these customs were still observed. |

288, 33     To Mortier, August 25, 1950 (unpublished).

288, 36     To R. de Terra, August 17, 1950 (*Letters to Two Friends*).

289, 5     To Leroy, August 29, 1950 (*Lettres familières*).

289, 15     To Leroy, November 11, 1950 (*Lettres familières*).

289, 33     Joseph Teilhard de Chardin's recollection of conversations he had had with his brother when they walked together in the evenings. Interviewed by the authors.

290, 10     Recollections of the relocation of the exiled Jesuits, given by Henri Brouillard, S.J., to the authors; Roquette's articles appeared in *Etudes* in May and October 1950.

290, 34     Letter to Bernard Gorostarzu, S.J., French Assistant at Rome, October 10, 1950. Archives of Les Fontaines, Chantilly.

290, 34     Mortier to the authors; also letter to Leroy, October 19, 1950 (*Lettres familières*).

291, 6     To Leroy, July 6, 1950, passage excised from *Lettres familières*.

291, 12     To Leroy, November 11, 1950 (*Lettres familières*); also d'Ouince to the authors.

291, 23     *New York Times*, November 2, 1950, ff.; *Documentation catholique*, vol. 47; The *Worker-Priests*; also, letter to Leroy, December 7, 1950 (*Lettres familières*).

292, 20     To Blanc, December 24, 1950 (unpublished).

292, 25     To Leroy, January 1, 1951 (*Lettres familières*).

292, 32     To Leroy, January 28, 1951 (*Lettres familières*).

292, 33 to     *Les Temps Modernes*, Vol. 6, 1951; *Documentation catholique*,
293, 9     vol. 48, 1951; d'Ouince to the authors.

293, 30 to     "De Executione Encyclici Humani Generis," Letter of Jean-Baptiste
294, 5     Janssens, S.J., *Textus authenticus: Acta Romana S.J.*, Vol. II; also, several Jesuits who had been at *Etudes* at the time, interviewed by the authors; additional material from a letter to Leroy, March 28, 1951 (*Lettres familières*).

294, 11     Quotation occurs in a letter from Valensin to Teilhard, February 24, 1948 (*Lettres intimes*).

294, 18 to     Teilhard's assessment of Valensin is contained in a letter to Leroy,
295, 5     March 28, 1951 (*Lettres familières*).

295, 12     Claude Cuénot, Mortier, and Leroy to the authors.

295, 19     D'Ouince to the authors; letter to Leroy, June 19, 1951 (*Lettres familières*).

295, 26     To Barbour, May 15, 1951. *In the Field with Teilhard de Chardin*; also, Dr. and Mrs. Barbour to the authors.

296–297,     D'Ouince and Mortier to the authors; also, description of Jouve
298, 20     from "Hommage" in *Etudes* at the time of his death in 1952, and from testimony given by de Lubac, LeCler and Leroy to the authors.

298, 21–36     D'Hauteville to the authors. One quotation from Solange Le Maitre's "Conference" on Teilhard in 1951.

301, 25     Barbour, *In the Field with Teilhard de Chardin*.

302, 8     Letter written by Barbour to his wife, August 4, 1951 (Barbour private collection).

302, 9 to     Barbour, *In the Field with Teilhard de Chardin*; letters to Leroy,
303, 15     August 15 and September 17, 1951 (*Lettres familières*); Dr. and

Mrs. Barbour to the authors; letters to Paul Fejos, August 10, 1951 and Joseph Teilhard de Chardin, August 18, 1951 (unpublished).

303, 16–29      To Mortier, September 10, 1951 (unpublished); to Andre Ravier, S.J., September 10, 1951 (*Lettres intimes*).

303, 30 ff.      To Mortier, November 30, 1951 (unpublished).

309, 4 ff.      To Joseph Teilhard de Chardin, February 10 and May 11, 1952 (unpublished).

310, 1–12      To Leroy, May 24, July 10 and July 30, 1952 (*Lettres familières*).

310, 34 to
312, 8      To Ravier, August 3, 1952 (*Lettres intimes*).

311, 31 to
312, 6      Mrs. Movius to the authors.

313, 36      Leroy to the authors.

314, 4–19      To Mortier, September 29, 1952 (unpublished); to Leroy, same date (*Lettres familières*).

315, 11      Father Gannon to the authors; letter to Mortier, September 7, 1952 (unpublished).

316, 1 ff.      To Leroy, October 14 and November 9, 1952 (*Lettres familières*).

317, 3      To François Russo, S.J., January 4, 1953 (unpublished).

317, 14      To Leroy, November 26, 1952 (*Lettres familières*).

317, 20      De Breuvery to the authors; letter to Mortier, November 9, 1952 (unpublished).

317, 15 ff.      To Mortier, September 9, 1952 (unpublished); to Leroy, October 14, 1952 (*Lettres familières*); de Breuvery to the authors.

317, 34 to
318, 8      Swann and Groning to the authors; Malvina Hoffman day books, 1952 (unpublished).

318, 9 ff.      To Leroy, September 29, 1952 (excised from *Lettres familières*); de Breuvery to the authors.

319      To Mortier, September 29, 1952 (unpublished); to de Solages, September 26, 1952 (*Lettres intimes*); to Leroy, November 20, 1952 (*Lettres familières*); to Russo, November 21, 1952 (unpublished); Nixon reference in letter to Joseph Teilhard de Chardin, December 14, 1952 (unpublished); Dansette, *Destin du catholicisme français*.

320, 11 to
321, 7      *Worker-Priests; Les Temps Modernes*, vols. 7–8, 1952, 1953; *Documentation catholique*, vols. 48–49, 1952, 1953.

321, 14      To Joseph Teilhard de Chardin, December 31, 1952 (unpublished); also, to Russo, December 23, 1952 (unpublished).

321, 16–30      To Leroy, December 24, 1952 (slightly excised in *Lettres familières*).

322, 6      To Russo, November 17, 1953 (unpublished).

322, 33      To Mortier, January 10, 1953 (unpublished); to Russo, May 29, 1953 (unpublished).

322, 34      To Leroy, March 6, April 28, 1952 (excised from *Lettres familières*).

323, 15      Dr. Albert Simard, Osmundsen, and de Breuvery to the authors; letter to Raphael, March 9, 1953 (unpublished); to Leroy, March 22, 1953 (*Lettres familières*); to Christian Burdo, S.J., February 14, 1953 (unpublished).

323, 5 ff.      To Leroy, March 1, 1953 (*Lettres familières*).

| | |
|---|---|
| 323, 16 ff. | Simard and Swan to the authors. |
| 323, 20 | To Leroy, January 13, 1952 (passage excised in *Lettres familières*). |
| 324, 13–17 | To Leroy, April 16, 1953 (*Lettres familières*). |
| 327, 20 ff. | Letters to Fejos, August 2 and September 6 (unpublished, in the archives of the Wenner-Gren Foundation). |
| 327, 20–30 | To Leroy, August 5, 1953 (*Lettres familières*). |
| 327, 32 to 328, 12 | To Leroy, September 9, 1953 (*Lettres familières*). |
| 329, 9 | To Ravier, September 7, 1953 (*Lettres intimes*). |
| 329, 16 ff. | To Leroy, November 9, 1953 (*Lettres familières*); to Marguerite Teillard-Chambon, November 8, 1953, in *Nouvelles Lettres de voyage* (Paris: Grasset, 1957). |
| 330, 5 | Letter from Oakley to Teilhard, November 19, 1953 (unpublished, in the Archives of the British Museum [Natural History]). |
| 330, 19 | Weiner, *The Piltdown Forgery.* |
| 330, 33 | To Breuil, December 14, 1953 (unpublished). |
| 331, 12 | Also to Leroy, March 7, 1954 (*Lettres familières*). |
| 331, 14 to 332, 20 | *The Worker-Priests: Les Temps modernes*, vol. 10, 1953; also, letters to Russo, January 14, February 7, 1954 (*Lettres intimes*), to Mortier, February 18, 1954 (unpublished). |
| 332, 33 | To de Solages, January 17, 1954 (*Lettres intimes*); to Mortier, January 10, 1954 (unpublished). |
| 333, 10 | To Leroy, January 5, February 9, 1954 (*Lettres familières*). |
| 333, 26 | To Leroy, March 16, 1954 (*Lettres familières*). |
| 333, 36 | Swan to the authors. |
| 334, 5 | Note to Swan, March 21, 1954. |
| 334, 19 | To Leroy, April 16, 1953 (excised from *Lettres familières*). |
| 334, 24 to 335, 2 | Leroy, d'Ouince, and de Lubac to the authors. |
| 335, 3–16 | To Ravier, July 11, 1954 (*Lettres intimes*); d'Ouince to the authors. |
| 335, 17–30 | To de Solages, July 11, 1954 (*Lettres intimes*); to Oakley, July 26, 1954 (unpublished); Jean Piveteau and Groning to the authors. |
| 335, 30 to 336, 9 | Leroy to the authors; Groning to the authors. |
| 336, 19 | Ravier to the authors. |
| 336, 21 to 337, 8 | Leroy to the authors. Incident recounted in less detail in connecting narrative in *Lettres familières*. |
| 337, 9–18 | D'Ouince and de Lubac, Cuenot and Alice Teillard-Chambon to the authors. |
| 338, 19–32 | D'Ouince and Ravier to the authors; also recounted in d'Ouince, *Prophet en procès*. Also, letter to Père Ravier, July 20, 1954 *Lettres intimes*. |
| 338, 15 | To Mortier, September 22, 1954 (unpublished); to Leroy, August 26, 1954 (*Lettres familières*). |

# Index

# Index

# Index